Operational Risk

New Frontiers Explored

Edited by Ellen Davis

Published by Risk Books, a Division of Incisive Media Investments Ltd

Incisive Media
32–34 Broadwick Street
London W1A 2HG
Tel: +44(0) 20 7316 9000
E-mail: books@incisivemedia.com
Sites: www.riskbooks.com
www.incisivemedia.com

© 2012 Incisive Media

ISBN 978-1-906348-85-4

British Library Cataloguing in Publication Data
A catalogue record for this book is available from the British Library

Publisher: Nick Carver
Commissioning Editor: Sarah Hastings
Managing Editor: Lewis O'Sullivan
Designer: Lisa Ling
Copy-edited and typeset by T&T Productions Ltd, London

Printed and bound in the UK by Berforts Group

Contents

About the Editor

Ellen Davis is the head of risk insight in Thomson Reuters' governance, risk and compliance division and is based in London. Previously, she spent 14 years at Incisive Media, where she worked with a cross-company team to shape the online editorial presence of the division that publishes *Risk* magazine, as divisional online editor. Prior to this she was the editor and publisher of *Operational Risk & Regulation* magazine, and editor of *AsiaRisk* magazine, based in Hong Kong. Originally from the US, she holds an MBA from NYU's Stern School of Business, and she wrote about capital markets, corporate finance, and emerging markets for various publications while living in New York City during the 1990s. Ellen continues to enjoy discussing the risk management challenges facing individuals, organisations and regulators around the world.

About the Authors

Nasreen al Qaseer is the general manager of risk management at the Kuwait International Bank. She earned her Doctorate in Business Administration from Liverpool John Moores University with her thesis "Examining the Magnitude of Operational Risk in the Lending Process: Application of Banks".

Devon E. Brooks is a senior vice president and head of global risk management audit at Northern Trust, where he is responsible for providing subject matter expertise on risk management and building a global audit team proficient in auditing topics related to enterprise risk management and the measurement and use of bank capital.

Alexander Cavallo is vice president and senior risk consultant at Northern Trust, where he is responsible for empirical analysis relating to operational risk assessment for compliance with the Basel II Capital Accord. Alexander has an MA in economics, and years of experience in economic, statistical and empirical analysis. He has supported expert witness testimony in litigation consulting for 10 years.

Andreas (Andy) A. Jobst is the chief economist of the Bermuda Monetary Authority. His work focuses on financial stability and macroprudential surveillance, risk analytics and financial regulation (banking and insurance). Previously, he was an economist at the monetary and capital markets department of the International Monetary Fund in Washington, DC. As a member of IMF Article IV missions Andy has been responsible for the financial sector coverage of several large mature and emerging market economies. He completed stress tests for Germany, Sweden, the UK and US as part of the IMF's Financial Stability Assessment Program. He also served as one of the main authors of the Spillover Report for the United States and the Global Financial Stability Report, with a focus on developing models for solvency and liquidity risk as well as macro-financial linkages. Andy has published more than 30 articles in, among others, *Journal of Banking and Finance*, *Journal of International Economics*, *Journal of Derivatives and Hedge Funds* and *World Economics*) as well as contributing to many books. He holds a PhD in finance from the London School of Economics.

Mikhail Makarov is managing partner and senior consultant at EVMTech. Mikhail's areas of expertise include risk modelling and computational finance. He has led numerous projects in the areas of operational, insurance and credit risk, and has led software implementation of AMA models for several Tier 1 banks. Mikhail has published a number of papers on mathematical methods in operational risk and is a regular speaker at operational risk conferences. He holds an MS degree in mathematics from Moscow State University as well as a PhD in mathematics and an MS in computer science from Ohio State University.

Roger Miles researches risk governance at King's College London, and is a Director of NudgeGlobal, devising behaviour-based controls for improved decision-making in uncertain conditions. He is special risk advisor to a global law firm and risk forum leader for GARP, the ICC and national/international government agencies. He has previously led corporate communications for organisations including the BBA in London and Brussels.

Bahram Mirzai is managing partner and senior advisor at EVMTech. Bahram has more than 10 years of experience in risk management with deep industry knowledge in banking and insurance, managing numerous projects in the areas of operational risk, stress-testing and Solvency II. He led the FSI seminar for senior regulators on operational risks for several years, and advised the Basel Committee during the consultation stage of Basel II. Bahram was previously with Swiss Re as senior vice president for global banking practice. He has an MS in Physics and a PhD in machine learning from ETH Zürich.

Marcel Monien is senior quantitative risk analyst at Nordeutsche Landesbank, Germany. He has worked for several years in the operational risk department developing and establishing methods for managing and measuring operational risks. He is responsible for the quantification and stress-testing of operational risks in the risk model department. As a member of national and international work groups, he is engaged in the further development of these topics. Marcel studied financial and business mathematics at the University of Braunschweig, Germany, and University of Manchester, UK.

J.D. Opdyke is a principal at Bates White LLC, an economic consulting firm, where he provides expert testimony and applied statistical and econometric analysis in large economic litigations. J.D. has over 20 years of experience as a quantitative consultant, most of this in the banking and credit sectors, where his clients include multiple Fortune and Global 50 banks and financial credit organisations. He has completed nine statistical operational risk modelling projects for these clients and has multiple publications treating the difficult statistical challenges of obtaining more robust, more precise and more accurate operational risk capital estimates. His other publications span statistical finance, number theory/combinatorics, computational statistics and applied econometrics. J.D. earned his undergraduate degree, with honours, from Yale University, his master's degree from Harvard University, where he was a Kennedy Fellow and a Social Policy Research Fellow, and completed post-graduate statistics work as an ASP Fellow in the graduate mathematics department at MIT.

Hansruedi Schütter was Credit Suisse Group's global head of operational risk and a member of the IIF Working Group on Operational Risk during the Basel II consultation period. He is the owner and managing director of hrs Risk Management Services. In association with RiskBusiness International he works with clients in Asia, the Middle East and Europe, and takes a particular interest in qualitative aspects of operational risk and pragmatic solutions.

Evan G. Sekeris is an assistant vice president in the bank supervision and regulation department at the Federal Reserve Bank of Richmond. He heads the policy analysis unit, which is responsible for bank supervision policy matters, research and the supervision of risk models at large banking institutions and for assessing their compliance with regulatory requirements, in particular the Basel II Capital Accord and operational risk. Evan's research focuses on information issues in asset pricing and on operational risk modelling. Prior to holding this position, Evan was a financial economist in the quantitative analysis unit at the Federal Reserve Bank of Boston and an associate professor at Pitzer College, part of the Claremont Colleges.

Andrew Sheen joined the UK Financial Services Authority in 2005, and is head of the risk frameworks team within the risk specialist division. This team's responsibilities include reviewing the operational risk frameworks of banks, asset managers and insurance firms, and reviewing AMA waiver applications. Before heading this team, Andrew led the FSA's operational risk policy team and was responsible for the operational risk rules and guidance produced during that time. While in industry, Andrew developed and implemented operational risk frameworks in the UK, Eastern Europe, Asia and the Isle of Man. He has experience in UK, international, investment and central banking.

Carsten Steinhoff is head of operational risk controlling at Norddeutsche Landesbank, Germany. He studied bank management and controlling at the University of Göttingen (Germany). After working with a bank in Italy, he changed to the risk-controlling department at Norddeutsche Landesbank, where he followed an on-the-job PhD programme. His thesis was on operational risk quantification, with focus on scenario analyses within loss distribution models. Before becoming head of department, Carsten created Norddeutsche Landesbank's internal OpRisk model and was engaged in the foundation of the German loss databases DakOR and ÖffSchOR. His research interest focuses on the development of holistic OpRisk management frameworks.

Johannes Voit is the director of internal models at the German Savings Banks Association (DSGV), where he is responsible for the quantitative and qualitative aspects of bank-wide risk modelling, eg, the development of holistic, bank-wide stress tests for german savings banks, the measurement and management of risk concentrations and the treatment of model risk. Previously, Johannes served as a professor of theoretical physics in many important universities and research institutions worldwide, before a career change leading the central development of operational risk management instruments for all German savings banks, and acting as head of operational risk for DSGV. He is the author of *The Statistical Mechanics of Financial Markets*.

Introduction

Scandals in the financial services industry seem to be popping up on a near-weekly basis as I write this introduction in the summer of 2012. The reason is simple enough: all of the work the regulators and the industry have undertaken since the financial crisis began has done almost nothing to address the underlying cause of the conflagration.

Poor operational risk management caused the global financial crisis. And good operational risk management is the answer to repairing the global financial crisis.

I believe that very, very strongly. When the dominos began to fall, I pointed this out in the pages of *Operational Risk & Regulation*. I said this to people over coffee, espoused it at conferences and generally tried to get people to pay attention to this fact.

I was not alone; there were quite a few people who were also saying this, and who continue to say it.

And yet, who listened? Certainly not the regulators. Or senior executives at banks, or even their boards of directors. All the focus since the crisis achieved lift-off has been on credit risk, market risk and liquidity risk. Some operational risk people – very brave ones – will clear their throats, cough a little and quietly suggest that perhaps liquidity risk is actually a form of operational risk. I can see the logic there, but liquidity risk has been well and truly claimed as a cousin to credit and market risk, and so I suppose there is little chance now of "op risk" claiming it as a close relative now.

So, is it any surprise that the front pages of the newspapers continue to be dominated by headlines about scandals at banks? As I write this, Barclays has just lost three of its top executives because it was caught fiddling Libor, the interest rate set by banks declaring what rate they are able to borrow money at, a process managed by the British Bankers' Association. Letters between the bank and the UK Financial Services Authority (FSA) have been released in which the FSA expressed concerns about the culture at Barclays Capital. And Barclays is not alone; several other banks will have taken their turn on the Libor scandal ducking stool before this is over.

In addition, HSBC has been fined by regulators because of huge holes in its money laundering compliance framework, which newspaper articles allege allowed terrorists and Mexican drug traffickers to launder money through the bank. HSBC was also hugely embarrassed by the US Senate's publication of emails that purported to show senior executives actively discussing how to ensure funds being transferred through the bank from Iran complied with US money laundering rules.

Weeks before that we had the so-called "London Whale", a trader at JP Morgan Chase, who built up giant positions seemingly by accident. It remains unclear whether this was the biggest model risk event ever witnessed in financial services, or whether it is a more complex tale perhaps involving a lack of transparency between the front office and the risk governance framework. At the end of the day, the truth is less important than the fact that it happened at a firm that was supposed to have a "best practice" risk framework in place. If it could happen at JP Morgan, many observers have said, it could happen anywhere.

And that is partly the point. Since the start of the crisis, operational risk as a discipline has been on the back foot. The crisis should have been operational risk's moment of glory, and instead we found that it was sidelined in favour of credit, market and liquidity risk, as well as plain old-fashioned firefighting.

I think a large part of the reason for this is the unsatisfactory way in which operational risk was shaped in Basel II. There is little argument from within these pages, and without, that the Basel II approach was misguided in some fundamental ways, from the levels at which the alphas and betas were set in the basic indicator and standardised approaches to the way the advanced measurement approach proved to be less risk sensitive than had been hoped for. In short, the Basel II approach to op risk barely creaks along as a regulatory framework, and does not work at all as a way for an organisation to measure and manage its operational risk.

This fundamental truth should not lead (and so far has not led) to a blame game within operational risk in quite the same way that problems in credit and market risk frameworks have since the mid 2000s, with regulators and the industry pointing the finger at each other. Nor should it. The industry and regulators both worked very hard to build the original op risk framework from scratch, and having watched this cooperation fairly closely, I think it is safe to say that the blame can be placed equally on all shoulders, even mine. I feel, for example, that I bought far too easily into the idea that operational risk quantification was something that would be quickly conquerable and that the naysayers who argued that it should not and could not be quantified were just out-of-touch doom-mongers. While I still feel strongly that operational risk modelling is a very worthy goal and that quantification has a range of benefits, I can now acknowledge that this is a much bigger challenge than I had previously hoped it would prove to be.

So, having expressed my *mea culpa*, why a new book that has a distinctive quantification angle? Am I falling into the same trap as I did before? Am I just a quantification groupie, who cannot give up her addiction to the hope that eventually the perfect distribution will be found, that scaling is a fundamental matter of faith and perhaps that the heterogeneous nature of loss data could be cleansed with the right application of a transfigurational tool?

No. Perhaps it is because I am writing this introduction on a quiet Sunday morning that I feel the need to "reaffirm my faith" in the quantification of operational risk in such terms, which somehow feel appropriate. When I came back to writing again on the subject in 2011, I discovered that in quiet corners of the discipline much work was going on around re-examining quantification. Much of this work has been taking place in the US, because this is where the majority of advanced measurement approach (AMA) banks reside. It is one of the bitter ironies of operational risk that it came to be perceived that it was the European banks who championed Basel II, and in particular the AMA, against the US infidel. And that, in the end, it is the US that has forced the greatest number of banks to adopt the AMA by fiat. Not only are a hefty number of US banks on the AMA, but they are forced to adopt a very strict version of that approach. European banks, on the other hand, are able to incorporate substantial amounts of scenario analysis into their operational risk frameworks, and even with this, at least to my mind, lower standard most have opted not to undertake the AMA.

So it is in the US that most of the dialogue around the AMA is taking place. For example, there is the work that is going on around stress-testing and factor modelling, championed by Marcelo Cruz, the editor of the *Journal of Operational Risk*, along with others. To my mind, factor modelling is one of the more exciting developments of the early years of the 21st century. US regulators' work around stress-testing and factor modelling is discussed briefly in the chapter written by the Federal Reserve Bank of Richmond's Evan G. Sekeris (Chapter 2). I know it is early days, and many people have said to me that they do not think that operational risk events can be correlated to economic factors or to internal data streams. There is still a large body of thought that believes operational risk is fundamentally uncorrelated to either market or credit risk. I would agree with this in so far as an earthquake is certainly uncorrelated to most happenings in the financial services sector. But I would disagree that operational risk in its entirety is uncorrelated to economic and internal data streams.

I suppose I stake this belief on the fact that human behaviour is often highly correlated within itself: groups of people, presented with the same set of incentives, will opt to behave in similar ways. For example, let us look at the chapter by Roger Miles (Chapter 9), which is derived in part from the work he did during his doctoral thesis at King's College London. Miles interviewed a number of chief risk officers at financial services firms for his work, and they speak with one voice: the majority of individuals and the firms they worked for viewed compliance with regulatory rules as a game that has to be played.

While regulators are busy trying to construct sets of rules that should make banks safer and more risk aware, these institutions are busy undermining those rules through their gaming. Chief Risk Officers and operational risk executives find themselves in the difficult position of being aware of the gaming, and sometimes the victim of it, but unable to do much to stop it. They are aware that such gaming undermines the risk position of their institution, but most are not empowered to alter this situation.

Another example of correlated human behaviour is the treatment of the operational risk components of lending; the doctoral thesis work by Nasreen Al Qaseer and Hansruedi Schütter covered in Chapter 11 shows that when many firms pause to think about it, they find that operational risk has a substantial role in the lending process. Yet, most firms put losses from lending in the credit risk box, and regulators are concerned that this is leading to a failure to manage those operational risks correctly. Many inside (and outside) the operational risk industry believe that the failure by firms to understand the operational risk components of the lending process led to a lack of controls, which in turn permitted widespread mortgage fraud, leading ultimately to the financial crisis.

So, to my mind, if human behaviours can be demonstrated to be correlated with other human behaviours and also with economic and financial factors, then can the results of such correlated behaviours ultimately be modelled? I am not pretending that we have the answers today, at this moment. Sociological modelling (say, attempting to model the behaviours of underprivileged children versus middle class children in terms of the outcome of going to university) is fraught with difficulty. Sociologists have spent years trying to pick apart the strands of what causes the massive gap in achievement and come to the conclusion that it is not just "one thing" that causes underperformance. Rather, they now conclude that a range of factors combine in a dynamic fashion to create an "emergent system", where the different challenges and cultural influences that underprivileged children face come together to create an environment that fosters underachievement in a way that is greater than simply the sum of the individual factors involved.

To my mind, the cultural problem in financial services – and I think we can all acknowledge that there is one, in that the culture at the time of writing has led to very negative outcomes for the firms themselves, for their customers and for the economy at large – is very similar. It may be difficult to model one strand or element as a "cause" of something like the financial crisis, because I would argue that the financial services system is ultimately an emergent system. However, if we can show correlations between the overall outcomes and specific patterns of human behaviour – in the same way that perhaps we know that there is a direct relationship between the time parents spend reading to their children or helping their children to read and overall literacy levels at the end of schooling – we can at least begin to understand some of the roots of the problem.

Ultimately, these improvements in understanding will hopefully morph into improvements in operational risk management that directly translate into benefits for the business, which is what the UK FSA's Andrew Sheen calls for in Chapter 4. Without improved operational risk management, all of the quantification and modelling is for naught.

In fact, Devon Brooks provides an excellent discussion (Chapter 10) on understanding model risk and how it applies to operational risk models: perhaps the ultimate way in which quantification and qualitative judgement connect on impact. Model risk in operational risk has been a topic that has drawn the attention of Basel's Standards Implementation Subgroup on Operational Risk, and Mitsutoshi Adachi, chair of that group, devoted much of his speech at the 2012 OpRisk North America Conference in New York to this subject. The upshot is, the large number of assumptions that firms have to make when they undertake their op risk modelling means that these models are particularly subject to model risk, and so executives should make sure they "kick the tyres" appropriately.

Other chapters in this book are also focused on quantitative best practices, and on the nexus between practical management tools and techniques and those best practices. I hope that readers will come away with a sense of how quantitative methods can add value to their operational risk management efforts.

The book includes two chapters on the use of external data, specifically from loss data consortiums, in the various stages of operational risk modelling. Chapter 8, by Carsten Steinhoff and Marcel Monien, looks at how loss consortiums' data can be used to improve scenario analysis, stress-testing and other techniques if the loss database is constructed correctly. Chapter 5, by Johannes Voit, looks specifically at how small German savings banks have used their loss databases to better understand the risks they face. I am a particular admirer of the work that Voit has done, which proves that these kinds of tools and techniques are just as valid for smaller firms as they are for larger ones.

Chapter 6 by Bahram Mirzai, seeks to improve our understanding of how operational risk could be better mapped into insurance products, in order to help advance the discussion with regulators and the insurance industry around improving the use of insurance as a capital substitute for operational risk. This is an important area that both the insurance and operational risk industries need to focus on further: there has to be a reward for firms that are able to better understand and manage their risks. While I understand the nature of the challenges around using insurance as a capital substitute, surely it is not beyond our grasp to find a real solution in this area sooner rather than later?

Chapter 3 by Andreas Jobst picks up on the theme of the need for incentives to better manage risk from a different angle. He explores the treatment of operational risk in both the insurance and banking regulatory frameworks and concludes that the incentives for the mitigation of operational risk do not exist under the standardised approach at present, and calls for financial services firms and regulators to develop a deeper understanding of the causality of operational risk and the embracing of the qualitative and quantitative balance that is inherent in the discipline.

Chapter 7, "A Unified Approach to Dependency Calibration in Operational Risk Models", by Mikhail Makarov, does exactly what it says on the tin. Basel II's construction forces banks to assume full dependency between risks, which can lead to high capital numbers. Makarov's chapter proposes a method to estimate dependence using internal or external data, which addresses some of the common challenges associated with attempting to estimate dependency.

Chapter 1, by J.D. Opdyke and Alexander Cavallo, is a thought-provoking piece on the use of the influence function as an analytical tool to enable the operational risk practitioner to use "existing AMA models to generate critical quantitative insights for direct business decision-making by users of operational risk capital estimates". Their words, but I could not have put it any better. This chapter has a higher mathematical content than the others, and incorporates elements of other work that Opdyke and Cavallo have engaged in, but I promise it is worth it. It is "outside the box" thinking like theirs that I believe will lead us to make the next series of breakthroughs in the operational risk discipline.

I would like to conclude this brief introduction by making a call for the kind of collaboration that operational risk executives and the regulatory community enjoyed during the creation of the operational risk discipline. I hope that this book can initiate the kind of dialogue that is needed around quantitative issues in order for the AMA to be effectively redrawn. While I know that collaboration between the regulators and the industry has not been perfect – the industry blames regulators for the lack of risk sensitivity in the AMA, and the regulators blame the industry for the low levels of the alphas and betas, among other things – my sense as an outside observer is that the regulators and the industry need each other on this. Neither side on its own has the resources or the experience to completely deal with the crucial issues that must be tackled if the AMA is to be reconfigured in a risk-sensitive way that regulators can have faith in, and that businesses can use to understand the challenges that they face. Operational risk as a discipline has broken new ground before in terms of collaboration between regulators and the industry, and it can do so again.

I am keen to get feedback from people in the industry about the chapters in this book, and further thoughts on issues around the quantification of operational risk. Readers can contact me at ellenldavis@hotmail.co.uk or via LinkedIn.

ACKNOWLEDGEMENTS

I thank my husband, Colin, who has always been so supportive of my work in so many ways and so helpful when I needed someone to talk things through with. Special thanks should go to my parents, because if it wasn't for their encouragement and love, I may never have found my way in the world.

Part I

Operational Risk Capital Estimation and Planning: Exact Sensitivity Analysis and Business Decision Making Using the Influence Function

John D. ("J.D.") Opdyke; Alexander Cavallo

Bates White LLC; Northern Trust

Financial institutions have invested tremendous resources in developing operational risk capital models within the framework of the advanced measurement approach (AMA) of the Basel II Accord. Most of their effort has focused on satisfying evolving regulatory requirements in the short term rather than risk-conscious business decision-making in the long term. However, a critical objective of the Basel II Accord is to move institutions beyond viewing operational risk capital modelling as a mere regulatory exercise to embedding operational risk awareness into risk-informed decision-making throughout the institution. To this end, we illustrate in this chapter the use of the influence function as a powerful analytical tool that allows the operational risk practitioner to leverage existing AMA models to generate critical quantitative insights for direct business decision-making by users of operational risk capital estimates.

The influence function (IF), which is borrowed from the robust statistics literature, is an extremely useful and relevant methodology that provides a theoretical basis for capital planning and business decision-making via exact sensitivity analysis. Because it is based on analytic derivations, the IF avoids the need to perform often resource-intensive, arguably subjective, and often inconclusive or inaccurate simulations. We clearly demonstrate how the IF utilises any given estimator of the severity model (easily the main driver of estimated capital requirements), the values of its parameter estimates and an assumed forward-looking frequency to define exact sensitivity curves for regulatory capital and economic capital. These curves can be used to conduct exact sensitivity analyses on the capital impacts of hypothetical changes to the underlying loss data. Hypothetical loss scenarios of interest to bank management may be current or prospective, such as assessing the potential capital impact of a single hypothetical "tail" event of differing magnitudes. Relevant loss scenarios may also be retrospective, providing "but for" and exact attribution analyses as to why capital changed from one quarter to another. The information generated from these sensitivity analyses can suggest potential enhancements to the estimation of severity model parameters, and, more broadly, better inform decision-making based on a more precisely defined risk profile.

1.1 BACKGROUND

The Basel II Accord represents a major step forward in the regulation and supervision of the international financial and banking system. The risk measurement and risk management principles and guidelines put forward in the Basel II Accord aim to increase the stability and soundness of the banking system through comprehensive capital adequacy regulation. The approach includes the "three pillars" concept, in which stability and soundness is enhanced through minimum capital requirements (Pillar 1), supervisory review (Pillar 2) and market discipline via public disclosure requirements (Pillar 3). Among the major changes in this second Basel Accord are a greater reliance on banks' internal data systems to provide inputs to capital calculations and the extension of capital requirements to a new risk class, operational risk. In this chapter we focus on the quantitative use of banks' internal data for assessing operational risk exposure.[1]

Operational risk is the risk of financial loss due to external events or due to inadequate or failed internal processes, people or systems, including legal risk but not reputational or strategic risk. Essentially, operational losses are the many different ways that a financial institution may incur a financial loss in the course of business, aside from market, credit or liquidity related exposure.[2] The Basel II Accord describes three potential methods for calculating capital charges for operational risk, and our focus in this chapter is on the most empirically sophisticated of the three – the advanced measurement approach (AMA).[3] National bank regulators typically require internationally active banks and banks with significant operational risk exposure (generally, the largest banks) to use the AMA.[4] Some of the advantages of the AMA are that it permits financial institutions to develop a customised quantification system that makes use of historical data (which may include both internal and external loss data), bank-specific information on internal controls and other relevant business factors, and the forward-looking assessments of potential risk generated by the bank's business experts via scenario analysis. The flexibility of the AMA is also arguably one of its major limitations: operational risk practitioners, regulators and academics have engaged in vigorous debates on issues of methodology and best practice, yet many challenges remain unresolved since the framework was finalised in 2004, despite more than eight years of concerted efforts.[5]

In the AMA framework, an institution attempts to quantify operational risk exposure at a very high percentile of the enterprise-level aggregate annual loss distribution. Using the value-at-risk (VaR) risk measure, regulatory capital for operational risk is estimated at the 99.9th percentile (which corresponds to the size of total annual loss that would be exceeded no more frequently than once in 1,000 years). Economic capital is estimated at an even higher percentile of the distribution (usually between the 99.95th and 99.98th percentiles).[6]

Within the AMA framework, the loss distribution approach (LDA) is the most commonly used method for estimating an aggregate annual loss distribution with parametric models. The LDA decomposes operational risk exposure into its frequency and severity components (ie, distributions of the number and magnitude of losses, respectively). Most institutions find a tractable solution to this empirical task by breaking the problem into a number of sequential stages, with the ultimate goal being the estimation of the enterprise level aggregate annual loss distribution from its underlying components.

Yet, even after carefully splitting the problem into distinct components (reviewed below), the fundamental statistical challenge remains: how can banks reliably estimate such a high percentile of the enterprise level aggregate annual loss distribution with sufficient precision, accuracy and robustness that it is actually useful in practice? To explain by way of example, a statistically correct estimate of required capital of US$250 million, based on LDA, that has a 95% confidence window of US$200 million on either side does not add much value: a range on the estimate of required capital from US$50 million to US$450 million is obviously not precise enough to use for making actual business decisions, but this range is actually narrower than many in practice. Even if the percentile was somehow estimated with greater precision, if a single, new loss that deviated somewhat from the parametric assumptions of the statistical model (not even necessarily a large loss) threw off the estimate by doubling it from one quarter to the next, and then dropping it by a factor of 3 in the following quarter, the estimator clearly is not robust enough to be considered reliable for actual business decision-making. Yet this, too, is very typical of the quarterly behaviour of many banks' capital estimates at the unit-of-measure level.[7] A number of the statistical challenges arising from both the LDA framework and its application to the limited amount of extant operational loss data were raised as early as 2001, during the initial consultative period for the Basel II Accord.[8] Research after the Basel II Accord was finalised has begun to provide a stronger theoretical and empirical understanding of the limitations of some of the widely used estimation methodologies when applied to operational risk capital quantification.[9]

The inescapable challenge, however, is that the 99.9th percentile is so far out-of-sample, even when pooling operational loss data across many institutions, that, in order to make any progress at all, the practitioner must make very far-reaching, out-of-sample extrapolations using parametric models: that is, they must fit an assumed statistical distribution as closely as possible to the existing data, and then use this "best fit" to presume what the losses look like far out into the right tail of the statistical distribution (even though no (or very, very little) observed loss data exists so far out into the right tail). Consequently, the component models that contribute to this estimated percentile receive a high level of scrutiny from internal auditors, model validators and regulatory supervisors. Of the empirical models and methods used in the AMA framework, the severity models generally pose much greater modelling challenges, have by far the largest impact on the ultimate estimates of economic and regulatory capital and are an active area of research among industry practitioners, academics and regulators.[10]

In this chapter, we demonstrate how, for a given set of parameter estimates of a severity model, the IF can be used to perform exact sensitivity analysis on capital requirements for various current, prospective and even retrospective changes to the underlying loss data. In other words, the IF can be used to inform us of exactly what the change in capital would be if the bank experienced a new loss of, say, US\$1 million, or US\$10 million or US\$500 million in the next quarter. The statistical theory behind the IF has been richly developed in the robust statistics literature for nearly half a century; only its application to operational risk is relatively new.[11] In this setting, the IF needs only three inputs to define exact capital sensitivity curves:

1. the estimator used in the severity model;

2. the values of its parameter estimates;

3. an assumed forward-looking frequency.

With these inputs the IF defines a deterministic, non-stochastic mathematical formula that exactly describes the impact of data changes (in the form of additional or changed losses) on the parameters of the severity distribution.[12]

Because these parameters directly define capital requirements, the IF formula directly determines the exact capital changes caused by hypothetical or actual changes in the loss data; hence, the IF provides exact capital sensitivity analyses. Consequently, the IF arms business users of operational risk capital estimates with relevant information about potential capital needs and precisely defined risks, as long as they carefully align the hypothetical data changes to realistic capital planning and business decisions.

A major benefit for business users lies in the fact that the IF is an exact formula, based on analytic derivations: to understand how capital changes under different scenarios, we need only use the formula, thus avoiding the need to perform extensive simulations that are often resource intensive, subjectively interpreted and inconclusive or inaccurate regarding capital outcomes. Simply put, the IF provides the definitive, exact answer to the question "how will capital requirements change if there is a new loss of US\$50 million in the next quarter? Or just US\$500,000? Or even US\$500 million?"

Fortunately, the IF has a very wide range of application. It can be used with any of the commonly used severity distributions as well as with virtually any estimator of the severity distribution parameters. We illustrate the use of the IF here with the most widely used operational risk severity estimator, the maximum likelihood estimator (MLE). In spite of its known limitations, the MLE continues to be most popular among practitioners and is almost universally accepted by regulatory authorities. The appeal of MLE for estimating the parameters of the severity distribution is its desirable statistical properties when the MLE modelling assumptions are satisfied, that is, when loss data is independent and identically distributed (iid).[13] Under these conditions, MLEs are accurate (asymptotically unbiased), asymptotically normal and maximally efficient (precise).

Under an extensive range of hypothetical changes in the loss data, we apply the IF to the MLEs of the parameters of multiple severity distributions to demonstrate, on both relative and absolute bases, the exact impacts of the data changes on the estimated capital requirements. These are the exact capital sensitivity curves mentioned above. This is extremely valuable information that is useful in two major ways: first, for capital planning, as they are, by definition, exact sensitivity analyses whereby the capital effects of different scenarios, based on hypothetical changes to the underlying loss data, can be seen directly. Scenarios of interest to bank management may be prospective, such as assessing the potential capital impact of hypothetical "tail" events of differing magnitudes, or retrospective, allowing for exact attribution or "but for" analysis to provide insight into the reasons why capital changed the way it did from one quarter to another. Second, statistically, the IF and the capital curves it generates can guide severity estimator choice and development to potentially increase both the robustness and efficiency of the capital distribution (as distinct from the distribution of the severity parameter estimates), while mitigating material bias via previously unidentified but important statistical effects, like Jensen's inequality (Opdyke and Cavallo 2012). Taken together, the IF and its associated exact capital sensitivity curves can not only suggest major potential enhancements to the severity model, but also better inform decision-making and capital planning based on a more precisely and accurately defined risk profile.

So the IF can be used

- as an essential tool to inform estimator choice and development when tackling the fundamental statistical problem of obtaining estimates of a very high percentile of the loss distribution that are more precise, less biased and more robust,

- directly in the capital planning process, once an estimator is selected, to generate corresponding exact capital sensitivity curves.

Opdyke and Cavallo (2012) focus on the former, but in this chapter we focus on the latter, while noting the many benefits associated with a unified methodological framework that relies on the IF for both uses.

In Section 1.2, we describe the basic capital estimation problem under LDA, including a discussion of the empirical challenges of estimating a severity distribution and operational risk capital from historical data. This is followed by a discussion of the M-class estimation framework, as the MLE is an M-class estimator. In Section 1.3, we discuss the IF and its central role in the robust statistics framework, with a focus on how the IF provides a widely accepted and well-established statistical definition of "robustness" (specifically, "B-robustness"). Here we also present the empirical influence function (EIF), and analytically derive the IFs of MLEs of parameters for some of the most commonly used medium-to-heavy-tailed loss severity distributions, both with and without data truncation.[14] In Section 1.4 we review a series of "case studies" to show how the exact capital sensitivity curves arise in real-world situations of relevance to business decision makers. Section 1.5 concludes the chapter with a summary and a discussion of the implications of the results, as well as suggested related topics for future applied research.

1.2 THE CAPITAL ESTIMATION PROBLEM IN OPERATIONAL RISK

The capital estimation problem is generally approached by segmenting risk into suitably homogeneous risk classes, applying the LDA to these risk classes, and then aggregating risk to the enterprise level. Typical stages of a modelling process may include the following.

1. **Unit of measure definition:** historical loss data (which may be internal to the bank or include external data as well) is partitioned or segmented into non-overlapping and homogeneous "units of measure" that share the same basic statistical properties and patterns.

2. **Frequency estimation:** empirical models are developed to describe or estimate the distribution of annual loss frequency in each unit of measure.

3. **Severity estimation:** empirical models for the severity of losses within each unit of measure are developed.

4. **Estimation of aggregate annual loss distributions:** by combining the frequency and severity components within each unit of measure, the distribution of the annual total value of operational losses is computed for each unit of measure.

5. **Top-of-house risk aggregation:** the aggregate annual loss distributions for each unit of measure are combined to represent the enterprise level aggregate annual loss distribution and related capital requirements. The Basel II framework presumes perfect dependence of risk across units of measure as a default assumption, which can be implemented for the VaR risk measures used at the time of this writing by simply summing all the VaR estimates of all the units of measure. A reduction in enterprise level capital can be obtained if an institution can successfully demonstrate that the risks of all the units of measure are less than perfectly dependent. This is often accomplished via correlation matrices or copula models.

1.2.1 The loss distribution approach

The LDA is an actuarial modelling technique widely used to estimate aggregate loss distributions for many types of risk, including operational risk. Total annual loss in unit of measure i is given by

$$S_i = \sum_{j=1}^{n_i} x_{ij}$$

where n_i is the total number of losses in the year for unit of measure i.

In order to estimate the probability distribution of total annual loss amounts, the LDA decomposes the distribution of S_i into its frequency and severity components. The application of the LDA within unit of measure i requires the following fundamental modelling assumptions.

- Annual loss frequency (n_{it}) is iid within unit of measure i with some probability distribution: $n_{it} \sim H_i(\lambda_i)$.

- Each of the n_i individual loss severities (x_{ij}) in unit of measure i are iid with some probability distribution: $x_{ij} \sim F_i(\theta_i)$ with $j = 1, \ldots, n_i$.

- Loss frequency is independent of loss severity.[15]

Existing industry practice is that banks use essentially all available data points for estimating the parameters of the severity distributions in each unit of measure. Some institutions exclude certain individual data points when they are not representative of operational risk exposure on a current or forward-looking basis. Typically, banking supervisors require a substantial level of documentation, justification and internal governance for the exclusion of historical loss events from the estimation samples.[16] The level of scrutiny for excluding external losses is substantially lower than for excluding internal losses.[17]

In contrast, the parameters of the frequency distributions are often estimated on subsets of the available data, for example, the five most recent years of data. Internal data quality considerations may also affect an institution's decision on how many years of loss frequency data to use in estimating frequency parameters.

1.2.2 The setting: empirical challenges to operational risk severity modelling

The very nature of operational loss data makes estimating severity parameters challenging for several reasons.

- **Limited historical data:** observed samples of historical data are quite limited in sample size since systematic collection of operational loss data by banks is a relatively recent development. Sample sizes for the critical low-frequency – high-severity loss events are even smaller.[18]

- **Heterogeneity:** obtaining reasonably large sample sizes for severity modelling necessarily requires making the unit of measure more heterogeneous, either by incorporating external loss data or by pooling internal loss data across multiple product lines, business units, etc.[19] Due to this inherent heterogeneity in the loss data, it is highly improbable that the critical MLE assumptions of iid data are satisfied.

- **Heavy-tailed severity distributions:** operational risk practitioners have observed that parameter estimates for heavy-tailed loss distributions are typically quite unstable and can be extremely sensitive to individual data points. The extreme sensitivity of parameter estimates and capital estimates to large losses is well documented, but the comparable sensitivity, and sometimes even greater sensitivity, of parameter estimates to small losses has been almost completely missed in the literature.[20]

- **Truncated severity distributions:** most institutions collect information on operational losses above a specific data collection threshold. The most common method of accounting for this threshold is to fit truncated severity distributions to the loss data, but truncation creates additional computational complexity and is a major source of parameter (and capital) instability. This is due at least in part to the fact that it creates much more heavy-tailed distributions. Additionally, for some estimators, such as MLE, truncation induces or augments existing covariance between the estimated parameters, which further heightens instability and non-robustness in the parameter estimates (Opdyke and Cavallo 2012).

- **Changing data:** an often underappreciated fact of real-world operational loss event databases is that the data itself evolves over time. Some institutions include specific provisions or reserves to account for this, because over time the severity of some losses may be adjusted upwards or downwards to reflect additional information about the event (events related to litigations of notable durations are common examples).[21] Also, due to the inherent application of judgment in interpreting and applying unit-of-measure classification schemes, individual loss events can even be reclassified into other business lines or event types as additional loss-event details are discovered or understood. As a result, business users of operational risk capital estimates have a strong need for a well-defined, theoretically justified and easily implemented tool to assess potential capital needs for certain hypothetical data changes, because in practice, such changes happen all the time, even without considering new loss events in each new quarter.

1.2.3   M-class estimation

Maximum likelihood estimation is among the class of M-class estimators, so called because they generalise "maximum" likelihood estimation. M-class estimators include a wide range of statistical models for which the optimal values of the parameters are determined by computing sums of sample quantities. The general form of the estimator in Equation 1.1 is extremely flexible and can accommodate a wide range of objective functions, including the MLE approach and various robust estimators

$$\hat{\theta}_M = \arg\min_{\theta \in \Theta} \sum_{i=1}^{n} \rho(x_i, \theta) \qquad (1.1)$$

Assuming the regularity conditions commonly assumed when using MLE,[22] all M-class estimators are asymptotically normal and consistent (asymptotically unbiased),[23] which are very useful properties for statistical inference.

Maximum likelihood estimation is considered a "classical" approach to parameter estimation from a frequentist perspective. In the Basel II framework, MLE is the typical choice for estimating the parameters of severity distributions in operational risk.[24] To maintain its desirable statistical properties (described below), MLE requires the following assumptions.

(A1) **Independence:** individual loss severities are statistically independent from one another.

(A2) **Homogeneity:** loss severities are identically distributed within a unit of measure (perfect homogeneity).

(A3) **Correct model:** the probability model of the severity distribution is correctly specified (this is distinct from the model's parameters, which must be estimated).

Under these restrictive and idealised textbook assumptions, MLE is known to be not only asymptotically unbiased ("consistent") and asymptotically normal, but also asymptotically efficient.[25] Given an iid sample of losses $(x_1, x_2, \ldots, x_n)$ and knowledge of the "true" family of the probability density function $f(x \mid \theta)$ (that is, knowledge of the probability density function (PDF), but not its parameter values), the MLE parameter estimates are the values of $\hat{\theta}_{MLE}$ that maximise the likelihood function, or equivalently, that minimise the objective function $\rho(x, \theta)$.

The MLE estimator is an M-class estimator with

$$\rho(x, \theta) = -\ln[f(x \mid \theta)]$$

so

$$\hat{\theta}_{\text{MLE}} = \arg\min_{\theta \in \Theta} \sum_{i=1}^{n} \rho(x_i, \theta) = \arg\min_{\theta \in \Theta} \sum_{i-1}^{n} -\ln f(x_i \mid \theta) \qquad (1.2)$$

An equivalent expression is obtained by maximising the usual log-likelihood function

$$\hat{l}(\theta \mid x_1, x_2, \ldots, x_n) = \ln[L(\theta \mid x)] = \sum_{i=1}^{n} \ln[f(x_i \mid \theta)]$$

so

$$\hat{\theta}_{\text{MLE}} = \arg\max_{\theta \in \Theta}[\hat{l}(\theta \mid x_1, x_2, \ldots, x_n)] \qquad (1.3)$$

An objective assessment of real-world operational risk data must acknowledge that each one of the key assumptions required for MLEs to retain their desirable statistical properties (asymptotic efficiency, asymptotic normality and consistency) is unlikely to hold in practice.

(A1) **Independence:** if the severity of operational losses has both deterministic and stochastic components, operational losses by definition fail to be independent due to common determinants. For example, systematic differences in loss severity may be explained by event characteristics such as geography, legal system, client segment, time period effects, etc.[26] The impact of potential failures of the independence assumption is beyond the scope of this chapter, but is known to be nontrivial (Van Belle 2002, pp. 7–11).

(A2) **Identically distributed:** because a unit of measure typically pools internal loss events from multiple business processes that undoubtedly have different data-generating processes, achieving perfect homogeneity, as required by MLE, is virtually impossible. The pooling of internal and external loss data for severity modelling further augments heterogeneity. Each institution's operational risk profile is unique and is moderated by its specific characteristics: the specific combination of products and service offerings, technology, policies, internal controls, culture, risk appetite, scale of operation, governance and other factors. Understanding the behaviour of severity estimates and capital estimates when confronted with both modest and extreme deviations from perfectly homogeneous data is the central focus of this chapter.

(A3) **Correctly specified model:** MLE has desirable asymptotic statistical properties only when the correct form of the loss distribution is "known" and correctly specified. Under idealised iid data conditions, MLE remains consistent, asymptotically efficient, and asymptotically normal, but if there is the possibility (probability) that some losses do not come from the statistical distribution assumed by the model, then MLE can perform poorly, losing most or all of these desirable statistical qualities. This has been shown in the literature (Dupuis 1999; Opdyke and Cavallo 2012) and is consistent with findings presented in the following sections of this chapter.

1.3 THE INFLUENCE FUNCTION AND THE "ROBUST STATISTICS" FRAMEWORK

Robust statistics is a general approach to estimation that explicitly recognises and accounts for the fact that all statistical models are by necessity idealised and simplified approximations of complex realities. As a result, a key objective of the robust statistics framework is to bound or limit the influence on parameter estimates of a small to moderate number of data points in the sample which happen to deviate from the assumed statistical model. Since actual operational loss data samples generated by real-world processes do not exactly follow mathematically convenient textbook assumptions (eg, all data points are not perfectly iid, and rarely, if ever, exactly follow parametric distributions), this framework would appear to be well suited for operational risk severity modelling.

The IF is central to the robust statistics framework, the theory behind which is very well developed and has been in use for almost half a century. Some of the seminal theoretical results that established the field of robust statistics include Tukey (1960), Huber (1964) and Hampel (1968). Classic textbooks on robust statistics such as Huber (1981) and Hampel *et al* (1986) have been widely used for more than 30 years. The dramatic increases in computing power since the 1990s have also enabled the theoretical development and practical use of computationally intensive methods for computing robust statistics.[27] Robust statistics have been widely used in many different applications, including the analysis of extreme values arising from both natural phenomena and financial outcomes.[28] These applications of robust statistics use many of the medium-to-heavy-tailed loss distributions of greatest relevance in operational risk. A unified approach to comparing the relative merits of robust statistics and classical statistics, both in terms of parameter estimation, directly, and capital estimation, ultimately, can be made with the IF. This is the focus of Opdyke and Cavallo (2012), but this chapter focuses on the application of the IF to MLE-based estimates of capital to better inform business decision-making.

1.3.1 The influence function

The IF is an essential tool from the robust statistics framework that allows researchers to analytically determine and describe the sensitivity of parameter estimates to arbitrary deviations from the assumed statistical model. The IF can be thought of as indicating the impact of a marginal deviation at severity amount x on the parameter estimates. Simply put, it answers the question: "how does the parameter estimate change when the data sample changes with a new loss of amount = USx?"

One requirement of the IF is that the estimator being assessed is expressed as a statistical functional, that is, as a function of the assumed distribution of the model $T(F(y, \theta)) = T(F)$, where $F(y, \theta)$ is the assumed severity distribution. Fortunately, almost all relevant estimators can be expressed as statistical functionals. Common examples are the first and second moments of a known distribution $F(y, \theta)$ as

$$m_1 = T_1(F(y, \theta)) = \int y \, dF(y, \theta) = \int y f(y, \theta) \, dy$$

and

$$m_2 = T_2(F(y, \theta)) = \int y^2 \, dF(y, \theta) = \int y^2 f(y, \theta) \, dy$$

respectively.

The IF is an analytic formula for assessing this impact of an infinitesimal deviation from the assumed distribution occurring at a severity amount of x

$$\begin{aligned} \text{IF}(x; T, F) &= \lim_{\varepsilon \to 0} \left[\frac{T\{(1 - \varepsilon)F + \varepsilon\delta_x\} - T(F)}{\varepsilon} \right] \\ &= \lim_{\varepsilon \to 0} \left[\frac{T(F_\varepsilon) - T(F)}{\varepsilon} \right] \end{aligned}$$ (1.4)

where

- $F(y, \theta) = F(\cdot)$ is the assumed severity distribution,
- $T(F(y, \theta)) = T(F)$ is the statistical functional for the specified estimator under the assumed distribution,
- x is the location of the deviation,
- ε is the fraction of data that is deviating,
- δ_x is the cumulative distribution function of the Dirac delta function D_x, a probability measure that puts mass 1 at the point x

$$D_x(y) = \begin{cases} 1 & \text{if } y = x \\ 0 & \text{otherwise} \end{cases}$$

and

$$\delta_x(y) = \begin{cases} 1 & \text{if } y \geqslant x \\ 0 & \text{otherwise} \end{cases}$$

- $T\{(1 - \varepsilon)F + \varepsilon\delta_x\} = T(F_\varepsilon)$ is simply the estimator evaluated with contamination.[29]

The IF has a simple and direct interpretation as the difference between the parameter estimates when the data sample is "contaminated", that is, having distribution F_ε which is "contaminated" by a new loss amount x, and the parameter estimates under the assumed distribution, F (with no "contamination"); this difference is then normalised by the amount of contamination, ε. This framework allows us to compare the exact asymptotic behaviour of a selected estimator across a range of arbitrary data deviations, or even make comparisons across multiple estimators, when faced with less-than-ideal, non-textbook data, regardless of the nature of the deviating data (ie, regardless of the distribution from which the "contamination" or "arbitrary deviation" came). By systematically varying the location of the arbitrary deviation (x) the impact of data contamination from any distribution can be assessed. The IF is an asymptotic result because it is the limiting value as the amount of deviating data approaches zero (or equivalently, as the sample size increases without bound, since ε is a function of the number of contaminated data points).[30] The IF is an extremely powerful tool with many uses and serves as the foundation for our analytic approach to capital sensitivity analysis using hypothetical scenarios based on changes in loss data.[31]

1.3.2 The empirical influence function

Often used in conjunction with the IF, the EIF is simply the finite sample approximation of the IF, that is, the IF applied to the empirical distribution of the data sample at hand. Arbitrary deviations, x, are used in the same way to trace the EIF as a function of x, and since the empirical distribution is used, typically $\varepsilon = 1/n$. So, to define the EIF, we use Equation 1.4 with the empirical cumulative distribution function, so $F(\cdot) = \hat{F}(\cdot)$

$$\text{EIF}(x; T, \hat{F}) = \lim_{\varepsilon \to 0} \left[\frac{T\{(1 - \varepsilon)\hat{F} + \varepsilon\delta_x\} - T(\hat{F})}{\varepsilon} \right]$$

$$= \lim_{\varepsilon \to 0} \left[\frac{T(\hat{F}_\varepsilon) - T(\hat{F})}{\varepsilon} \right] \quad (1.5)$$

where all terms agree with Equation 1.4 except that practical application dictates that $\varepsilon = 1/n$ (so $\varepsilon \to 0$ still as $n \to \infty$)

Because EIF converges to IF quickly, that is, even with relatively small sample sizes, EIF is a good practical tool for validating IF derivations, or for approximating IF for other reasons (we show examples of this in practice later in the chapter, and this is one of the reasons it is good practice to implement EIF and IF simultaneously).

1.3.3 B-robustness

The entire point of robust statistics is to obtain reliable estimates of a parametric model even when the assumed model is only approximately correct, specifically, when some of the data may come from a different underlying distribution than the bulk of the data. The definitions of the IF suggest a simple and useful definition of "robustness" to such deviating data points. An estimator is said to be "B-robust" for the distribution $F(\cdot)$ if the IF is bounded (meaning it does not diverge towards $\pm\infty$) over the domain of $F(\cdot)$. If the IF is not bounded, then the estimator is not "B-robust" for a particular parameter of distribution $F(\cdot)$.[32] When the IF is unbounded, on the other hand, an arbitrary deviant data point can result in meaningless or practically unusable parameter estimates, such as when parameter estimates become arbitrarily large or small (ie, divergent toward $\pm\infty$). This type of extreme sensitivity of parameter estimates is precisely the type of "bias" that can result from heterogeneous data.

A comparison of the influence functions of two estimators of central tendency, the mean and the median, is useful for illustrating the concept of B-robustness. Assume that the data follows a standard normal distribution, $F = \Phi$. The statistical functional for the mean is

$$T(F) = \int y \, dF(y) = \int yf(y) \, dy$$

so to derive the IF of the mean, we have

$$
\begin{aligned}
\mathrm{IF}(x; T, F) &= \lim_{\varepsilon \to 0} \left[\frac{T(F_\varepsilon) - T(F)}{\varepsilon} \right] \\
&= \lim_{\varepsilon \to 0} \left[\frac{T\{(1 - \varepsilon)F + \varepsilon\delta_x\} - T(F)}{\varepsilon} \right] \\
&= \lim_{\varepsilon \to 0} \left[\frac{\int y \, d\{(1 - \varepsilon)\Phi + \varepsilon\delta_x\}(y) - \int y \, d\Phi(y)}{\varepsilon} \right] \\
&= \lim_{\varepsilon \to 0} \left[\frac{(1 - \varepsilon)\int y \, d\Phi(y) + \varepsilon \int y \, d\delta_x(y) - \int y \, d\Phi(y)}{\varepsilon} \right] \\
&= \lim_{\varepsilon \to 0} \left[\frac{\varepsilon x}{\varepsilon} \right]
\end{aligned}
$$

because

$$\int u \, d\Phi(u) = 0$$

so

$$\mathrm{IF}(x; T, F) = x \tag{1.6}$$

From the mathematical derivation above, it is evident that the IF for the mean of a standard normal random variable is unbounded. As the point of arbitrary deviation (x) increases to $+\infty$, so does the IF and, as a result, the mean becomes arbitrarily large and meaningless. Similarly, as the point of deviation decreases to $-\infty$, the IF does as well, and the mean becomes arbitrarily small and meaningless.

Figure 1.1 displays the IFs of the mean and median of a standard normal distribution.[33] Consistent with the mathematical derivation above, the IF for the mean has a positive slope of 1 and increases without bound in both directions. In contrast, the IF for the median is bounded and never tends to $\pm\infty$.

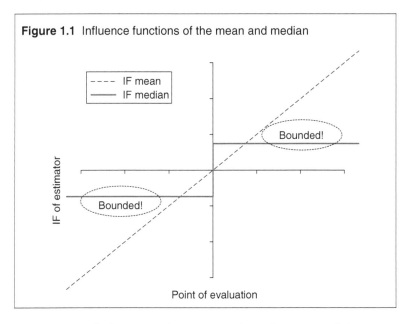

Figure 1.1 Influence functions of the mean and median

As expected, the non-robustness and B-robustness of the mean and median, respectively, hold even when the $F(\cdot)$ is not the standard normal distribution, as shown below for the mean

$$
\begin{aligned}
\text{IF}(x; T, F) &= \lim_{\varepsilon \to 0} \left[\frac{(1 - \varepsilon) \int y \, dF(y) + \varepsilon \int y \, d\delta_x(y) - \int y \, dF(y)}{\varepsilon} \right] \\
&= \lim_{\varepsilon \to 0} \left[\frac{\varepsilon x - \varepsilon \mu}{\varepsilon} \right] \\
&= x - \mu
\end{aligned}
$$

where μ is the mean, so

$$
\text{IF}(x; T, F) = x - \mu
$$

As should now be apparent from the above, estimators that are not B-robust run the very real risk of generating capital estimates that, due to unanticipated, unmeasured, or unmeasurable heterogeneity (even if it is relatively small), are extremely "biased" relative to those that would be generated by the assumed severity distribution of the model, and potentially grossly inflated. The IF is the analytic tool to use to identify such conditions. In the next section, we present the formula for the IF for M-class estimators generally and MLE specifically. We use this to derive and present the MLE IFs of parameters of specific and widely used severity distributions in operational risk.

The capital estimates based on these estimators are then generated and assessed, with one criterion for evaluation being whether they are B-robust, and how this robustness, or lack thereof, affects capital estimation from the standpoint of practical implementation.

1.3.4 The influence function for M-class estimators

M-class estimators generally are defined as any estimator

$$T_n = T_n(X_1, \ldots, X_n)$$

whose optimised objective function satisfies $\sum_{i=1}^{n} \varphi(X_i, T_n) = 0$ or, equivalently,

$$\sum_{i=1}^{n} \rho(X_i, T_n) = \min_{T_n}!$$

where

$$\varphi(x, \theta) = \frac{\partial \rho(x, \theta)}{\partial \theta}$$

is the derivative of ρ, which is defined over $\wp \times \Theta$, the sample space and parameter space, respectively.

The first-order conditions for this optimisation problem are

$$\varphi(x, \theta) = \frac{\partial \rho(x, \theta)}{\partial \theta} = 0$$

The second-order conditions are satisfied when the Hessian of the objective function

$$\varphi'_\theta(x, \theta) = \frac{\partial \varphi_\theta(x, \theta)}{\partial \theta}$$

is positive definite.[34]

Hampel *et al* (1986) show that, conveniently, the IF for all M-class estimators is

$$\text{IF}_\theta(x; \theta, T) = \frac{\varphi_\theta(x, \theta)}{- \int_a^b \varphi'_\theta(y, \theta) \, dF(y)} \tag{1.7}$$

where a and b are the end points of support for the distribution. When multiple parameters are being estimated, as with most operational risk severity distributions, the possibility of (non-zero) parameter covariance must be taken into account with the matrix form of

Equation 1.7 as shown in

$$\text{IF}_\theta(x; \theta, T) = A(\theta)^{-1} \varphi_\theta$$

$$= \begin{bmatrix} -\int_a^b \dfrac{\partial \varphi_{\theta_1}}{\partial \theta_1} dF(y) & -\int_a^b \dfrac{\partial \varphi_{\theta_1}}{\partial \theta_2} dF(y) \\ -\int_a^b \dfrac{\partial \varphi_{\theta_2}}{\partial \theta_1} dF(y) & -\int_a^b \dfrac{\partial \varphi_{\theta_2}}{\partial \theta_2} dF(y) \end{bmatrix}^{-1} \begin{bmatrix} \varphi_{\theta_1} \\ \varphi_{\theta_2} \end{bmatrix}$$

$$(1.8)$$

(Stefanski and Boos 2002).

1.3.5 The influence function for maximum likelihood estimators

MLE is an M-class estimator with objective function

$$\rho(x, \theta) = -\ln[f(x, \theta)]$$

In this case, the derivative of the objective function with respect to the parameters is simply the negative of the score function

$$\varphi_\theta(x, \theta) = \frac{\partial \rho(x, \theta)}{\partial \theta} = -\left(\frac{\partial f(x, \theta)}{\partial \theta}\right) \frac{1}{f(x, \theta)}$$

and the Hessian is

$$\varphi'_\theta(x, \theta) = \frac{\partial \varphi_\theta(x, \theta)}{\partial \theta}$$

$$= \frac{\partial^2 \rho(x, \theta)}{\partial \theta^2}$$

$$= \left(-\frac{\partial^2 f(x, \theta)}{\partial \theta^2} f(x, \theta) + \left[\frac{\partial f(x, \theta)}{\partial \theta}\right]^2\right) \frac{1}{[f(x, \theta)]^2}$$

So for the specific case of MLE, the IF shown in Equation 1.7 and Equation 1.8 is simply the score function normalised by its variance (the negative of the expected value of the second-order derivative, or the Fisher information). And, as noted above, in this setting it is important to note and account for potential covariance of the severity distribution's parameters by evaluating the cross-partial-derivative terms for each parameter in Equation 1.8. This is shown below to sometimes have very large and even counterintuitive effects on the estimators under common conditions. The IF is the tool that can establish such effects, definitively, as the analytic behaviour of the estimators, and not as an uncertain function of simulations that can be misspecified or subjectively interpreted, with inferences resting largely on the specific and narrow ranges of input parameter values. This is one of the tremendous advantages of using IF: it is an analytic derivation describing the exact behaviour of the estimator under any degree of arbitrary deviation from the assumed severity distribution. Not only is the more accurate than any simulation could be, but it makes behavioural simulations moot because it is the formulaic answer to the question: "exactly how does the parameter estimate change when loss event x is added to my sample of loss data?" And regarding the possible "B-robustness" of the MLE(s) for a specific distribution, this can be determined, based on the above, simply by determining whether the score function is bounded, as long as it is monotonic over the relevant domain (Huber 1981).

1.3.6 The influence function for MLEs of truncated severity distributions

Most banks record losses only above a certain threshold H (typically $H = $ US\$5,000, US\$10,000 or €20,000 for the case of some external consortium data), so data on smaller losses generally is not available. The reason for this is that many business processes at a financial institution generate large numbers of operational loss events with *de minimis* impact that do not threaten bank solvency. It is much more efficient for banks to gather operational loss data on the smaller set of operational loss events that have material impact on earnings, may threaten bank solvency, may generate reputational risk and/or may be preventable with appropriate changes in bank policies and procedures.

When data is collected subject to a data collection threshold, the most widely accepted and used method to account for incomplete observation of the data sample is to assume that losses below the threshold follow the same parametric loss distribution, $f(\cdot)$, as those above it, whereby the severity distribution becomes $g(\cdot)$, a (left) truncated distribution, with PDF and cumulative distribution function (CDF)

$$g(x, \theta, H) = \frac{f(x, \theta)}{1 - F(H, \theta)} \quad \text{and} \quad G(x, \theta, H) = 1 - \frac{1 - F(x, \theta)}{1 - F(H, \theta)}$$

Under truncation, the terms of the IF for the MLE estimator now become

$$\rho(x, \theta) = -\ln(g(x, \theta)) = -\ln\left(\frac{f(x, \theta)}{1 - F(H, \theta)}\right)$$
$$= -\ln(f(x, \theta)) + \ln(1 - F(H, \theta))$$

$$\varphi_\theta(x, H, \theta) = \frac{\partial \rho(x, \theta)}{\partial \theta}$$

$$= -\frac{1}{f(x, \theta)} \left(\frac{\partial f(x, \theta)}{\partial \theta} \right) - \frac{1}{1 - F(H, \theta)} \left(\frac{\partial F(H, \theta)}{\partial \theta} \right)$$

and

$$\varphi'_\theta(x, H, \theta) = \frac{\partial \varphi_\theta(x, H, \theta)}{\partial \theta} = \frac{\partial^2 \rho(x, \theta)}{\partial \theta^2}$$

$$= \frac{-\dfrac{\partial^2 f(x, \theta)}{\partial \theta^2} f(x, \theta) + \left[\dfrac{\partial f(x, \theta)}{\partial \theta} \right]^2}{[f(x, \theta)]^2}$$

$$+ \frac{-\dfrac{\partial^2 F(H, \theta)}{\partial \theta^2} [1 - F(H, \theta)] - \left[\dfrac{\partial F(H, \theta)}{\partial \theta} \right]^2}{[1 - F(H, \theta)]^2}.$$

When the severity distribution has only one parameter, the general form of the IF is

$$\text{IF}_\theta(x; \theta, T)$$
$$= \left(-\frac{\partial f(x, \theta)/\partial \theta}{f(x, \theta)} - \frac{\partial F(H, \theta)/\partial \theta}{1 - F(H, \theta)} \right)$$
$$\times \left(-\frac{1}{1 - F(H, \theta)} \int_a^b \frac{[\partial f(y, \theta)/\partial \theta]^2 - (\partial^2 f(y, \theta)/\partial \theta^2) f(y, \theta)}{f(y, \theta)} \, dy \right.$$
$$\left. + \frac{[\partial F(H, \theta)/\partial \theta]^2 + (\partial^2 F(H, \theta)/\partial \theta^2)[1 - F(H, \theta)]}{[1 - F(H, \theta)]^2} \right)^{-1}$$

$$(1.9)$$

where a and b define the end points of support, which are now H and (for all relevant severity distributions) $+\infty$, respectively. When the severity distribution has more than one parameter, the IF has the general form

$$\text{IF}_\theta(x; \theta, T) = A(\theta)^{-1} \varphi_\theta$$

$$= \left[\begin{matrix} -\int_a^b \dfrac{\partial \varphi_{\theta_1}}{\partial \theta_1} \, dG(y) - \int_a^b \dfrac{\partial \varphi_{\theta_1}}{\partial \theta_2} \, dG(y) \\ -\int_a^b \dfrac{\partial \varphi_{\theta_2}}{\partial \theta_1} \, dG(y) - \int_a^b \dfrac{\partial \varphi_{\theta_2}}{\partial \theta_2} \, dG(y) \end{matrix} \right]^{-1} \begin{bmatrix} \varphi_{\theta_1} \\ \varphi_{\theta_2} \end{bmatrix}$$

$$(1.10)$$

The structure of the multi-parameter (typically two-parameter) version of the IF does not change from Equation 1.8 except that the differential, of course, corresponds with the CDF of the truncated severity distribution, $G(\cdot)$.

Comparing Equations 1.7 and 1.9, we can see that the numerator of the IF of a truncated distribution is simply a shift of the score function for the non-truncated distribution, and the magnitude of the shift depends on the threshold H and the parameter values θ, but not on the location of the arbitrary deviation x. The denominator of the IF for a truncated distribution differs substantially from that of its non-truncated distribution. The expected value of the Hessian is computed over the truncated domain (H, ∞), multiplied by a truncation constant, and added to an additional constant term in each second derivative. As is the case for the φ function, the constant terms depend on the threshold H and the parameter values θ, but not on the location of the arbitrary deviation x. These changes in the Fisher information matrix (relative to the non-truncated case) fundamentally alter the correlation structure of the parameters of the distribution, introducing dependence or magnifying it if already present before truncation.

Even when analysing data collected with a data collection threshold, the MLE IF is an analytically determined function given an assumed distribution and parameter values. With it, no simulation is required to assess the behaviour of MLE parameter estimators because this remains a definitive, analytic result. All that is required to perform the analysis is the calculation of the derivatives and integration in Equations 1.7 and 1.8 or Equations 1.9 and 1.10, and these derivatives, of course, differ for each different severity distribution. So for each severity distribution, we must calculate

$$\frac{\partial f(y;\theta)}{\partial \theta_1}, \quad \frac{\partial f(y;\theta)}{\partial \theta_2}, \quad \frac{\partial^2 f(y;\theta)}{\partial \theta_1 \partial \theta_2}, \quad \frac{\partial^2 f(y;\theta)}{\partial \theta_1^2} \quad \text{and} \quad \frac{\partial^2 f(y;\theta)}{\partial \theta_2^2}$$

and under truncation, also calculate

$$\frac{\partial F(H;\theta)}{\partial \theta_1}, \quad \frac{\partial F(H;\theta)}{\partial \theta_2}, \quad \frac{\partial^2 F(H;\theta)}{\partial \theta_1 \partial \theta_2}, \quad \frac{\partial^2 F(H;\theta)}{\partial \theta_1^2} \quad \text{and} \quad \frac{\partial^2 F(H;\theta)}{\partial \theta_2^2}$$

(the derivatives of the cumulative distribution function with respect to the parameters can be computed using Leibniz's rule). Once this is done, Equations 1.8 and 1.10 apply to all non-truncated and truncated severity distributions, respectively, which is very convenient as it makes calculations and testing for multiple severity distributions considerably easier.

1.3.7 The IF for lognormal, log-Gamma and GPD distributions, with and without truncation

Using the analytic formulas for the IF under MLE estimation in Equation 1.8 and Equation 1.10, we summarise below the key mathematical results to obtain the IF for the parameters of the lognormal, log-Gamma and GPD distributions when there is no truncation. The same results under truncation can be found in the appendix. Complete derivations for all IFs can be found in Opdyke and Cavallo (2012). Below we also present figures, for all six truncated and non-truncated cases, of all the IFs and the EIFs, so the behaviour of the former and the convergence of the latter are clear.

Lognormal

The PDF and CDF of the lognormal distribution are defined as

$$f(x; \mu, \sigma) = \frac{1}{\sqrt{2\pi}\sigma x} \exp\left(-\frac{1}{2}\left(\frac{\ln(x) - \mu}{\sigma}\right)^2\right)$$

and

$$F(x; \mu, \sigma) = \frac{1}{2}\left[1 + \mathrm{erf}\left(\frac{\ln(x) - \mu}{\sqrt{2\sigma^2}}\right)\right]$$

for $0 < x < \infty, 0 < \sigma$.

Inserting the derivatives of

$$\frac{\partial f(y; \theta)}{\partial \theta_1}, \quad \frac{\partial f(y; \theta)}{\partial \theta_2}, \quad \frac{\partial^2 f(y; \theta)}{\partial \theta_1 \partial \theta_2}, \quad \frac{\partial^2 f(y; \theta)}{\partial \theta_1^2} \quad \text{and} \quad \frac{\partial^2 f(y; \theta)}{\partial \theta_2^2}$$

into the Fisher information yields

$$A(\theta) = \begin{bmatrix} \dfrac{-1}{\sigma^2} & 0 \\ 0 & \dfrac{-2}{\sigma^2} \end{bmatrix}$$

and into the psi function yields

$$\varphi_\theta = \begin{bmatrix} \dfrac{\mu - \ln(x)}{\sigma^2} \\ \dfrac{1}{\sigma} - \dfrac{(\ln(x) - \mu)^2}{\sigma^3} \end{bmatrix}$$

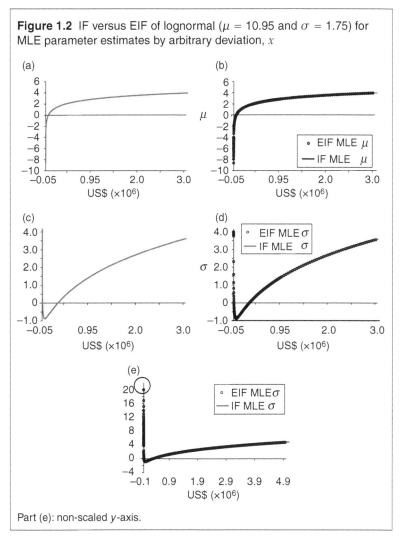

Figure 1.2 IF versus EIF of lognormal ($\mu = 10.95$ and $\sigma = 1.75$) for MLE parameter estimates by arbitrary deviation, x

Part (e): non-scaled y-axis.

So, via Equation 1.8 the IF of the MLE parameters of the lognormal severity is

$$\mathrm{IF}_\theta(x; \theta, T) = A(\theta)^{-1}\varphi_\theta = \begin{bmatrix} -\sigma^2 & 0 \\ 0 & \dfrac{-\sigma^2}{2} \end{bmatrix} \begin{bmatrix} \dfrac{\mu - \ln(x)}{\sigma^2} \\ \dfrac{1}{\sigma} - \dfrac{(\ln(x) - \mu)^2}{\sigma^3} \end{bmatrix}$$

$$= \begin{bmatrix} \ln(x) - \mu \\ \dfrac{(\ln(x) - \mu)^2 - \sigma^2}{2\sigma} \end{bmatrix} \qquad (1.11)$$

Importantly, note that the zero cross derivatives in $A(\theta)$ indicate parameter independence in x, which is discussed further below.

This result (see Equation 1.11) for the lognormal is well known. Graphs of the IF for the MLE parameters of the lognormal severity (with $\mu = 10.95$ and $\sigma = 1.75$), compared with their EIF counterparts, are shown in Figure 1.2.

First, note, as mentioned above, the quick convergence of EIF to IF even for not very large n (here, $n = 250$). Second, note the asymptotic behaviour of both μ and σ as $x \to 0^+$: according to Equation 1.11, $\mu \to -\infty$ and $\sigma \to +\infty$. But note that $\sigma \to +\infty$ at a much faster rate because of the squared term in the numerator of its IF, so this would indicate a capital estimate tends to $+\infty$ as $x \to 0^+$, that is, a larger and larger capital estimate caused by smaller and smaller arbitrary deviations in the left tail. This is an important, counter-intuitive result shown previously only in Opdyke and Cavallo (2012), which we shall explore more in the next section when we present the exact capital sensitivity curves.

Log-Gamma

We present the same derivations below for the log-Gamma[35]

$$f(x; a, b) = \frac{b^a (\log(x))^{a-1}}{\Gamma(a) x^{b+1}}$$

and

$$F(x; a, b) = \frac{b^a}{\Gamma(a)} \int_{\ln(0^+)}^{\ln(x)} y^{a-1} \exp(-yb) \, dy$$

for $0 < x < \infty, 0 < a, 0 < b$.

Inserting the derivatives of

$$\frac{\partial f(y; \theta)}{\partial \theta_1}, \quad \frac{\partial f(y; \theta)}{\partial \theta_2}, \quad \frac{\partial^2 f(y; \theta)}{\partial \theta_1 \partial \theta_2}, \quad \frac{\partial^2 f(y; \theta)}{\partial \theta_1^2} \quad \text{and} \quad \frac{\partial^2 f(y; \theta)}{\partial \theta_2^2}$$

into the Fisher information yields

$$A(\theta) = \begin{bmatrix} -\psi_1(a) & \dfrac{1}{b} \\ \dfrac{1}{b} & \dfrac{-a}{b^2} \end{bmatrix}$$

and into the psi function yields

$$\varphi_\theta = \begin{bmatrix} -\ln(b) - \ln(\ln(x)) + \psi_0(a) \\ -\dfrac{a}{b} + \ln(x) \end{bmatrix}$$

where ψ_0 is the digamma function and ψ_1 is the trigamma function. So via Equation 1.8 the IF of the MLE parameters of the log-Gamma severity is

$$\text{IF}_\theta(x; \theta, T)$$
$$= A(\theta)^{-1}\varphi_\theta$$

$$= \frac{1}{(-a/b^2)(-\psi_1(a)) - 1/b^2} \begin{bmatrix} \dfrac{-a}{b^2} & \dfrac{-1}{b} \\ \dfrac{-1}{b} & -\psi_1(a) \end{bmatrix}$$

$$\times \begin{bmatrix} -\ln(b) - \ln(\ln(x)) + \psi_0(a) \\ -\dfrac{a}{b} + \ln(x) \end{bmatrix}$$

$$= \begin{bmatrix} \dfrac{a/b^2[\ln(b) + \ln(\ln(x)) - \psi_0(a)] - (1/b)[\ln(x) - (a/b)]}{\psi_1(a)(a/b^2) - (1/b^2)} \\ \\ \dfrac{(1/b)[\ln(b) + \ln(\ln(x)) - \psi_0(a)] - \psi_1(a)[\ln(x) - (a/b)]}{\psi_1(a)(a/b^2) - 1/b^2} \end{bmatrix}$$

$$(1.12)$$

Importantly, note that the non-zero cross derivatives in $A(\theta)$ indicate parameter dependence in x, the effects of which are discussed below.

Graphs of the IF for the MLE parameters of the log-Gamma severity (with $a = 35.5$ and $b = 3.25$), compared with their EIF counterparts, are shown in Figure 1.3.

Note again the quick, if imperfect, convergence of EIF to IF even for not very large n ($n = 250$). Secondly, note the asymptotic behaviour of both a and b as $x \to 1^+$: $a \to -\infty$ and $b \to -\infty$, which we can see in Figures 1.3 and 1.4, where the y-axis is not scaled. But note that, while smaller a indicates smaller quantiles for the log-Gamma, smaller b indicates larger quantiles for the log-Gamma. What does this mean for capital estimation (which is essentially a high quantile estimate of the severity distribution)? The effect of the b term in Equation 1.12 ends up dominating that of the a term because of the relative size of the constants in the numerators of both terms, and estimated capital tends to $+\infty$ as $x \to 1^+$; that is, like the lognormal, a larger and larger capital estimate results from a smaller and smaller arbitrary deviation in the left tail: again, a counterintuitive result and, as we shall see in the next section, a very important one.

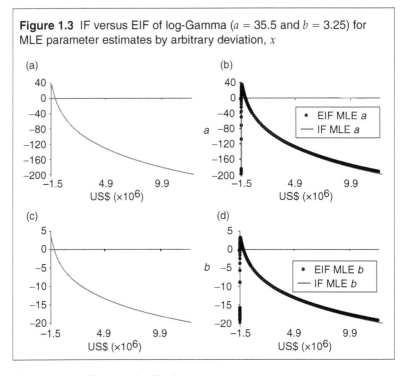

Figure 1.3 IF versus EIF of log-Gamma ($a = 35.5$ and $b = 3.25$) for MLE parameter estimates by arbitrary deviation, x

Generalised Pareto distribution

For the GPD severity, we have

$$f(x; \varepsilon, \beta) = \frac{1}{\beta}\left[1 + \varepsilon\frac{x}{\beta}\right]^{[-(1/\varepsilon)-1]}$$

and

$$F(x; \varepsilon, \beta) = 1 - \left[1 + \varepsilon\frac{x}{\beta}\right]^{[-1/\varepsilon]}$$

for $0 \leqslant x < \infty$, $0 < \beta$ assuming $\varepsilon > 0$ (which is appropriate in this setting).

Inserting the derivatives of

$$\frac{\partial f(y; \theta)}{\partial \theta_1}, \quad \frac{\partial f(y; \theta)}{\partial \theta_2}, \quad \frac{\partial^2 f(y; \theta)}{\partial \theta_1 \partial \theta_2}, \quad \frac{\partial^2 f(y; \theta)}{\partial \theta_1^2} \quad \text{and} \quad \frac{\partial^2 f(y; \theta)}{\partial \theta_2^2}$$

into the cells of the Fisher information

$$A(\theta) = \begin{bmatrix} -\int_a^b \frac{\partial \varphi_{\theta_1}}{\partial \theta_1}\, \mathrm{d}F(y) & -\int_a^b \frac{\partial \varphi_{\theta_1}}{\partial \theta_2}\, \mathrm{d}F(y) \\ -\int_a^b \frac{\partial \varphi_{\theta_2}}{\partial \theta_1}\, \mathrm{d}F(y) & -\int_a^b \frac{\partial \varphi_{\theta_2}}{\partial \theta_2}\, \mathrm{d}F(y) \end{bmatrix}$$

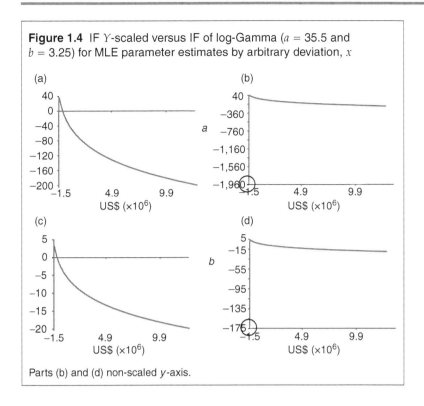

Figure 1.4 IF Y-scaled versus IF of log-Gamma ($a = 35.5$ and $b = 3.25$) for MLE parameter estimates by arbitrary deviation, x

Parts (b) and (d) non-scaled y-axis.

yields

$$-\int_0^\infty \frac{\partial \varphi_\varepsilon}{\partial \varepsilon} \, \mathrm{d}F(x)$$

$$= -\int_0^\infty \left[\frac{x\beta + 2\varepsilon x^2 + \varepsilon^2 x^2}{(\beta\varepsilon + \varepsilon^2 x)^2} \right.$$

$$\left. + \frac{x}{(\beta + \varepsilon x)\varepsilon^2} - \frac{2\ln(1 + \varepsilon x/\beta)}{\varepsilon^3} \right] f(x) \, \mathrm{d}x$$

$$-\int_0^\infty \frac{\partial \varphi_\beta}{\partial \beta} \, \mathrm{d}F(x)$$

$$= -\int_0^\infty \left[\frac{1}{\beta^2} - \frac{x(1 + \varepsilon)(2\beta + \varepsilon x)}{(\beta^2 + \beta\varepsilon x)^2} \right] f(x) \, \mathrm{d}x$$

$$-\int_0^\infty \frac{\partial \varphi_\varepsilon}{\partial \beta} \, \mathrm{d}F(x)$$

$$= -\int_0^\infty \frac{\partial \varphi_\beta}{\partial \varepsilon} \, \mathrm{d}F(x)$$

$$= -\int_0^\infty \left[\frac{x}{\beta\varepsilon(\beta + \varepsilon x)} - \frac{\varepsilon x(1 + \varepsilon)}{(\beta\varepsilon + \varepsilon^2 x)^2} \right] f(x) \, \mathrm{d}x$$

and into the psi function yields

$$\varphi_\theta = \left[\begin{array}{c} \dfrac{1}{\beta}\left[\dfrac{\beta - x}{\beta + \varepsilon x}\right] \\[2ex] -\left[\left(\dfrac{-x(1 + \varepsilon)}{\beta\varepsilon + \varepsilon^2 x}\right) + \dfrac{\ln(1 + (\varepsilon x/\beta))}{\varepsilon^2}\right] \end{array} \right] \qquad (1.13)$$

Via Equation 1.8, the IF of the MLE parameters of the GPD severity

$$\mathrm{IF}_\theta(x; \theta, T) = A(\theta)^{-1}\varphi_\theta$$

is solved numerically. However, note that Smith (1987),[36] for the GPD specifically, was able to conveniently simplify the Fisher information to yield

$$A(\theta)^{-1} = (1 + \xi)\begin{bmatrix} 1 + \xi & -\beta \\ -\beta & 2\beta^2 \end{bmatrix} \qquad (1.14)$$

(Ruckdeschel and Horbenko (2010) later re-present this result in the operational risk setting.) This gives the exact same result, as shown in Figure 1.5, as the numerical implementation of Equation 1.13 above, and provides further independent validation of the more general framework presented herein (which, of course, can be used with all commonly used severity distributions).

Importantly, note that the non-zero cross derivatives in Equation 1.13, as well as in Equation 1.14, indicate parameter dependence in x, the effects of which are discussed below.

Graphs of the IF for the MLE parameters of the GPD severity (with $\xi = 0.875$ and $\beta = 57,500$), compared with their EIF counterparts, are given in Figure 1.5.

Again note the quick, if imperfect, convergence of EIF to IF even for not very large n ($n = 250$). Also, note that as $x \to +\infty$ apparently $\xi \to +\infty$ and $\beta \to -\infty$, which will undoubtedly be reflected in the exact capital sensitivity curves in the following sections.

The mathematical results for the IFs of the lognormal, log-Gamma and GPD severities under truncation all are presented in the appendix. Their corresponding figures, for thresholds (H) of US$0, US$10,000 and US$25,000, are presented in Figure 1.6, with IFs presented side-by-side with EIFs.

Truncated lognormal

For the truncated lognormal, we have Figure 1.6.

Again, EIF converges to IF even for not very large n ($n = 250$). Note also that the effects of a data collection threshold on parameter

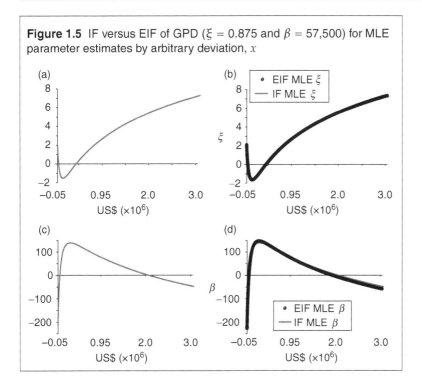

Figure 1.5 IF versus EIF of GPD ($\xi = 0.875$ and $\beta = 57,500$) for MLE parameter estimates by arbitrary deviation, x

estimation can be unexpected, and even counterintuitive, in both the magnitude of the effect and its direction. For the lognormal, truncation causes not only a change in the shape but also a change in the direction of $\mu(x)$ as x increases. Many would call this unexpected, if not counter-intuitive: when arbitrary deviations increase, what many consider the location parameter, μ, actually decreases.[37] Note that this is not true for σ, which still increases as x increases, so truncation induces negative covariance between the parameters. Many have thought this finding, when it shows up in simulations, to be numeric instability in the convergence algorithms used to obtain MLEs, but as the IF definitively shows, this is the right result. And of course, neither the definition of the lognormal density nor that of the truncated lognormal density prohibits negative values for μ. This is probably the source, at least in part, of the extreme sensitivity reported in the literature of MLE parameter estimates of the truncated lognormal.

This is but one example of the ways in which the IF can provide definitive answers to difficult statistical questions, about which

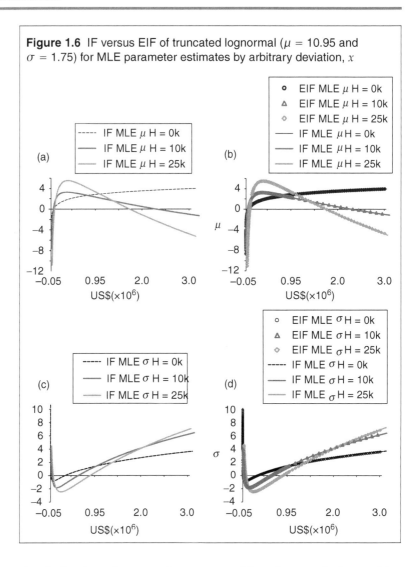

Figure 1.6 IF versus EIF of truncated lognormal ($\mu = 10.95$ and $\sigma = 1.75$) for MLE parameter estimates by arbitrary deviation, x

simulation-based approaches can provide only speculation and inconclusive musing.

Truncated log-Gamma

For the Truncated log-Gamma, we have Figure 1.7.

Note again the quick, if imperfect, convergence of EIF to IF even for not very large n ($n = 250$). Also note that the extreme asymptotic behaviour of both parameters as $x \to 1^+$ is mitigated somewhat by truncation, just as with the lognormal. However, both parameters

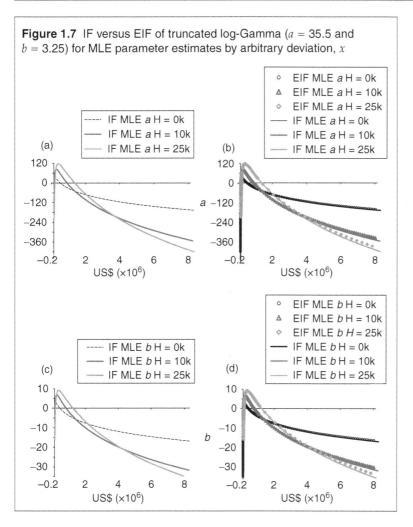

Figure 1.7 IF versus EIF of truncated log-Gamma ($a = 35.5$ and $b = 3.25$) for MLE parameter estimates by arbitrary deviation, x

diverge much more quickly to negative infinity as $x \rightarrow +\infty$, and this more rapid divergence is also like the lognormal (but in the opposite direction for μ). So while in the case of the lognormal truncation caused parameter dependence, in the case of the log-Gamma it augmented dependence that was already there, as shown in the non-zero cross derivative terms of $A(\theta)$ in Equation 1.12.

Truncated GPD

For the GPD, we have Figure 1.8.

EIF again converges to IF fairly quickly, if imperfectly, even for not very large n ($n = 250$). Unlike the lognormal and the log-Gamma,

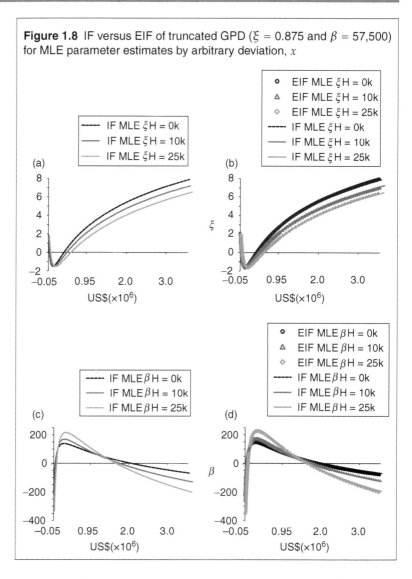

Figure 1.8 IF versus EIF of truncated GPD ($\xi = 0.875$ and $\beta = 57,500$) for MLE parameter estimates by arbitrary deviation, x

truncation does not mitigate parameter variance as $x \to 0^+$ (perhaps because there was somewhat less to begin with), but like the other two severity distributions it does cause much more rapid divergence to negative infinity for β as $x \to +\infty$, while ξ mostly just shifts to the right, which is consistent with its role as the tail index. So the negative parameter covariance in x that was already present in the non-truncated case, as seen in Equations 1.13 and 1.14, remains in the truncated case, as seen in Equation 1.21 in the appendix.

1.3.8 Capital estimation

The entire point of the statistical exercise of estimating severity distribution parameters is to estimate a capital requirement. As the convolution of the frequency and severity distributions, the aggregate loss distribution, for which we must obtain a VaR, has no general closed-form solution, so large-scale Monte Carlo simulations are the gold standard for obtaining the "true" capital requirement for a given set of frequency and severity distribution parameters. However, a number of less computationally intensive methods exist, the most convenient of which is the mean-adjusted single loss approximation (SLA) of Degen (2010).[38] Given a desired level of statistical confidence (α), an estimate of forward-looking annual loss frequency (λ), an assumed severity distribution ($F(\cdot)$) and values for the parameters of the severity distribution (θ), capital requirements are approximately given by

$$C_\alpha \approx F^{-1}\left(1 - \frac{1-\alpha}{\lambda}\right) + \lambda\mu \qquad (1.15)$$

where α is the single-year loss quantile (0.999 for regulatory capital; 0.9997 for economic capital), λ is the average number of losses occurring within one year (the frequency estimate) and μ is the mean of the estimated severity distribution.

This provides us with a very accurate approximation of the VaR of the aggregate loss distribution without having to simulate it.[39] Note that from Equation 1.15 we can see that the VaR of the aggregate loss distribution is essentially just a high quantile of the severity distribution on a single loss (the first term) with a mean adjustment that typically is small (the second term) relative to the first term (in the remainder of the chapter, our use of "SLA" refers to the mean-adjusted SLA of Equation 1.15). And for the case of severity distributions with infinite mean, say, a GPD severity with $\xi \geqslant 1$, Degen derives an SLA approximation that is not dependent upon the mean of the distribution

$$C_\alpha \approx F^{-1}\left(1 - \frac{1-\alpha}{\lambda}\right) - (1-\alpha)F^{-1}\left(1 - \frac{1-\alpha}{\lambda}\right)\left(\frac{c_\xi}{1 - 1/\xi}\right) \qquad (1.16)$$

where

$$c_\xi = \begin{cases} (1-\xi)\dfrac{\Gamma^2(1 - 1/\xi)}{2\Gamma(1 - 2/\xi)} & \text{if } 1 < \xi < \infty \\ 1 & \text{if } \xi = 1 \end{cases}$$

So the capital estimates, based on Equations 1.15 and 1.16, are functions of the severity distribution parameter estimates θ (via MLE or some other estimator) which define $F^{-1}(x, \theta)$. Since the IFs define the exact behaviour of the parameter estimator, and the parameter estimator defines the exact behaviour of capital estimates, all as a function of new losses, the exact capital sensitivity curve can thus be drawn as a function of new losses, based directly on the IF. We now have a way to perform exact sensitivity analyses (no simulations required) based on hypothetical new losses: simply evaluate the IF at the value of the new loss, then multiply IF by ε (typically $1/n$) and subtract the parameter estimate based on the original sample to get the value of the new parameter estimate. Then use the new parameter estimate to obtain the new capital requirement (this is shown in Equation 1.17). This provides a capital estimate with no additional estimation error (beyond that of the original frequency and severity parameter estimation), and is described in more detail below.

1.4 USING THE INFLUENCE FUNCTION TO INFORM BUSINESS DECISIONS

In this section we demonstrate how the IF is directly used to define, under a wide range of scenarios, exact capital requirements for business decision makers. The basic framework begins with a set of baseline parameters for the loss severity distribution $F(x, \theta_0)$ using a particular estimator on a sample of size n. The mean-adjusted single loss approximation can be used to generate a baseline estimate of capital given the relevant forward-looking annual loss frequency (λ) and the required percentile of the aggregate annual loss distribution (eg, $\alpha = 99.9\%$ for regulatory capital and, typically, $\alpha = 99.95\%$ to 99.98% for economic capital).

The exact asymptotic behaviour of the MLE estimator when faced with potential deviating data, ie, a new loss event, x, is given by the analytic formulas presented in Section 1.3.7 and in the appendix. The exact capital impact of the new loss event can be assessed by using these analytic formulas in combination with the specific information for the hypothetical data change scenario. For example, for a data change scenario in which an additional loss is to be included in the sample, the IF describes the impact of adding an infinitesimal fraction of deviating data at severity amount x, so we obtain the new parameter estimates via

$$T(F_\varepsilon) \approx \varepsilon \, \text{IF}(x; T, F) + T(F) \qquad (1.17)$$

where $\varepsilon = 1/n$ is used in practice.

This new parameter estimate is then used in the SLA formula to generate a new estimate of capital, and the difference between this new capital and the baseline capital is the change in capital resulting from the new (or dropped) loss event.

The examples that follow represent some of the real-world business situations whose changing capital requirements can be informed, directly and exactly, by the IF via Equation 1.17. The specific values for the parameters of the severity distributions and the hypothetical loss events in each scenario have been modified to protect confidential and proprietary information. The examples apply the IF approach to samples of 250 loss events from lognormal, log-Gamma and GPD distributions, with data collection thresholds of US\$0, US\$10,000, and US\$25,000. By examining the resulting exact capital sensitivity curves we can see how deviations from the assumed distributions differentially affect the capital estimates based on different severity distributions, and (very) differentially affect capital estimates over different ranges of deviating loss values. A summary of the baseline parameters from the samples and the resulting capital estimates based on the SLA Equation 1.15, assuming an annual loss frequency of $\lambda = 25$, are presented in Table 1.1.

A very important finding to remember when considering the following capital results is the MLE's apparent lack of B-robustness. Although we have left mathematical proofs for the less obvious cases for future work, based on the derivations and results shown in Section 1.3.7 and the appendix, all evidence points to non-robustness of the MLE for all of the parameters of all of the severity distributions examined. More important, however, is that this lack of robustness is reflected in the behaviour of the capital estimates shown in the next section. Across the entire domain of relevant loss events, this MLE non-robustness directly affects capital estimates in very material, sometimes unexpected and even completely counter-intuitive ways.

1.4.1 Case study 1: new right tail loss of different possible severity amounts

Operational losses associated with litigation are a common occurrence in the banking industry. The existence of potential litigation

Table 1.1 Baseline parameter and capital estimates

Distribution	Parameter names	Data collection threshold (H)	"Historical" loss (n=250) (US$ million)	Parameter 1	Parameter 2	Capital (US$ million) Regulatory (α = 0.999)	Economic (α = 0.9997)
Lognormal	μ, σ	0	61.2	10.953	1.749	63.3	99.0
Lognormal	μ, σ	10,000	77.6	10.954	1.750	69.1	107.4
Lognormal	μ, σ	25,000	77.3	10.917	1.749	73.5	113.0
Log-Gamma	α, β	0	71.0	35.484	3.252	359.0	755.4
Log-Gamma	α, β	10,000	94.0	35.513	3.263	387.3	809.3
Log-Gamma	α, β	25,000	146.2	35.410	3.252	464.8	960.7
GPD	ξ, β	0	48.9	0.8713	57,584	459.8	1,291.8
GPD	ξ, β	10,000	64.8	0.8825	57,484	583.1	1,670.3
GPD	ξ, β	25,000	77.1	0.8798	57,340	680.8	1,939.6

brings an element of uncertainty into the capital planning process on the part of management. In some cases, management may request information on the potential capital requirements assuming alternative outcomes for the litigation.

Suppose that the institution faces a legal claim for an alleged operational loss related to the advisory services event subtype of clients, products and business practices (CPBP), and that on the advice of counsel it is determined that a loss reserve of US$100 million be established in accordance with US GAAP accounting rules (so, based on available information, a loss of US$100 million is probable and reasonably estimable). Suppose that this loss is recognised after the regular quarterly cycle of capital modelling and reporting has been completed. Although the best estimate of the potential loss is US$100 million at the time the loss is financially recognised, suppose that it is determined that the loss could be as low as US$15 million if the litigation were to resolve favorably and could be as high as US$200 million in the case of very adverse discovery or motion rulings. Management could very reasonably request an assessment of the potential capital implications of the three alternative loss scenarios.

The loss scenarios are the addition of a single individual loss with severity of US$15 million, US$100 million or US$200 million. This can be evaluated within the IF framework via Equation 1.17, or using the EIF by augmenting the baseline data sample with the additional hypothetical loss and re-estimating the severity parameters. An updated set of capital estimates is then calculated, making use of the revised severity parameter estimates. If this process is repeated over a range of relevant loss severities, then the capital curves as in Figures 1.9–1.11 can be plotted. Table 1.2 summarises overall US dollar impact of the hypothetical loss scenarios for Case 1 (addition of a right tail loss).

The results above make clear that the sensitivity of capital to a new large loss is greatly affected by the assumed distribution of losses. The more heavy-tailed the loss distribution (ie, having a larger data collection threshold within a distributional family or for log-Gamma and GPD compared with the lognormal), the greater the impact of an additional loss in the right tail. Moreover, the impact relative to the total loss in the loss sample can be extremely large, often 10, 20 and even more than 30 times the size of all previous losses put together!

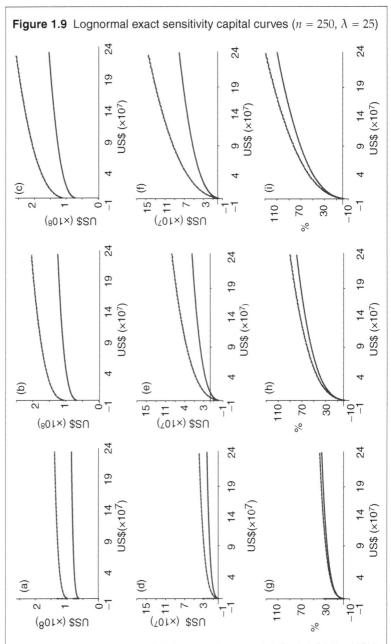

Figure 1.9 Lognormal exact sensitivity capital curves ($n = 250$, $\lambda = 25$)

Dashed line: economic capital. Solid line: regulatory capital. Capital: (a) H = US$0, (b) H = US$10k, (c) H = US$25k. Change in capital: (d) H = US$0, (e) H = US$10k, (f) H = US$25k. Percentage change in capital: (g) H = US$0, (h) H = US$10k, (i) H = US$25k.

Figure 1.10 Log-Gamma exact sensitivity capital curves ($n = 250$, $\lambda = 25$)

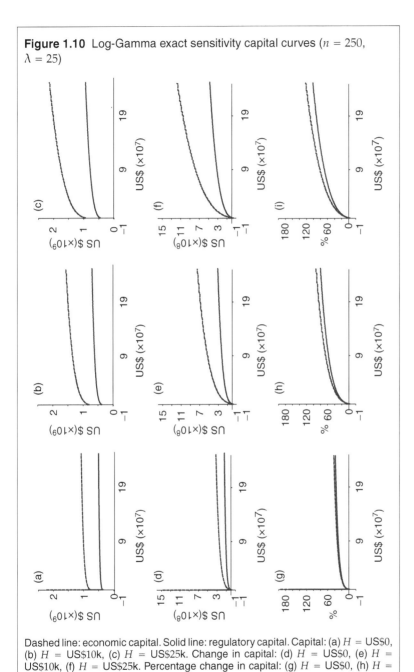

Dashed line: economic capital. Solid line: regulatory capital. Capital: (a) H = US$0, (b) H = US$10k, (c) H = US$25k. Change in capital: (d) H = US$0, (e) H = US$10k, (f) H = US$25k. Percentage change in capital: (g) H = US$0, (h) H = US$10k, (i) H = US$25k.

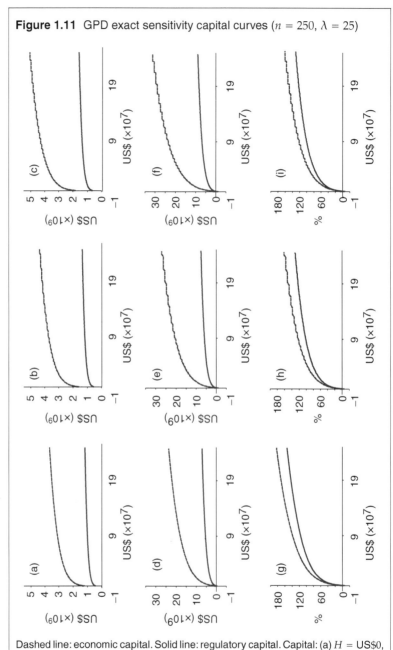

Figure 1.11 GPD exact sensitivity capital curves ($n = 250$, $\lambda = 25$)

Dashed line: economic capital. Solid line: regulatory capital. Capital: (a) H = US$0, (b) H = US$10k, (c) H = US$25k. Change in capital: (d) H = US$0, (e) H = US$10k, (f) H = US$25k. Percentage change in capital: (g) H = US$0, (h) H = US$10k, (i) H = US$25k.

This brings into question the plausibility of the LDA framework, or, at the very least, the use of MLE as a severity estimator, as the severity distributions above are widely used in this setting.

1.4.2   Case study 2: new left tail loss

As financial institutions increase the business use of operational risk quantification models, operational risk practitioners are increasingly asked to explain to management why capital has changed from the prior period estimate. Many business users of operational risk capital estimates reasonably believe that capital estimates should be stable from quarter to quarter when the institution's risk profile is stable, should increase when the institution's risk profile increases (eg, due to an increase in the scale of operations through acquisition, or due to the realisation of losses in the right tail of the distribution) and should decrease when the institution's risk profile decreases (eg, due to a decrease in loss frequency). Operational risk practitioners note that satisfactory attribution analysis of capital changes for the business audience can be quite elusive, because even though mathematical or statistical explanations can be provided, the resulting capital impacts can be quite unexpected to all constituents, both business users and operational risk quantitative experts. This case study demonstrates how the influence function can be used as a statistical tool to explain changes in capital, especially when such changes are counter-intuitive, and simulation approaches, unlike the IF, provide no definitive answers as to why.

Suppose that an institution has observed a total of 250 loss events within the unit of measure and that only one additional loss is expected to enter the loss database in the next period. Suppose that this individual event happened to be very close to the data collection threshold, specifically, the data collection threshold plus US$1,000 (which is generally below the fifth percentile of each of the loss distributions, but certainly not extremely unlikely).

The loss scenarios are the addition of a single individual loss with severity of US$1,000, US$11,000 or US$26,000 (for H equal to US$0, US$10,000 and US$25,000, respectively). As in Case 1, this can be studied within the IF framework by using Equation 1.17 or augmenting the baseline data sample with the additional hypothetical loss and re-estimating the severity parameters. An updated set of capital estimates is then calculated, making use of the revised severity parameter estimates.

Table 1.2 Dollar impact of an additional hypothetical loss in the right tail

| Estimator | Distribution | Data collection threshold (H) | Total loss (US$ mn) | Change from MLE baseline due to additional loss | | | | | | | |
| | | | | US$15 million | | US$100 million | | US$200 million | |
				RC	EC	RC	EC	RC	EC
MLE	Lognormal	0	61.2	9.5	16.0	17.9	30.6	21.8	37.4
MLE	Lognormal	10,000	77.6	17.2	30.0	38.9	67.8	50.5	89.7
MLE	Lognormal	25,000	77.3	21.5	37.9	54.4	97.4	73.4	132.6
MLE	Log-Gamma	0	71.0	62.5	144.6	109.3	254.9	129.5	302.8
MLE	Log-Gamma	10,000	94.0	110.0	254.3	229.4	551.3	289.6	695.0
MLE	Log-Gamma	25,000	146.2	140.2	335.7	332.9	814.5	433.9	1,082.4
MLE	GPD	0	48.9	298.5	987.1	550.8	1,844.7	666.7	2,229.2
MLE	GPD	10,000	64.8	331.5	1,127.8	609.7	2,083.2	724.8	2,541.6
MLE	GPD	25,000	77.1	374.7	1,280.7	700.9	2,427.0	844.7	2,961.9

Table 1.2 Continued

Estimator	Distribution	Data collection threshold (H)	Total loss (US$ mn)	Percentage change from MLE baseline due to additional loss					
				US$15 million		US$100 million		US$200 million	
				RC (%)	EC (%)	RC (%)	EC (%)	RC (%)	EC (%)
MLE	Lognormal	0	61.2	15	16	28	31	34	38
MLE	Lognormal	10,000	77.6	25	28	56	63	73	83
MLE	Lognormal	25,000	77.3	29	34	74	86	100	117
MLE	Log-Gamma	0	71.0	17	19	30	34	36	40
MLE	Log-Gamma	10,000	94.0	28	31	59	68	75	86
MLE	Log-Gamma	25,000	146.2	30	35	72	85	93	113
MLE	GPD	0	48.9	65	76	120	143	145	173
MLE	GPD	10,000	64.8	57	68	105	125	124	152
MLE	GPD	25,000	77.1	55	66	103	125	124	153

Table 1.2 Continued

Estimator	Distribution	Data collection threshold (H)	Total loss (US$ mn)	Percentage of total loss					
				US$15 million		US$100 million		US$200 million	
				RC (%)	EC (%)	RC (%)	EC (%)	RC (%)	EC (%)
MLE	Lognormal	0	61.2	15	26	29	50	36	61
MLE	Lognormal	10,000	77.6	22	39	50	87	65	116
MLE	Lognormal	25,000	77.3	28	49	70	126	95	172
MLE	Log-Gamma	0	71.0	88	204	154	359	183	427
MLE	Log-Gamma	10,000	94.0	117	270	244	586	308	739
MLE	Log-Gamma	25,000	146.2	96	230	228	557	297	740
MLE	GPD	0	48.9	610	2,018	1,126	3,771	1,363	4,557
MLE	GPD	10,000	64.8	512	1,742	942	3,217	1,119	3,925
MLE	GPD	25,000	77.1	486	1,661	909	3,148	1,096	3,842

Table 1.3 Dollar impact of an additional hypothetical loss in the left tail (US$ millions)

Estimator	Distribution	Data collection threshold (H)	Total loss (US$ million)	Change from MLE baseline due to additional loss						
				US$15 million		US$100 million		US$200 million		
				RC	EC	RC	EC	RC	EC	
MLE	Lognormal	0	61.2	2.6	4.5	−0.5	−0.8	−0.8	−1.4	
MLE	Lognormal	10,000	77.6	—	—	2.3	4.2	0.0	0.0	
MLE	Lognormal	25,000	77.3	—	—	—	—	2.4	4.2	
MLE	Log-Gamma	0	71.0	29.4	70.4	−5.2	−11.5	−7.8	−17.9	
MLE	Log-Gamma	10,000	94.0	—	—	21.6	52.6	−0.1	−0.1	
MLE	Log-Gamma	25,000	146.2	—	—	—	—	24.0	66.9	
MLE	GPD	0	48.9	25.9	85.7	10.1	34.1	−4.2	−12.8	
MLE	GPD	10,000	64.8	—	—	28.8	95.5	4.8	19.1	
MLE	GPD	25,000	77.1	—	—	—	—	38.4	133.7	

Table 1.3 Continued

Estimator	Distribution	Data collection threshold (H)	Total loss (US$ million)	Percentage change from MLE baseline due to additional loss					
				US$15 million		US$100 million		US$200 million	
				RC (%)	EC (%)	RC (%)	EC (%)	RC (%)	EC (%)
MLE	Lognormal	0	61.2	4	5	−1	−1	−1	−1
MLE	Lognormal	10,000	77.6	—	—	3	4	0	0
MLE	Lognormal	25,000	77.3	—	—	—	—	3	4
MLE	Log-Gamma	0	71.0	8	9	−1	−2	−2	−2
MLE	Log-Gamma	10,000	94.0	—	—	6	7	0	0
MLE	Log-Gamma	25,000	146.2	—	—	—	—	5	7
MLE	GPD	0	48.9	6	7	2	3	−1	−1
MLE	GPD	10,000	64.8	—	—	5	6	1	1
MLE	GPD	25,000	77.1	—	—	—	—	6	7

Table 1.3 Continued

Estimator	Distribution	Data collection threshold (H)	Total loss (US$ million)	Percentage of total loss					
				US$15 million		US$100 million		US$200 million	
				RC (%)	EC (%)	RC (%)	EC (%)	RC (%)	EC (%)
MLE	Lognormal	0	61.2	4	7	−1	−1	−1	−2
MLE	Lognormal	10,000	77.6	—	—	3	5	0	0
MLE	Lognormal	25,000	77.3	—	—	—	—	3	5
MLE	Log-Gamma	0	71.0	41	99	−7	−16	−11	−25
MLE	Log-Gamma	10,000	94.0	—	—	23	56	0	0
MLE	Log-Gamma	25,000	146.2	—	—	—	—	16	46
MLE	GPD	0	48.9	53	175	21	70	−9	−26
MLE	GPD	10,000	64.8	—	—	44	148	7	29
MLE	GPD	25,000	77.1	—	—	—	—	50	173

As Table 1.3 shows, in Case 2 the story is less the change in capital relative to the baseline and more the change relative to the size of the new loss. These results are quite dramatic: a US$4.5 million increase in economic capital results from a US$1,000 loss under a lognormal model; a US$21 million increase in regulatory capital results from a US$11,000 loss under a truncated log-Gamma (H = US$10k) model; and a US$133.7 million increase in economic capital results from a US$26,000 loss under a truncated GPD (H = US$25k) model. These capital increases appear extremely disproportionate with the new loss amount, and yet they are completely consistent with the IFs derived in Section 1.3.7 and in the appendix. For example, recall the IF of the MLE lognormal parameters in Equation 1.11

$$\text{IF}_\theta(x; \theta, T) = \begin{bmatrix} \ln(x) - \mu \\ \dfrac{(\ln(x) - \mu)^2 - \sigma^2}{2\sigma} \end{bmatrix} \qquad (1.18)$$

As seen in Equation 1.11, and as Figure 1.2 showed, when $x \rightarrow 0^+$, $\sigma \rightarrow +\infty$ much faster than $\mu \rightarrow -\infty$, because $\ln(x)$, which becomes a very large negative number as $x \rightarrow 0^+$, is squared in IF_σ, but not in IF_μ. So σ will increase without bound, causing the entire log-normal severity (all of its percentiles) to increase without bound. This causes the capital estimate based on Equation 1.15 to increase without bound, because Equation 1.15 is a direct function of the specified percentile of the lognormal severity. So if a new loss was even smaller than US$1,000, say US$10, capital would increase even more; increases of US$19,019,123 and US$33,292,687, in fact, for regulatory and economic capital, respectively. The same increases under the log-Gamma, which is characterised by an even more extreme asymptotic behaviour as $x \rightarrow 1^+$, would be US$590,889,232 and US$1,469,816,763, respectively. Of course these numbers are absurd, but they are inescapable mathematical consequences of using MLEs. And while few, if any, banks would include US$10 losses in their severity models, every single one, by definition, will be conducting severity modelling on loss event datasets with losses within a few thousand dollars of their respective data collection thresholds. Truncation does mitigate to some degree the extreme asymptotic behaviour of the MLEs and the capital estimates based on them, but, as shown in Table 1.3, it certainly does not eliminate it altogether.

These extreme results are actually shown in the full exact capital sensitivity curves in Figures 1.9–1.11 but they are difficult to

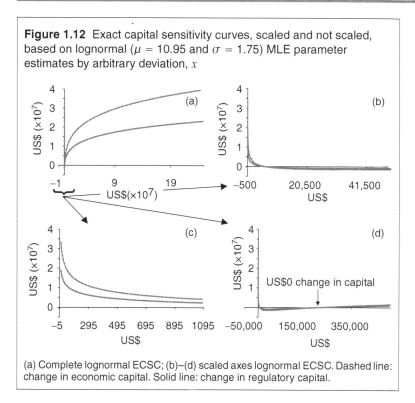

Figure 1.12 Exact capital sensitivity curves, scaled and not scaled, based on lognormal ($\mu = 10.95$ and $\sigma = 1.75$) MLE parameter estimates by arbitrary deviation, x

(a) Complete lognormal ECSC; (b)–(d) scaled axes lognormal ECSC. Dashed line: change in economic capital. Solid line: change in regulatory capital.

see because of the large scales of the axes. In Figures 1.12–1.14 we reproduce the same figures, for changes in capital, with expanded scales for the lognormal as an example, to highlight the counterintuitive and dramatic affect that small left-tail losses have on capital estimation.

Given Table 1.3 and Figure 1.12, it is no wonder that most banks relying on MLE-based LDA experience tremendous quarter-to-quarter instability in their capital requirements. All it takes is a few losses near, say, the US$10,000 threshold to add many tens of millions of dollars to estimates of required capital – and this is a "correct" result, based on maximum likelihood estimation!

1.4.3   Case study 3: removal of a current loss

In practice, operational loss event databases evolve over time and financial institutions estimate capital requirements using the state of the database at a particular point in time. Depending on an institution's data recording policies and internal governance, individual loss events may appear in the loss event database only for a particular period of time. Many institutions have a thorough data review and approval process for entries to the loss event database but include events in "draft" status in the modelling dataset while the review and approval process is underway. A loss event may be removed from the loss event database for any of number of potential reasons. We now give some examples.

- **Change to loss severity:** the severity of an operational loss may exceed the data collection threshold at the time the record was first entered into the loss event database, but may be found to fall below the threshold during the review process.

- **Reclassification of loss event:** the precise determination of whether a particular event is an operational risk or represents some other type of risk such as credit risk, business risk or strategic risk can take some time to complete. Modelling datasets include only losses due to operational risk, and such events are removed when they have been determined to represent a different risk class.

This type of data change can affect individual loss events across the entire range of the loss distribution.

Suppose that an institution has observed a total of 250 loss events within the unit of measure and that one event in draft status will be removed from the loss event database in the subsequent quarter. Suppose that this individual event is either a left-tail event (very close to the data collection threshold) or a right-tail event. Since these hypothetical data-change scenarios reflect the removal of a loss, we simply change the sign of the usual IF to capture the impact of removing data with arbitrary loss amount x. The resulting capital curves are the same as in Figures 1.9–1.11, but the change in capital is multiplied by -1. For purposes of brevity, only one illustrative example, that of the IF of the MLEs of the truncated log-Gamma, is shown below.

1.4.4 Case study 4: reclassification of an individual loss

Since operational loss event databases evolve over time, any number of important data fields may change as more information is learned about an individual loss event. Any number of issues may result in the reclassification of a loss in such a way that it no longer belongs in a particular unit of measure. Some examples include the following.

Figure 1.13 Exact capital sensitivity curves, loss added/dropped, based on truncated log-Gamma ($a = 35.5$ and $b = 3.25$) MLE parameter estimates by arbitrary deviation, x

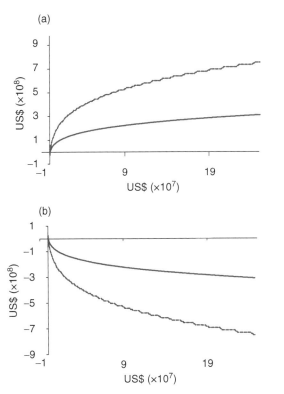

(a) Loss added; (b) loss dropped. Dashed line: change in economic capital. Solid line: change in regulatory capital.

- **Reclassification of loss event type:** when a particular operational loss is first financially recognised, the details of the loss pathway may be unclear. For example, a business unit may recognise an operational loss for an event believing it to result from a type of improper business practice (a subclass of Basel loss event type CPBP), while subsequent review identifies the loss as a transaction error event (a subclass of execution delivery and process management (EDPM)).

- **Reclassification of business line:** individual business units or subgroups may dispute which business is responsible for a particular operational loss. Subsequent internal discussions may result in a shared allocation of a loss event or even complete reassignment from one business to another.

- **Treatment of corporate events:** in some cases, an operational loss may initially be recognised by a particular business unit, but upon further internal review may be reassigned to the corporation as a whole.

Such reclassifications can affect individual loss events across the entire range of the loss distribution. For the unit of measure that receives the reclassified loss event, the IF analysis follows the form of Case 1 or Case 2. For the unit of measure from which the loss event is removed, the IF analysis follows the form of Case 3. The aggregate effect is calculated when the VaRs are combined across all units of measure.

1.4.5 Case study 5: revision of a current loss

As previously explained, there are a variety of reasons why the characteristics of an operational loss event may change over time in the database. The examples above have focused on the capital impacts of adding or removing data points from the estimation sample, but it is quite common for the severity of individual loss events to change during the current period. This can occur for events that are in "draft" status, or due to updates of certain components of the loss amount (such as transaction fees, taxes, penalties, attorney fees). Suppose the original loss severity is an amount x_0, and the revised loss amount is x_1. To accommodate this type of data change in the IF framework, Equation 1.17 is simply applied using x_0 and a new capital requirement is calculated; then Equation 1.17 is applied a second time using x_1 and another capital requirement is calculated. The difference between these two capital requirements is the difference in the expected capital effect.

Suppose that an institution has observed a total of 250 loss events within the unit of measure and that, under a GPD ($\xi = 0.875$ and $\beta = 57,500$) severity model, a US\$1 million loss event has its severity revised to US\$10 million. For such data changes, the resulting difference in expected change in capital is just the difference between the two points on the capital curve; that is, the change in capital associated with the US\$1 million loss subtracted from the change in capital associated with the US\$10 million loss, as described above. This is shown in Figure 1.14. Regulatory capital would have increased

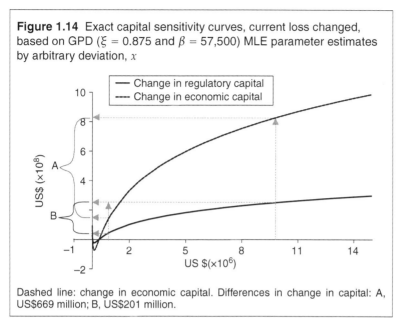

Figure 1.14 Exact capital sensitivity curves, current loss changed, based on GPD ($\xi = 0.875$ and $\beta = 57{,}500$) MLE parameter estimates by arbitrary deviation, x

Dashed line: change in economic capital. Differences in change in capital: A, US$669 million; B, US$201 million.

by US$52.1 million due to the US$1 million loss, but it changed by US$253.5 million because the loss was really US$10 million, for a difference of about US$201 million. Economic capital would have increased by US$166.3 million, but it actually changed by US$834.9 million for a difference of about US$668.5 million.

1.4.6 Case study 6: a retrospective exact attribution/"but for" analyses

Due in part to the quarter-to-quarter instability in capital estimation, bank management may request an attribution analysis in an attempt to understand why capital requirements changed from the previous period. This is especially true when no major new losses were recorded and the bank's risk profile did not change in any notable way, but nonetheless a dramatic movement in estimated required capital is observed (Case 2 is one way this can happen).

Suppose that an institution has observed a total of 250 loss events within the unit of measure and that three losses were recorded in the previous quarter. Management could reasonably ask what capital requirements would have been "but for" the second loss. This is simply Case 3 above, where the loss dataset used is the one that existed at the time of the quarter in question, and the dropped loss is the second loss. Or management could ask, "what would capital requirements have been if only the first loss, only the second loss or only the third loss occurred?" This is simply Case 1 or 2, applied to each loss separately, and the loss dataset used is the one that existed at the time of the quarter in question excluding the other two losses. The three resulting capital estimates can then be compared to provide some measure of the contribution of each to the overall change in capital. The effects of each could be offsetting, or in the same direction, all augmenting the overall change in capital, but either way such an analysis would identify whether, for example, one small left tail loss event was driving 99% of the change in capital; or whether a loss of, say, about US$220,000 actually had no effect on capital whatsoever, as shown in part (d) of Figure 1.12.

This type of "but for" exact sensitivity analysis is particularly helpful in explaining the surprising capital response to a cluster losses of similar severity that are very near the data collection threshold, which is not an uncommon occurrence. When a bank's internal constituents (such as senior management or other business users of operational risk capital estimates) or external constituents (regulatory supervisors) find quarter-to-quarter capital changes to be "out of proportion" to the underlying data changes (eg, Case 2 above), there may be calls for independent validation of the results by the bank's internal audit group or the bank's model validation group. The IF and its associated exact capital sensitivity curves, however, can immediately make apparent the sources of the "out of proportion" effects, and demonstrate definitively and absolutely how capital estimates using MLE-based severity parameter estimates can very easily display unexpected, material and even "counter-intuitive" capital requirements.

1.5 CONCLUSIONS

Given the well-documented and extensive empirical challenges of operational risk loss data and the methodological challenges inherent in the AMA framework (specifically, estimating very high percentiles of the aggregate loss distribution), reliable estimation of both economic and regulatory capital without bias, with acceptable precision, and with reasonable robustness remains a very formidable exercise. In this chapter, we demonstrated how the IF can be used in this effort as a definitive, analytic tool for two essential purposes:

1. to inform the development and choice of severity estimators, which unarguably remain the main drivers of capital estimation in the LDA framework;

2. to perform direct capital planning, once an estimator has been selected, that permits the exact determination of capital needs under alternative hypothetical changes to the loss data used in severity modelling.

For the former objective, we demonstrated how the IF can very effectively highlight the failure of the most widely used estimator (namely, MLE) to provide robust, reliable and stable capital estimates under a wide range of commonly encountered conditions. But our main focus in this chapter has been on the latter objective. The main advantage of the IF for capital planning lies in the fact that it is an analytically derived, deterministic formula. As such, it is the superior alternative, when assessing the behaviour of capital estimates under varying conditions, to simulation-based approaches that are often resource-intensive, arguably subjective and often inconclusive as they are unable to definitively confirm or invalidate counter-intuitive results. The IF literally provides the definitive answer to the question, "if my bank is subjected to a new US$10 million loss, or a US$50 million loss or even a US$200 million loss, what will be the exact effect on my capital requirements?" As a relatively straightforward formula, the IF provides this exact answer with no additional estimation error beyond that of the already estimated severity and frequency parameters.

The IF is readily programmed in most software systems for statistical or mathematical modelling, and in fact this was done to provide the results presented herein. We provide the blueprint for doing this by presenting the derivations for the IFs of the MLEs for the parameters of some of the most commonly used loss distributions, namely, the lognormal, log-Gamma and generalised Pareto distributions. We also provide the derivations for each of these distributions when they are truncated on the left, which is the most common and accepted method for dealing with loss data recorded subject to a data collection threshold. In addition, we describe how the EIF can be used as a very simple yet accurate approximation of the asymptotic IF. It is good practice to use the IF and the EIF simultaneously, to both know definitively the behaviour of the estimator over the entire domain of possible loss events and have a useful and easily implemented verification of the more involved calculations required for some IFs.

Finally, we illustrated the practical use of the IF for capital planning by using its results to generate exact capital sensitivity curves. These demonstrate the definitive, exact capital impacts under six realistic data-change scenarios that might arise within a financial institution. Through these scenarios, we demonstrate the inherent instability of capital estimates using the LDA with MLE-estimated severity parameters. Unfortunately, MLE's non-robustness directly translates into non-robustness in its capital estimates. The instability of MLE-based capital estimates is sometimes very dramatic and, worse, occurs under unexpected conditions (eg, new, small left-tail losses) and in counter-intuitive ways, increasing dramatically and without bound as the severity of a new loss actually decreases dramatically. This behaviour is exactly the opposite of the business requirements for operational risk capital estimates: stability, reliability, robustness and precision. Given the potentially material changes in capital that can result from changes to the underlying data using the LDA/MLE method, it may be prudent for operational risk practitioners to inform management and business users of operational risk capital estimates about the range of potential capital outcomes for different data change scenarios. Management and other business users need a better understanding of how capital requirements under LDA/MLE may be affected by data changes, as capital instability may negatively affect medium to long term strategic plans. And we believe there is no more effective tool to communicate this than the IF.

Regarding next steps, as described above, the IF can be used to assess the behaviour of virtually any estimator, applied to any of the commonly used severity distributions in operational risk modelling. Alternatives to MLE should be sought out and/or developed. In fact, Opdyke and Cavallo (2012) present initial results of similar tests on a widely used B-robust estimator, the optimally bias-robust estimator (OBRE).[40] Preliminary results of OBRE-based capital estimates show a respectable mitigation of MLE's extreme sensitivity versus new, small, left-tail loss events. However, under some conditions, OBRE-based capital estimates can exhibit what is arguably too much robustness on the other extreme, with relatively flat capital requirements over large ranges of very large new losses. The optimally bias-robust estimator's robustness tuning parameter may provide an effective method for getting around this possible limitation, and this is currently being researched. Regardless of the estimators ultimately used, given the depth of the challenges in estimating operational risk capital (both empirical and methodological), and the inherent limitations of the LDA framework, it is unlikely that any estimator will serve as a panacea under all possible severity distributions, all possible data conditions and all possible new or revised loss scenarios, providing universally reasonable capital estimates and a capital distribution that is robust, unbiased and reasonably precise. However, we have demonstrated that, under the complete domain of data-change conditions, for any estimator and any severity distribution, the IF is an absolutely essential tool in this effort that will guide and improve estimator development and choice as well as direct capital planning.

APPENDIX: INFLUENCE FUNCTIONS OF LOGNORMAL, LOG-GAMMA AND GPD PARAMETERS UNDER TRUNCATION

Truncated lognormal

The truncated lognormal distribution is defined as

$$g(x; \mu, \sigma) = \frac{f(x; \mu, \sigma)}{1 - F(H; \mu, \sigma)}$$

and

$$G(x; \mu, \sigma) = 1 - \frac{1 - F(x; \mu, \sigma)}{1 - F(H; \mu, \sigma)}$$

for $0 < H \leqslant x < \infty$, $0 < \sigma < \infty$, where $f(\cdot)$ and $F(\cdot)$ are the PDF and CDF of the lognormal (see Section 1.3.7).

Inserting the derivatives of

$$\frac{\partial f(y; \theta)}{\partial \theta_1}, \quad \frac{\partial f(y; \theta)}{\partial \theta_2}, \quad \frac{\partial^2 f(y; \theta)}{\partial \theta_1 \partial \theta_2}, \quad \frac{\partial^2 f(y; \theta)}{\partial \theta_1^2}, \quad \frac{\partial^2 f(y; \theta)}{\partial \theta_2^2},$$

$$\frac{\partial F(H; \theta)}{\partial \theta_1}, \quad \frac{\partial F(H; \theta)}{\partial \theta_2}, \quad \frac{\partial^2 F(H; \theta)}{\partial \theta_1 \partial \theta_2}, \quad \frac{\partial F^2(H; \theta)}{\partial \theta_1^2}, \quad \frac{\partial F^2(H; \theta)}{\partial \theta_2^2}$$

into the Fisher information

$$A(\theta) = \begin{bmatrix} -\int_a^b \frac{\partial \varphi_{\theta_1}}{\partial \theta_1} \, dK(y) & -\int_a^b \frac{\partial \varphi_{\theta_1}}{\partial \theta_2} \, dK(y) \\ -\int_a^b \frac{\partial \varphi_{\theta_2}}{\partial \theta_1} \, dK(y) & -\int_a^b \frac{\partial \varphi_{\theta_2}}{\partial \theta_2} \, dK(y) \end{bmatrix}$$

yields

$$-\int_H^\infty \frac{\partial \varphi_\mu}{\partial \mu}\, dG(y)$$

$$= -\frac{1}{\sigma^2} + \frac{1}{[1 - F(H; \mu, \sigma)]^2}$$

$$\times \left(\left[\int_0^H \frac{\ln(y) - \mu}{\sigma^2} f(y)\, dy \right]^2 + \int_0^H \frac{(\ln(y) - \mu)^2}{\sigma^4} \right.$$

$$\left. - \frac{1}{\sigma^2} f(y)\, dy [1 - F(H; \mu, \sigma)] \right)$$

$$-\int_H^\infty \frac{\partial \varphi_\sigma}{\partial \sigma}\, dG(y)$$

$$= -\frac{1}{[1 - F(H; \mu, \sigma)]} \int_H^\infty \frac{3(\ln(y) - \mu)^2}{\sigma^4} f(y)\, dy$$

$$+ \frac{1}{\sigma^2} + \frac{1}{[1 - F(H; \mu, \sigma)]^2}$$

$$\times \left(\left[\int_0^H \frac{(\ln(y) - \mu)^2}{\sigma^3} - \frac{1}{\sigma} f(y)\, dy \right]^2 \right.$$

$$+ \int_0^H \left[\frac{1}{\sigma^2} - \frac{3(\ln(y) - \mu)^2}{\sigma^4} \right]$$

$$\left. + \left[\frac{(\ln(y) - \mu)^2}{\sigma^3} - \frac{1}{\sigma} \right]^2 f(y)\, dy [1 - F(H; \mu, \sigma)] \right)$$

$$-\int_H^\infty \frac{\partial \varphi_\mu}{\partial \sigma}\, dG(y)$$

$$= -\int_0^\infty \frac{\partial \varphi_\sigma}{\partial \mu}\, dF(y)$$

$$= -\frac{1}{[1 - F(H; \mu, \sigma)]} \int_H^\infty \frac{-2(\ln(y) - \mu)}{\sigma^3} f(y)\, dy$$

$$+ \frac{1}{[1 - F(H; \mu, \sigma)]^2} \left(\left[\int_0^H \frac{\ln(y) - \mu}{\sigma^2} f(y)\, dy \right] \right.$$

$$\left. \times \left[\int_0^H \frac{(\ln(y) - \mu)^2}{\sigma^3} - \frac{1}{\sigma} f(y)\, dy \right] \right) + \frac{1}{[1 - F(H; \mu, \sigma)]^2}$$

$$\times \left(\int_0^H \frac{-2(\ln(y) - \mu)}{\sigma^3} f(y)\, dy \right.$$

$$+ \int_0^H \left[\frac{\ln(y) - \mu}{\sigma^2} \right] \left[\frac{(\ln(y) - \mu)^2}{\sigma^3} - \frac{1}{\sigma} \right] f(y)\, dy$$

$$\left. \times [1 - F(H; \mu, \sigma)] \right)$$

and into the psi function yields

$$\varphi_\theta = \begin{bmatrix} -\left[\dfrac{\ln(x) - \mu}{\sigma^2}\right] \\ -\dfrac{1}{1 - F(H; \mu, \sigma)} \displaystyle\int_0^H \left[\dfrac{\ln(y) - \mu}{\sigma^2}\right] f(y; \mu, \sigma)\, dy \\ -\left[\dfrac{(\ln(x) - \mu)^2}{\sigma^3} - \dfrac{1}{\sigma}\right] \\ -\dfrac{1}{1 - F(H; \mu, \sigma)} \displaystyle\int_0^H \left[\dfrac{(\ln(y) - \mu)^2}{\sigma^3} - \dfrac{1}{\sigma}\right] f(y; \mu, \sigma)\, dy \end{bmatrix}$$

(1.19)

So, via Equation 1.10, the IF of the MLE parameters of the truncated lognormal severity, $\text{IF}_\theta(x; \theta, T) = A(\theta)^{-1}\varphi_\theta$, is computed numerically.

As seen in the figures in Section 1.3.7, note that the non-zero cross derivatives in $A(\theta)$ above introduce parameter dependence in x, which dramatically changes the behaviour of the parameters and the resulting capital estimates as a function of x.

Truncated log-Gamma

For the truncated log-Gamma, we have

$$g(x; \mu, \sigma) = \frac{f(x; \mu, \sigma)}{1 - F(H; \mu, \sigma)}$$

and

$$G(x; \mu, \sigma) = 1 - \frac{1 - F(x; \mu, \sigma)}{1 - F(H; \mu, \sigma)}$$

for $0 < H \leqslant x < \infty$, $0 < a$, $0 < b$, where $f(\cdot)$ and $F(\cdot)$ are the PDF and CDF of the log-Gamma (see Section 1.3.7).

Inserting the derivatives of

$$\frac{\partial f(y; \theta)}{\partial \theta_1}, \quad \frac{\partial f(y; \theta)}{\partial \theta_2}, \quad \frac{\partial^2 f(y; \theta)}{\partial \theta_1 \partial \theta_2},$$

$$\frac{\partial^2 f(y; \theta)}{\partial \theta_1^2}, \quad \frac{\partial^2 f(y; \theta)}{\partial \theta_2^2}, \quad \frac{\partial F(H; \theta)}{\partial \theta_1},$$

$$\frac{\partial F(H; \theta)}{\partial \theta_2}, \quad \frac{\partial^2 F(H; \theta)}{\partial \theta_1 \partial \theta_2}, \quad \frac{\partial F^2(H; \theta)}{\partial \theta_1^2}, \quad \frac{\partial F^2(H; \theta)}{\partial \theta_2^2}$$

into the Fisher information

$$A(\theta) = \begin{bmatrix} -\int_a^b \dfrac{\partial \varphi_{\theta_1}}{\partial \theta_1}\, dK(y) & -\int_a^b \dfrac{\partial \varphi_{\theta_1}}{\partial \theta_2}\, dK(y) \\[2mm] -\int_a^b \dfrac{\partial \varphi_{\theta_2}}{\partial \theta_1}\, dK(y) & -\int_a^b \dfrac{\partial \varphi_{\theta_2}}{\partial \theta_2}\, dK(y) \end{bmatrix}$$

yields

$$-\int_H^\infty \frac{\partial \varphi_a}{\partial a}\, dG(x)$$

$$= -\psi_1(a) + \frac{1}{[1 - F(H; a, b)]^2}$$

$$\times \left[\int_1^H \ln(b) + \ln(\ln(x)) - \psi_0(a) f(x)\, dx \right]^2 + \frac{1}{[1 - F(H; a, b)]^2}$$

$$\times \left([1 - F(H; a, b)] \right.$$

$$\times \left. \int_1^H [\ln(b) + \ln(\ln(x)) - \psi_0(a)]^2 - \psi_1(a) f(x)\, dx \right)$$

$$-\int_H^\infty \frac{\partial \varphi_b}{\partial b}\, dG(x)$$

$$= -\frac{a}{b^2} + \frac{1}{[1 - F(H; a, b)]^2}$$

$$\times \left(\left[\int_1^H \left(\frac{a}{b} - \ln(y) \right) f(x)\, dx \right]^2 + [1 - F(H; a, b)] \right.$$

$$\times \left. \int_1^H \frac{a(a-1)}{b^2} - \frac{2a \ln(y)}{b} + [\ln(y)]^2 f(x)\, dx \right)$$

$$-\int_H^\infty \frac{\partial \varphi_a}{\partial b}\, dG(x)$$

$$= -\int_H^\infty \frac{\partial \varphi_b}{\partial a}\, dG(x)$$

$$= \frac{1}{b} + \frac{[1 - F(H; a, b)](1/b)F(H; a, b)}{[1 - F(H; a, b)]^2} + \frac{1}{[1 - F(H; a, b)]^2}$$

$$\times \left([1 - F(H; a, b)] \int_1^H [\ln(b) + \ln(\ln(x)) - \psi_0(a)] \right.$$

$$\times \left. \left[\frac{a}{b} - \ln(x) \right] f(x)\, dx \right) + \frac{1}{[1 - F(H; a, b)]^2}$$

$$\times \left(\int_1^H \ln(b) + \ln(\ln(x)) - \psi_0(a) f(x)\, dx \right.$$

$$\times \left. \int_1^H \left(\frac{a}{b} - \ln(x) \right) f(x)\, dx \right)$$

and into the psi function yields

$$
\varphi_\theta = \begin{bmatrix} -\left[\ln(b) + \ln(\ln(y)) - \psi_0(a)\right] \\ \quad - \dfrac{\int_1^H \left[\ln(b) + \ln(\ln(y)) - \psi_0(a)\right] f(y; a, b)\, dy}{1 - F(H; \mu, \sigma)} \\[2ex] -\left[\dfrac{a}{b} - \ln(y)\right] - \dfrac{\int_1^H \left[\frac{a}{b} - \ln(y)\right] f(y; a, b)\, dy}{1 - F(H; \mu, \sigma)} \end{bmatrix}
$$

$$(1.20)$$

So via Equation 1.10, the IF of the MLE parameters of the truncated log-Gamma severity, $\mathrm{IF}_\theta(x; \theta, T) = A(\theta)^{-1} \varphi_\theta$, is computed numerically.

As seen in the figures in Section 1.3.7, note that the non-zero cross derivatives in $A(\theta)$ above augment parameter dependence in x, which changes the behaviour of the parameters and the resulting capital estimates as a function of x.

Truncated GPD

For the truncated GPD, we have

$$
g(x; \mu, \sigma) = \frac{f(x; \mu, \sigma)}{1 - F(H; \mu, \sigma)}
$$

and

$$
G(x; \mu, \sigma) = 1 - \frac{1 - F(x; \mu, \sigma)}{1 - F(H; \mu, \sigma)}
$$

for $0 < H \leqslant x < \infty$; $0 < \beta$, assuming $\varepsilon > 0$ (which is appropriate in this setting) where $f(\cdot)$ and $F(\cdot)$ are the PDF and CDF of the GPD (see Section 1.3.7).

Inserting the derivatives of

$$
\frac{\partial f(y; \theta)}{\partial \theta_1}, \quad \frac{\partial f(y; \theta)}{\partial \theta_2}, \quad \frac{\partial^2 f(y; \theta)}{\partial \theta_1 \partial \theta_2}, \quad \frac{\partial^2 f(y; \theta)}{\partial \theta_1^2}, \quad \frac{\partial^2 f(y; \theta)}{\partial \theta_2^2},
$$

$$
\frac{\partial F(H; \theta)}{\partial \theta_1}, \quad \frac{\partial F(H; \theta)}{\partial \theta_2}, \quad \frac{\partial^2 F(H; \theta)}{\partial \theta_1 \partial \theta_2}, \quad \frac{\partial F^2(H; \theta)}{\partial \theta_1^2}, \quad \frac{\partial F^2(H; \theta)}{\partial \theta_2^2}
$$

into the Fisher information

$$
A(\theta) = \begin{bmatrix} -\int_a^b \dfrac{\partial \varphi_{\theta_1}}{\partial \theta_1}\, dK(y) & -\int_a^b \dfrac{\partial \varphi_{\theta_1}}{\partial \theta_2}\, dK(y) \\[2ex] -\int_a^b \dfrac{\partial \varphi_{\theta_2}}{\partial \theta_1}\, dK(y) & -\int_a^b \dfrac{\partial \varphi_{\theta_2}}{\partial \theta_2}\, dK(y) \end{bmatrix}
$$

yields

$$-\int_0^\infty \frac{\partial \varphi_\varepsilon}{\partial \varepsilon}\, dG(x)$$

$$= -\frac{1}{[1 - F(H; \beta, \varepsilon)]}$$

$$\times \int_H^\infty \left[\frac{x\beta + 2\varepsilon x^2 + \varepsilon^2 x^2}{(\beta \varepsilon + \varepsilon^2 x)^2} \right.$$

$$\left. + \frac{x}{(\beta + \varepsilon x)\varepsilon^2} - \frac{2\ln(1 + (\varepsilon x/\beta))}{\varepsilon^3} \right] f(x)\, dx$$

$$+ \frac{1}{[1 - F(H; \beta, \varepsilon)]^2}$$

$$\times \left(\int_0^H \left[\left(\frac{-x(1 + \varepsilon)}{\beta \varepsilon + \varepsilon^2 x} \right) + \frac{\ln(1 + (\varepsilon x/\beta))}{\varepsilon^2} \right] f(x; \beta, \varepsilon)\, dx \right)^2$$

$$+ \frac{1}{[1 - F(H; \beta, \varepsilon)]^2} \left([1 - F(H; \beta, \varepsilon)] \right.$$

$$\times \int_0^H \left(\left[\frac{x\beta + 2\varepsilon x^2 + \varepsilon^2 x^2}{(\beta \varepsilon + \varepsilon^2 x)^2} + \frac{x}{(\beta + \varepsilon x)\varepsilon^2} - \frac{2\ln(1 + (\varepsilon x/\beta))}{\varepsilon^3} \right] \right.$$

$$\left. \left. + \left[\left(\frac{-x(1 + \varepsilon)}{\beta \varepsilon + \varepsilon^2 x} \right) + \frac{\ln(1 + (\varepsilon x/\beta))}{\varepsilon^2} \right]^2 \right) f(x; \beta, \varepsilon)\, dx \right)$$

$$-\int_0^\infty \frac{\partial \varphi_\beta}{\partial \beta}\, dG(x)$$

$$= -\frac{1}{[1 - F(H; \beta, \varepsilon)]} \int_H^\infty \left[\frac{1}{\beta^2} - \frac{x(1 + \varepsilon)(2\beta + \varepsilon x)}{(\beta^2 + \beta \varepsilon x)^2} \right] f(x)\, dx$$

$$+ \frac{1}{[1 - F(H; \beta, \varepsilon)]^2} \left(\int_0^H -\frac{1}{\beta} \left[\frac{\beta - x}{\beta + \varepsilon x} \right] f(x; \beta, \varepsilon)\, dx \right)^2$$

$$+ \frac{1}{[1 - F(H; \beta, \varepsilon)]^2}$$

$$\times \left([1 - F(H; \beta, \varepsilon)] \int_0^H \left(\left[\frac{1}{\beta^2} - \frac{x(1 + \varepsilon)(2\beta + \varepsilon x)}{(\beta^2 + \beta \varepsilon x)^2} \right] \right. \right.$$

$$\left. \left. + \frac{1}{\beta^2} \left[\frac{\beta - x}{\beta + \varepsilon x} \right]^2 \right) f(x; \beta, \varepsilon)\, dx \right)$$

$$-\int_0^\infty \frac{\partial \varphi_\varepsilon}{\partial \beta}\, dG(x)$$

$$= -\int_0^\infty \frac{\partial \varphi_\beta}{\partial \varepsilon}\, dG(x)$$

$$= -\frac{1}{[1 - F(H; \beta, \varepsilon)]} \int_H^\infty \left[\frac{x}{\beta \varepsilon (\beta + \varepsilon x)} - \frac{\varepsilon x(1 + \varepsilon)}{(\beta \varepsilon + \varepsilon^2 x)^2} \right] f(x)\, dx$$

$$+ \frac{1}{[1 - F(H; \beta, \varepsilon)]^2}$$

$$\times \left(\int_0^H \left[\left(\frac{-x(1 + \varepsilon)}{\beta\varepsilon + \varepsilon^2 x} \right) + \frac{\ln(1 + (\varepsilon x/\beta))}{\varepsilon^2} \right] f(x; \beta, \varepsilon)\, dx \right)$$

$$\times \left(\int_0^H -\frac{1}{\beta} \left[\frac{\beta - x}{\beta + \varepsilon x} \right] f(x; \beta, \varepsilon)\, dx \right) + \frac{1}{[1 - F(H; \beta, \varepsilon)]^2}$$

$$\times \Bigg([1 - F(H; \beta, \varepsilon)]$$

$$\times \int_0^H \left(\left[\frac{x\beta + 2\varepsilon x^2 + \varepsilon^2 x^2}{(\beta\varepsilon + \varepsilon^2 x)^2} + \frac{x}{(\beta + \varepsilon x)\varepsilon^2} - \frac{2\ln(1 + (\varepsilon x/\beta))}{\varepsilon^3} \right] \right.$$

$$\left. + \left[\left(\frac{-x(1 + \varepsilon)}{\beta\varepsilon + \varepsilon^2 x} \right) + \frac{\ln(1 + (\varepsilon x/\beta))}{\varepsilon^2} \right]^2 \right) f(x; \beta, \varepsilon)\, dx \Bigg)$$

and into the psi function yields

$$\varphi_\theta = \begin{bmatrix} - \left[-\frac{1}{\beta} \left[\frac{\beta - x}{\beta + \varepsilon x} \right] \right] - \frac{1}{1 - F(H; \mu, \sigma)} \\ \times \int_0^H -\frac{1}{\beta} \left[\frac{\beta - x}{\beta + \varepsilon x} \right] f(x; \beta, \varepsilon)\, dx \\ - \left[\left(\frac{-x(1 + \varepsilon)}{\beta\varepsilon + \varepsilon^2 x} \right) + \frac{\ln(1 + (\varepsilon x/\beta))}{\varepsilon^2} \right] - \frac{1}{1 - F(H; \mu, \sigma)} \\ \times \int_0^H \left[\left(\frac{-x(1 + \varepsilon)}{\beta\varepsilon + \varepsilon^2 x} \right) + \frac{\ln(1 + (\varepsilon x/\beta))}{\varepsilon^2} \right] f(x; \beta, \varepsilon)\, dx \end{bmatrix}$$

$$(1.21)$$

So via Equation 1.10, the IF of the MLE parameters of the truncated GPD severity, $IF_\theta(x; \theta, T) = A(\theta)^{-1}\varphi_\theta$, is computed numerically. As seen in the figures in Section 1.3.7, note that the non-zero cross derivatives in $A(\theta)$ above indicate parameter independence in x, as existed in the non-truncated case.

The views expressed in this chapter are solely those of the authors and do not necessarily reflect the opinions of Bates White LLC or Northern Trust Corporation. All analyses were performed by J.D. Opdyke using SAS.

The first author (corresponding author), J.D. Opdyke (jd.opdyke @bateswhite.com), wishes to thank his colleague at Bates White LLC, Randal Heeb, PhD, for his encouragement and support, and expresses his sincere gratitude to Toyo R. Johnson and Nicole A. J. Opdyke for their thoughtful insights.

Alexander Cavallo gratefully acknowledges the assistance and encouragement of colleagues at Northern Trust including Benjamin

Rosenthal, Regina Desler, David Humke, Shang Xue and Devon Brooks, and the patient support of Giovanna, Allison, Natalie and Nicholas Cavallo.

1 The methods examined and developed herein are readily applicable to the use of external loss data as well, such as that proffered by any of several banking consortiums. But the capital management and business planning that are informed by these methods would, in all likelihood, take place at the level of the individual bank or financial organisation, whose policies would affect all internal data but only a fraction of the external data (if the bank was a member of the data consortium).

2 Additional information about the Basel II Accord and its specific framework for operational risk, including the definition of operational risk and standardised classification schemes for loss events according to business line (Annex 8) and event type (Annex 9), can be found in Basel Committee on Banking Supervision (2006).

3 The other two approaches in the Basel II framework are the standardised approach (TSA) and the basic indicator approach (BIA) (Basel Committee on Banking Supervision 2006).

4 Some institutions benchmark their AMA capital estimates against estimates generated from the simpler and less risk sensitive BIA or TSA.

5 The Basel II framework for operational risk was first formally proposed by the Basel Committee on Banking Supervision in June 1999, with substantial revisions released in January 2001 and April 2003, and was finalised in June 2004. The regulations implementing the Basel II Accord in the US were finalised in 2007.

6 Economic capital is defined as the amount of capital required to support an institution's risk in alignment with the institution's financial strength or creditworthiness. The enterprise level aggregate annual loss distribution is estimated using the institution's capital quantification system. The institution then selects a solvency standard (probability of default due to operational losses) that is acceptable, often referring to external benchmarks of credit risk. For example, over a one-year time horizon, firms with a Moody's credit rating of Aa have a historical probability of default of 0.03%. To support a solvency standard equivalent to a Moody's Aa rating, economic capital could be determined with a VaR percentile of 99.97% (see McNeil *et al* (2005) for further discussion).

7 A unit of measure is a grouping of loss event data for which a bank estimates a distinct operational risk exposure.

8 In a May 2001 report on Basel II, Daníelson *et al* (2001) argue that operational risk simply cannot be measured reliably due to the lack of comprehensive operational loss data. At that point in time, few financial institutions were systematically collecting operational loss data on all business lines and all operational risk event types. Because of this, operational risk analysis made extensive use of external loss events from vended database products. De Fontnouvelle *et al* (2003) developed empirical models to address the substantial biases that can arise when modelling operational risk with such data including data capture bias (because only losses beyond a specific threshold are recorded) and reporting bias (because only losses above some randomly varying threshold become public knowledge or are claimed against an insurance policy).

9 Using the Operational Riskdata eXchange database (an extensive database of operational losses occurring at member institutions) Cope *et al* (2009) demonstrate that data sufficiency and the regulatory requirements to extrapolate to the 99.9th percentile of the loss distribution are major sources of instability and sensitivity of capital estimates. Opdyke and Cavallo (2012) demonstrated that the inherent non-robustness of MLE is exacerbated by the use of truncated distributions, and that the extrapolations required for estimating regulatory and especially economic capital systematically and, in many cases, materially, overstate capital requirements due to Jensen's inequality.

10 Frachot *et al* (2004) demonstrate that the vast majority of variation in capital estimates is due to the variation of the estimated severity parameters, as opposed to the variation of the estimated frequency parameter(s).

11 Some applications of robust statistics to operational risk severity estimation include Opdyke and Cavallo (2012), Ruckdeschel and Horbenko (2010) and Horbenko *et al* (2011). Older publications include Chernobai and Rachev (2006) and Dell'Aguila and Embrechts (2006).

12 Another way of stating this is that, as an exact formula, the IF introduces no additional estimation error beyond what has been estimated already, namely, the severity and frequency parameters.

13 The iid assumption describes two important aspects of a data sample. First, an observed sample of data points is independent "when no form of dependence or correlation is identifiable across them" (Basel Committee on Banking Supervision 2011, Footnote 29). Second, an observed sample of data points is identically distributed (homogeneous) when the data is generated by exactly the same data-generating process, such as one that follows a parametric probability density function or "are of the same or similar nature under the operational risk profile" (Basel Committee on Banking Supervision 2011, Footnote 29). These textbook conditions are mathematical conveniences that rarely occur with actual, real-world data, let alone "messy" operational risk loss event data.

14 Most institutions collect information on operational losses only above a specified data collection threshold. The most common method of accounting for this threshold is to fit truncated severity distributions to the available loss data.

15 However, Ergashev (2008) notes that this assumption is violated for truncated distributions. Whether this violation is material to the estimation of either severity parameters or capital estimates is not explored.

16 Both industry practitioners and banking supervisors appear to accept the notion that some external loss events may not reflect an institution's risk profile for a variety of reasons. Filtering of external data for relevance according to business lines, geographic areas and other salient characteristics is widely accepted. Scaling models are sometimes used to make external losses more representative of an institution's risk profile. Banking supervisors also appear to be receptive to arguments that specific individual external loss events may be excluded, but banks must typically acquire very detailed information in order to make acceptable arguments. For example, certain types of events are "industry" events that occur at multiple institutions in the same general time period, such as the wave of legal settlements related to allegations of mutual fund market timing. An institution that itself incurred one or more such losses may be justified in excluding other institutions' losses (if they can be identified in the external data), since that specific industry event is already represented by an internal loss in the bank's loss database.

17 There is greater industry range of practice across the different national banking jurisdictions with respect to the exclusion of internal loss events from estimation samples. Some jurisdictions permit wholesale exclusion of losses for disposed businesses (ie, when business units or business lines are no longer part of the institution). Some jurisdictions require more detailed analysis to determine which losses may be excluded (eg, banking supervisors may require the inclusion of loss events related to employment practices, since these policies are typically established at a corporate level).

18 Pooling data from multiple financial institutions in the 2002 Loss Data Collection Exercise, Moscadelli (2004) estimates GPD distributions on as few as 42 data points. Chapelle *et al* (2008) estimate GPD distributions with sample sizes of only 30 to 50 losses, and other parametric distributions with sample sizes of approximately 200, 700 and 3,000 losses. The smaller sizes are in stark contrast to important publications in the literature, both seminal (Embrechts *et al* 1997) and directly related to operational risk VaR estimation (Embrechts *et al* 2003), which make a very strong case, via "Hill horror plots" and similar analyses, for the need for sample sizes much larger in order to even begin to approach stability in parameter estimates.

19 Heterogeneity of operational loss data has been flagged as a major problem by a number of authors. Danielson *et al* (2001, p. 13) state "the loss intensity process will be very complicated, depending on numerous economic and business related variables". For example, Cope and Labbi (2008) and Cope (2010) make use of country-level characteristics and bank gross income to build location-scale models that define more homogeneous units of measure, without which, of course, the units of measure would have been (much more) heterogeneous.

20 Cope (2011) documents the substantial sensitivity of MLE parameter estimates to large losses using a mixture approach to induce misspecification in the right tail. The analysis does not examine the ultimate impact on operational risk capital, nor does it examine misspecification in the left tail. Opdyke and Cavallo (2012) is the only paper known to these authors that does all three and it finds, under certain circumstances, potentially massive instability due to left tail misspecification, both in terms of parameter estimation and in terms of capital estimation.

21 AMA-related guidance states that banks must have a process for updating legal event exposure after it is financially recognised on the general ledger until the final settlement amount is established (Basel Committee on Banking Supervision 2011).

22 A discussion of the regularity conditions required for the application of MLE is included in many statistics and econometrics textbooks (see Greene (2007) for one example).

23 A summary of the regularity conditions needed for the consistency and asymptotic normality of M-class estimators generally can be found in many textbooks on robust statistics, such as Huber and Ronchetti (2009).

24 The recent AMA guidance from the Basel Committee acknowledges the recent application of robust statistics in operational risk, but refers to maximum likelihood estimation and probability weighted moments as "classical" methods (Basel Committee on Banking Supervision 2011, Paragraph 205).

25 The term "efficient" here is used in the absolute sense, indicating an estimator that achieves the Cramér–Rao lower bound: the inverse of the information matrix, or the negative of the expected value of the second-order derivative of the log-likelihood function. This is the minimal variance achievable by an estimator (see Greene (2007) for more details). The term "efficient" can also be used in a relative sense, when one estimator is more efficient, ie, all else being equal, it achieves a smaller variance (typically assuming unbiasedness), than another.

26 Cope *et al* (2011) find systematic variation in loss severity by region, country characteristics and certain macroeconomic variables.

27 See Huber and Ronchetti (2009) for a discussion of these more recent advances.

28 A detailed summary table of applications of robust statistics across many disciplines is available from the authors upon request.

29 The term "statistical contamination" does not indicate a problem with data quality per se, but instead reflects the realistic possibility (probability) that most of the data follows the assumed distribution, but some fraction of the data comes from a different distribution (this portion is called "contaminated"). In the remainder of this chapter, we use the more neutral term "arbitrary deviation" synonymously with "statistical contamination".

30 The conditions required for the existence of the IF are detailed in Hampel *et al* (1986) and Huber (1981). The IF is a special case of a Gâteaux derivative and it requires even weaker conditions for existence than a Gâteaux derivative. The IF can be defined for any of the commonly used operational risk severity distributions.

31 See Hampel *et al* (1986) for an extensive and detailed description of the many uses of the influence function.

32 Note that the "B" in "B-robust" signifies limiting the bias of an estimator, because if the estimator itself is bounded, so too must be its bias (if any).

33 See Hampel *et al* (1986) for a derivation of the influence function of the median.

34 This is the second partial derivative test for more than one variable (in this case, more than one parameter). The Hessian is positive definite if all eigenvalues are positive, in which case $f(\cdot)$ attains a local minimum at x, the point at which it is evaluated.

35 A common definition of the log-Gamma distributed random variable, z, is $z = \exp(q)$, where q is a random variate that follows the Gamma distribution with end points of support $0 < q < \infty$. This inconveniently makes the end points of support for the log-Gamma $1 < z < \infty$. Conventional practice, when using this definition, is to subtract the value 1 *ex post* so that the end points of support for the log-Gamma become $0 < z < \infty$.

36 Smith (1987) is the earliest example of this result that we were able to find in the literature.

37 In fact, $\exp(\mu)$ is the scale parameter of the lognormal.

38 The formula of Degen (2010) is supported by analytic derivations, whereas that of Böcker and Sprittulla (2006), which is commonly used, is based on empirical observation (although the two are very similar).

39 Capital estimates based on fully simulated aggregate loss distributions, with both frequency and severity parameters simulated (which is the gold standard here) are compared with SLA approximations in Opdyke and Cavallo (2012) and are shown to be very accurate for practical purposes.

40 OBRE is a B-robust estimator that is essentially a constrained MLE. As such, it preserves efficiency under data-change conditions consistent with the presumed severity distribution, but is resistant to extreme data-change conditions inconsistent with the presumed severity distribution.

REFERENCES

Alaiz, M. P., and M. Victoria-Feser, 1996, "Modelling Income Distribution in Spain: A Robust Parametric Approach", DARP Discussion Paper 20, STICERD, LSE, URL: http://papers.ssrn.com/sol3/papers.cfm?abstract_id=1094765.

Basel Committee on Banking Supervision, 2006, "Basel II: International Convergence of Capital Measurement and Capital Standards: A Revised Framework", Bank for International Settlements, June, URL: http://www.bis.org/publ/bcbs128.pdf.

Basel Committee on Banking Supervision, 2011, "Operational Risk: Supervisory Guidelines for the Advanced Measurement Approaches", Bank for International Settlements, June, URL: http://www.bis.org/publ/bcbs196.pdf.

Böcker, K., and J. Sprittulla, 2006, "Operational VaR: Meaningful Means", *Risk* 19(12), pp. 96–8.

Chapelle A., Y. Crama, G. Hubner and J. P. Peters, 2008, "Practical Methods for Measuring and Managing Operational Risk in the Financial Sector: A Clinical Study", *Journal of Banking and Finance* 32, pp. 1049–61.

Chernobai, A., and S. Rachev, 2006, "Applying Robust Methods to Operational Risk Modelling", *The Journal of Operational Risk* 1(1), pp. 27–41.

Cope, E., 2010, "Modelling Operational Loss Severity Distributions from Consortium Data", *The Journal of Operational Risk* 5(4), pp. 35–64.

Cope, E., 2011, "Penalized Likelihood Estimators for Truncated Data", *Journal of Statistical Planning and Inference* 141(1), pp. 345–58.

Cope, E., and A. Labbi, 2008, "Operational Risk Scaling by Exposure Indicators: Evidence from the ORX Database", *The Journal of Operational Risk* 3(4), pp. 25–46.

Cope, E., G. Mignola, G. Antonini and R. Ugoccioni, 2009, "Challenges and Pitfalls in Measuring Operational Risk from Loss Data", *The Journal of Operational Risk* 4(4), pp. 3–27.

Cope, E., M. Piche and J. Walter, 2011, "Macroenvironmental Determinants of Operational Loss Severity", *Journal of Banking and Finance* 36(5), pp. 1362–80.

Daníelson, J., P. Embrechts, C. Goodhart, C. Keating, F. Muennich, O. Renault and H. S. Shin, 2001, "An Academic Response to Basel II", LSE Financial Markets Group, Special Paper No 130, URL: http://www.bis.org/bcbs/ca/fmg.pdf.

De Fontnouvelle, P., V. DeJesus-Rueff, J. Jordan and E. Rosengren, 2003, "Capital and Risk: New Evidence on Implications of Large Operational Losses", Working Paper 03-5, Federal Reserve Bank of Boston. URL: http://www.bos.frb.org/economic/wp/wp2003/wp035.htm.

De Fontnouvelle, P., J. Jordan and E. Rosengren, 2006, "Implications of Alternative Operational Risk Modelling Techniques", in M. Carey and R. Stulz (eds), *The Risks of Financial Institutions* (NBER/University of Chicago Press).

Degen, M., 2010, "The Calculation of Minimum Regulatory Capital Using Single-Loss Approximations", *The Journal of Operational Risk* 5(4), pp. 3–17.

Dell'Aguila, R., and P. Embrechts, 2006, "Extremes and Robustness: A Contradiction?" *Financial Markets and Portfolio Management* 20, pp. 103–18.

Dupuis, D. J., 1999, "Exceedances over High Thresholds: A Guide to Threshold Selection", *Extremes* 1(3), pp. 251–61.

Embrechts, P., C. Klüppelberg and T. Mikosch, 1997, *Modelling Extremal Events for Insurance and Finance* (Springer).

Embrechts, P., H. Furrer and R. Kaufmann, 2003, "Quantifying Regulatory Caiptal for Operational Risk", Working Paper, URL: http://www.bis.org/bcbs/cp3/embfurkau.pdf.

Ergashev, B., 2008, "Should Managers Rely on the Maximum Likelihood Estimation Method while Quantifying Operational Risk?" *The Journal of Operational Risk* 3(2), pp. 63–86.

Frachot, A., O. Moudoulaud and T. Roncalli, 2004, "Loss Distribution Approach in Practice", in M. Ong (ed), *The Basel Handbook: A Guide for Financial Practitioners* (London: Risk Books).

Greene, W., 2007, *Econometric Analysis*, Sixth Edition (Upper Saddle River, NJ: Prentice Hall).

Hampel, F. R., 1968, "Contributions to the Theory of Robust Estimation", PhD Thesis, University of California, Berkeley.

Hampel, F. R., E. Ronchetti, P. Rousseeuw and W. Stahel, 1986, *Robust Statistics: The Approach Based on Influence Functions* (Chichester: John Wiley & Sons).

Horbenko, N., P. Ruckdeschel and T. Bae, 2011, "Robust Estimation of Operational Risk", *The Journal of Operational Risk* 6(2), pp. 3–30.

Huber, P. J., 1964, "Robust Estimation of a Location Parameter", *Annals of Mathematical Statistics* 35, pp. 73–101.

Huber, P. J., 1981, *Robust Statistics* (Chichester: John Wiley & Sons).

Huber, P. J., and E. Ronchetti, 2009, *Robust Statistics*, Second Edition (Chichester: John Wiley & Sons).

Jensen, J. L. W. V., 1906, "Sur les Fonctions Convexes et les Inégalités entre les Valeurs Moyennes", *Acta Mathematica* 30(1), pp. 175–193.

McNeil, A. J., R. Frey and P. Embrechts, 2005, *Quantitative Risk Management: Concepts, Techniques and Tools* (Princeton University Press).

Moscadelli, M., 2004, "The Modelling of Operational Risk: The Experience from the Analysis of the Data Collected by the Risk Management Group of the Basel Committee", Working Paper No. 517, Bank of Italy.

Opdyke, J.D., and A. Cavallo, 2012, "Estimating Operational Risk Capital: The Challenges of Truncation, the Hazards of MLE, and the Promise of Robust Statistics", *The Journal of Operational Risk*, 7(3).

Ruckdeschel, P., and N. Horbenko, 2010, "Robustness Properties of Estimators in Generalized Pareto Models", Technical Report ITWM 182, URL: http://www.itwm.fraunhofer.de/presse/berichte-des-itwm.html.

Smith, J., 1987, "Estimating the Upper Tail of Flood Frequency Distributions", *Water Resources Research*, 23, (8), pp. 1657–66.

Stefanski, L., and D. Boos, 2002, "The Calculus of M-Estimation", *The American Statistician*, 56(1), pp. 29–38.

Tukey, J. W., 1960, "A Survey of Sampling from Contaminated Distributions", in I. Olkin (ed), *Contributions to Probability and Statistics*, pp. 448–85 (Stanford University Press).

Van Belle, G., 2002, *Statistical Rule of Thumb* (New York: John Wiley & Sons).

New Frontiers in the Regulatory Advanced Measurement Approach

Evan G. Sekeris

Federal Reserve Bank of Richmond

2.1 INTRODUCTION

At the end of the 1990s, operational risk was elevated to the status of a distinct risk and was institutionalised as a risk category warranting management and regulatory attention. Until this point, operational risk had been considered a "residual category, something left over from market and credit risk" (Power 2003). The establishment of operational risk as a fully fledged risk discipline[1] occurred progressively throughout the 1990s and culminated with its establishment as an independent risk in the Basel II Accord in the early 2000s, alongside market and credit risk (Basel Committee on Banking Supervision 2006). Firstly, the collapse of Barings Bank in 1995 due to unauthorised trading by Nick Leeson was a turning point in the history of operational risk and the magnitude of the loss underscored its importance. The dissolution of one of the oldest banking institutions in the world, one which had survived numerous booms and busts over the centuries, showed that no institution was immune to operational risk. Secondly, and most importantly, the largest operational risk loss up to that point in time occurred as the industry and regulators were paying closer attention to the risk and henceforth the collapse of Barings has often been referred to as the event that gave birth to the field of operational risk. While this is likely an overstatement, it is clear that Leeson's actions drew even more attention to operational risk and accelerated the ascension of the risk to its status at the time of writing.

The institutionalisation of operational risk in the Basel Accord (Basel Committee on Banking Supervision 2006) brought about the need for adequate resources to effectively manage it. Effective risk management and modelling is one of the main objectives of the Accord. The Accord puts operational risk on equal footing with market and credit risk. By imposing a capital requirement for operational risk, the Accord ensures that this type of operational risk will receive the same level of attention from risk managers and bank executives more established forms of credit and market risk. Operational risk modelling is a young discipline compared with market and credit risk modelling, but it is maturing rapidly. Operational risk modelling has mainly developed in response to Basel II in order to estimate capital needs according to the advanced measurement approach (AMA). The most common approach to comply with the AMA is the loss distribution approach (LDA), and this is now considered the operational risk modelling standard. The fact that the implementation of LDA may appear obvious to many readers illustrates how far the field has come. When the banking industry first grappled with developing AMA frameworks, it was not clear at all that the LDA was the natural modelling choice. Despite advances, numerous operational risk professionals are still suspicious of the capital numbers generated by the models and, most importantly, of their use to risk management. Despite these suspicions, operational risk models have the potential to be valuable tools for risk management as well as for capital estimation.

Common criticisms levelled against operational risk models include their seemingly "black box" nature and their insensitivity to changes in an institution's risk profile. These criticisms are valid. Operational risk models were developed for capital estimation, not for risk management. Banks have been exposed to operational risk and have managed it for as long as banks have existed; operational risk models were mainly developed in response to Basel II to estimate capital needs rather than to manage operational risk. This perception of models as being simply a capital calculation tool is still widespread. The comments by Ludwig Van Wemmel, director of operational risk management at Dexia's Belgian banking arm, reported in Meek (2012), are very telling:

> Last year, the opportunity for Dexia to move from the standardized approach to the AMA for operational risk management was

examined. The final proposal was not to do it for a number of reasons, most of them financial: additional resources to be deployed without the assurance that the perceived benefits – *reduced regulatory capital* needs – would at least compensate for the additional costs [emphasis added].

In his comments, Van Wemmel does not make any reference to the potential risk management benefits of adopting the AMA. Because operational risk models are seen as nothing more than a tool to calculate capital, the move to adopt AMA is seen as an investment in potential capital reduction and nothing more.

The fact that the development of operational risk models has mainly been driven by regulatory requirements rather than risk management needs has determined the nature of the models and their relationship to the risk management function. Modelling teams and risk managers often work in separate silos. As a result, models are being developed by people who have not managed operational risks and who do not always adequately understand the nature of these risks. The worlds of operational risk management and modelling coexist but do not communicate sufficiently. The existence of these silos will adversely affect the evolution of operational risk models and their usefulness for the foreseeable future. In principle, operational risk models should be valuable risk management tools.

The AMA framework and operational risk models, even in their current form, can provide useful information to risk managers. The primary benefit of the adoption of an AMA framework is the rigour it imposes on data collection frameworks, the comprehensiveness of the coverage it requires and the increased awareness of operational risk it produces in senior management. The systematic collection and analysis of loss data provides valuable information about the hotspots in a bank and the evolution of risks. The quantitative models, for all their weaknesses, are nonetheless useful tools. The capital numbers they estimate are certainly approximations, but they do give a fairly accurate picture of the relative materiality of different activities. Through their modelling efforts, some banks have been able to identify activities that were significantly riskier than a cursory review of their history suggested. Even if the exact causes of the risk are not captured by the models and if risk managers and business leaders do not fully understand the inner workings of the models, they can help institutions make better strategic decisions.

Two key developments are needed for AMA models to gain wider acceptance and to bridge the gap between modelling and risk management. First, managers and modellers need to recognise that models are not a replacement for risk management, but they can provide meaningful input to risk management. Second, models need to evolve in order to become more sensitive to changes in the underlying causes of risk and to become more transparent to non-quant users.

Models, because of their mathematical rigour, are often taken too literally and are seen as an alternative to human analysis with all its biases. It is often forgotten that models are a simplification of reality and that they are a local approximation of a phenomenon. Blind faith in models can result in catastrophic decisions, which naturally leads to scepticism about the soundness of the models and often a backlash against the use of models. *Wired*'s article on the role of Gaussian copulas in the 2008 crisis (Salmon 2009) is a perfect example of the industry's struggle with the appropriate role of models. Salmon blames the Gaussian copula for the financial meltdown. A more accurate explanation is that misuse and blind belief in the copula were root causes of the crisis. The copula is just a tool like all models used in finance and in the banking industry. It is the users' responsibility to understand the limits of the tool and to communicate those clearly to management. As David Li is quoted as saying about the Gaussian copula model in *Wired*: "the most dangerous part is when people believe everything coming out of it" (Salmon 2009). The adversarial relationship between models and risk management in operational risk is partly the result of this perception that models are a substitute for risk management. Reaffirming the role of models as one of the numerous pieces of information that should be used as inputs by risk managers will help to decrease the suspicion with which model outputs are viewed.

Operational risk models need to evolve and address their main weakness: lack of sensitivity to changes in the institution's controls or business environment. A main drawback of the LDA is that it does not identify and consider the risk factors driving losses. This drawback has led to the treatment of operational risk models as "black boxes". The consequences of actions by risk managers will not be reflected in the output of LDA models for years after data reflecting the consequences of those actions has been collected. This delayed reflection of consequences in model outputs undermines the credibility of the models, especially because credit and market risk models are much more reactive to changes.

In the next section we look at the four data elements, the role each one plays in operational risk modelling and their limitations. In Section 2.3 we give a brief overview of the loss distribution approach and, drawing mostly from experience in the US, we discuss the limits of the approach as implemented at the time of writing. In Section 2.4 we look at the nascent field of factor modelling in operational risk. The potential of this new generation of models as a bridge between modelling and risk management and as a tool for stress-testing is discussed. Section 2.5 concludes.

2.2 DATA ELEMENTS

When the Basel Accord was finalised, operational risk was still in its infancy from a modelling standpoint, and few institutions, if any, had been collecting data systematically. Data availability was seen as a potential obstacle to the successful modelling of operational risk, and the Basel Committee required four data elements – internal data, external data, scenario analysis and business environment and control factors (BEICFs) – to be considered with the hope that they would complement each other. Scenario analysis and BEICFs were added to the more "traditional" (from a modelling point of view) internal and external data elements not only in order to address the lack of data but also to prevent a situation where AMA models would be used solely as tools for capital calculation with little value from a risk management perspective. Internal data and external data are often described as the backward-looking data elements, whereas scenario analysis and, to a lesser degree, BEICFs are referred to as the forward-looking data elements. This distinction has its roots in the types of models now in use, which try to extrapolate the magnitude of future losses based on historical losses but with no consideration for the environment in which they occurred. Scenarios have earned the forward-looking label because of their focus on the environment and on the mechanisms that led to the losses. This focus also makes scenarios a very valuable tool from a risk management perspective. All four elements have their strengths and weaknesses, not all of which were anticipated when the Accord was drafted. As the field has matured, the relative importance of the elements has evolved.

Internal data has emerged as the key data element for quantification purposes in most jurisdictions. Use of external data, while very promising, still needs to overcome the daunting challenge of scaling. Scenario data is subject to biases and imprecisions that make it a very difficult data element to use for modelling purposes, even though it is still the best bridge between modelling and risk management. BEICFs, for their part, have taken a back seat to the other elements because of the difficulty of quantifying them.

2.2.1 Internal data

Internal data is the most critical data element from a quantification point of view. No solid quantification framework can be put in place without a credible model based on internal data. Loss history is the best indication a modeller has of the true riskiness of an institution. However, despite the importance of this data element, the most significant obstacle facing operational risk modellers is without doubt that of data availability. Prior to the Accord, banks did not have comprehensive data collection systems in place for operational losses. When banks collected data they focused on large losses, and only in specific areas; the data collected was mostly anecdotal with little or no value for quantification. The industry launched the first serious data collection efforts in the early 2000s when it became clear to the industry that operational risk had become an established risk category. Not only was comprehensive data collection a recent development, but the industry had to learn how to collect data. Initial attempts at data collection were not suitable for modelling. Consequently, the data sets that lend themselves to modelling contain at most 10 years of loss history, and most institutions have data sets often covering no more than five years of losses. Does this mean that operational risk modellers must develop models to calculate a 1-in-1,000-year loss using 5 or, at best, 10 years of data? Fortunately not. The LDA standard does not require a direct estimate of the loss distribution (numerous losses are observed in a given year, sometimes in the hundreds, which the LDA leverages to estimate the severity distribution) but it gives a sense of the magnitude of the challenge.

2.2.1.1 Data for fat tails

Data sufficiency is particularly problematic when the processes being estimated are fat tailed. The heavier the tail of a process, the larger the sample needed to achieve a certain level of confidence in the esti-mates. Unfortunately, low-frequency–high-severity losses, by their very nature, do not occur frequently, resulting in samples that are often insufficient for estimating the severity with reasonable preci-sion. At this point a clarification of the concept of "low-frequency, high-severity" and of its usage in operational risk is warranted. It is common to hear practitioners use the terms "fat tailed" and "low-frequency, high-severity" interchangeably. While it is true that the most heavy-tailed processes tend to also be characterised by low frequencies, a fat-tailed process can also exhibit a high frequency. The high/low severity nature of losses is a reference to the tail of the severity distribution, while the high/low frequency refers to the number of draws from the severity observed over a time interval. One of the basic assumptions of the LDA is the independence of severity and frequency. There is no reason to expect a unit of mea-sure (UoM) with a fat-tailed severity to have a low frequency. In reality, every UoM in operational risk is modelled using some type of fat-tailed distribution! The fact that a process is fat tailed makes it particularly important to have a good fit of the tail but it does not imply that only tail data is important. A good fit of the tail can only be achieved through a good fit of the overall distribution, and requires data covering the full spectrum of losses.

A popular modelling technique used to model operational risk is extreme value theory (EVT). At first this seems like a very reason-able and obvious choice given the nature of operational risk losses. However, EVT is a data-intensive technique that in most cases is not usable in operational risk because of the limited sample sizes. It is fairly common to have samples of 100 or 200 losses, which is far too small for EVT to be used effectively. Coles and Tawn (1996) put this problem in perspective. They developed a Bayesian framework for EVT, which they present as a tool to address the lack of data for the process that they were trying to model. This process was daily rain-fall in London, for which they have more than 30,000 observations, orders of magnitude more data than the typical sample in opera-tional risk and significantly more homogeneous than operational risk data. The data-generating process for rainfall has probably not changed since the early 20th century (except possibly since the early 2000s as a result of global warming), the same cannot be said for operational risk data over much shorter time horizons. After scarcity, data homogeneity is the second biggest problem facing operational risk modellers.

2.2.1.2 Homogeneity

Lack of homogeneity is another problem in operational risk modelling. Financial institutions face different types of operational risks generated by different statistical processes. The purpose of UoMs is to separate losses coming from these different processes in homogeneous samples. When modelling a UoM it is assumed that the data in the sample was generated by the same process. This is a very strong assumption. First, because of data limitations UoMs are not always granular enough to guarantee that different processes have not been mixed. Second, data is collected over multiple years during which an institution can change significantly because of growth, implementation of new controls, changes in environment, etc.

How likely is it that the processes generating the loss data have not themselves changed during this time? If the data-generating process is changing, the samples collected will not be homogeneous as assumed by modellers when fitting severity distributions. The LDA assumes that there is a single severity distribution independent from the frequency distribution. To apply the LDA it is crucial to work with data representative of a unique statistical process, otherwise a unique distribution will be fitted to data generated by two or more processes and yield erroneous capital numbers. The Basel Accord addresses this issue by requiring institutions to consider multiple units of measure using the line of business and the event type categorisation. It is unrealistic for institutions to segment their data at the most granular level, ie, at the event type/business line level, because of the insufficient number of observations that would be in some of the buckets. Most institutions choose to work with data segmented along one of the two above-mentioned dimensions and to apply some form of LDA model to it.

2.2.1.3 Data collection threshold

Most institutions opt to collect only those losses that are above a certain amount, known as the data collection threshold. This is done because the cost of collecting data about small losses outweighs the benefits of including them in the model. The fat-tailed nature of operational risk losses led to the common perception in the field that only large losses matter. This is essentially a misconception that has also contributed to the poor performance of operational risk models as risk management tools. It is a misconception because it puts the emphasis on the large, attention-grabbing tail losses, as opposed to an understanding of the process that generates all losses.

One explanation for this misconception is that these large tail losses may be fundamentally different from the other losses. If this is indeed the case, then the pooling of data in UoMs is not appropriate, since it assumes that all losses in a given UoM are homogeneous. Another weakness of this focus on large tail events is that not all types of operational risk losses are fat tailed. A number of UoMs have relatively thinner tails and are often referred to in the industry as high-frequency, low-severity UoMs. For such UoMs, even a relatively low data collection threshold can result in a large number of losses not being collected (some institutions report up to 90% of their data missing), leading to significant challenges when fitting severity distributions. These challenges have been dismissed by some as unimportant because of the immateriality of these UoMs. This perception is inaccurate; UoMs with very high frequency and relatively fat tails can contribute significantly to a firm's risk exposure. Furthermore, as argued earlier, these are the UoMs for which improved controls can have the most meaningful impact.

The data collection threshold gives rise to two related problems. First, not taking accounting correctly for the data collection threshold when estimating the severity distribution will result in biased estimates of the severity parameters. Two commonly used techniques fall in this category: the naive approach, which ignores the threshold altogether, and the shifted approach, which subtracts the threshold amount from every loss prior to fitting the distribution. The magnitude and direction of the bias will depend on the particulars of the data, but can in some cases be very significant. Second, as mentioned above, for certain UoMs a significant amount of data can sit below the data collection threshold. Ignoring those losses can also lead to a large underestimation of the capital. In order to correctly address the existence of the threshold, the correct fitting methodology is to use a conditional maximum likelihood estimator (MLE), which takes into account the threshold. A common criticism of the conditional MLE is that the standard errors of the estimates are significantly larger than those obtained with either the naive or the shifted approach.

This criticism is misleading in that it suggests that the larger standard errors indicate a less accurate estimator. In reality the larger standard errors simply reflect the fact that a significant amount of information (the data under the threshold) is missing, which is ignored by the other two techniques and hence results in artificially lower standard errors. Unfortunately, the conditional MLE is no panacea either. If the proportion of data below the threshold is too significant, the technique fails and either provides no solution or leads to unrealistic estimates. Alternative techniques will have to be developed to address this problem. Bayesian estimators seem to be a potentially fruitful research direction because of the ability to leverage alternative sources of information to complement the information available in the internal data set. Rozenfeld (2010) explores another approach, which leverages alternative sources of information about the data below the threshold, such as the general ledger, to correct for the missing data, but does not address the parameter bias resulting from the shifting of the data. In later, as yet unpublished, research Rozenfeld uses these alternative sources of information to resolve the bias problem by constraining the parameter space in a conditional MLE setting.

2.2.2 External data

In order to address internal data insufficiency, banks are required to consider external data. The use of external data, however, is not as straightforward as many had envisioned when the Basel Accord was being drafted, although it is a common practice for other risk categories. For example, in market risk, even if a bank has not traded a specific asset but decides to do so, it can purchase historical data on that asset and similar assets to build models to assess the riskiness of the investment. Because of the significant data limitations that exist in operational risk, adopting this practice appears, at first, to be a sensible solution. But there are problems.

The first problem is that of the availability of external data. Because no bank had historically collected data prior to the end of the 1990s, there was no data in the industry. A number of vendors tried to fill this gap by building databases of data collected from public sources. Such data can be very useful to inform risk managers about what risks have materialised at other institutions, but are typically too inaccurate to be useable in a model. Institutions also tried to address this problem by setting up consortiums such as the Operational Risk eXchange (ORX) or the American Bankers' Association (ABA) consortium. Data from these consortiums does not suffer from the inaccuracies of the public databases but because of the sensitivity of the data it is anonymised to protect the identity of the reporting banks.

The second problem is that losses from one institution are not necessarily directly applicable to another institution and require scaling. Without any information about the institution that incurred a specific loss, it is impossible to scale the data. Furthermore, even if institutions had access to more information, it is unclear how successful scaling will be. Operational Risk eXchange has developed a scaling tool for its members, but it is still in its early stages of development.

Scaling is a difficult problem because of a fundamental problem with operational risk losses when compared with credit and market risk losses: the operational risk losses of a bank are uniquely a function of the bank's processes and its controls. When a creditor defaults, the risk sits with the obligor and is a result of the obligor's action, it is not the result of actions taken by the bank. When a bank incurs an operational risk loss it is the result of the bank's actions. There are no known metrics to assess a bank's exposure to operational risk. Simple metrics such as asset size or revenue can potentially explain some of the operational risk but metrics that capture a bank's risk appetite will be crucial to the development of any scaling methodology.

2.2.3 Scenarios

The use of scenarios in operational risk management is popular across the industry. In certain countries regulators go so far as to prefer the use of scenarios over models for capital calculation. Despite the popularity of scenarios as a risk management tool, risk managers have raised concerns about the focus on generating loss estimates in scenario workshops. The fear is that if a scenario workshop focuses on producing loss estimates, which qualify them for inclusion in a model, the workshop will overemphasise refining the numbers and underemphasise understanding and analysing the risks and root causes. From a risk management perspective, understanding of the risk is significantly more important than the estimation of a semi-accurate loss number that at best gives a sense of materiality. Ironically, scenarios exist today because in the AMA framework scenario analysis is one of the required elements, but some practitioners see this requirement as detrimental to the quality of scenarios. However, the problem is not that scenarios are a requirement in the AMA framework but rather that this requirement has been interpreted to mean that scenarios must be data inputs to the model.

2.2.3.1 Scenarios and quantitative models

When the Basel Accord was written, little was known about operational risk. Operational loss data, particularly tail data, was scarce. Scenarios and external data were seen as the ideal complements to internal data to inform the behaviour of losses in the tail, which led to the interpretation of scenarios as data. It is common to refer to scenarios as the "forward-looking" element because they include estimates of the potential size of future losses, with the implication that internal data is the "backward-looking" element. Unfortunately this characterisation has framed thinking about the usage of scenarios, with the consequences just described. Models based on solid internal data need not be any less forward-looking than models based on scenarios. The objective of these two types of models is exactly the same: to use available information to estimate future exposure. The techniques used are different but complementary. A quantitative model uses a mathematical structure based on the modeller's intuition about the risk, the "soft knowledge" to estimate future losses based on observed losses. A scenario is a mental model that leverages workshop participants' knowledge of and experience with risk to achieve the same objective as the quantitative model. Because it is a mental non-quantitative model, a scenario is less constrained than a quantitative model. It allows risk managers to evaluate the processes that drive risks but less constraint comes at the cost of less precision and significant behavioural biases. Consequently, scenarios should not be seen as inputs to a quantitative model but as a parallel process trying to achieve a similar objective through different, less rigorous means. However, it is true that modelling techniques at the time of writing are inherently backward looking. Many models currently in use simply try to fit statistical distributions to the data and then use these distributions to extrapolate future losses in the tail. These approaches completely ignore the causes of the losses and the environment in which they occurred. Consequently, if the environment were to change, models currently in use would not be able to capture those changes and their impact on future losses, whereas a scenario workshop would focus on these environmental changes to understand future losses, even though inaccurately. While this distinction between models and scenario analysis currently holds, hopefully it will fade as new generations of models are developed that take into account risk drivers and environmental factors making them more forward looking.

Despite these concerns about the current development and use of scenarios, there is no doubt that they are a crucial element of the AMA framework. Scenarios make use of sources of knowledge about risks not used in quantitative models; most importantly, they are one of the few tools that risk managers currently have at their disposal to affect models. However, their development and usage need to be rethought to improve their effectiveness both as a risk management tool and as a complement to modelling.

2.2.3.2 The appropriate role of scenarios

The industry faces a balancing act in choosing the appropriate role for scenarios in the AMA framework. On the one hand, the industry needs to avoid completely excluding scenarios from their operational risk models used for capital estimation. Such exclusion would further separate risk management from modelling and encourage the perpetuation of the silos that so many institutions are trying to eliminate. Risk managers would feel that they have no impact on the capital number allocated to their business and would lose interest in the scenario process. On the other hand, the industry needs to avoid any inclusion of scenarios in the modelling framework in an artificial way. Doing so will not break down silos; it will instead impair the usefulness of scenarios as a risk management tool and the quality and reliability of the model output.

The US inter-agency guidance[2] issued in 2011 attempts to solve the problem of the appropriate role of scenarios by promoting their use as a benchmark. This solution acknowledges that scenarios are a parallel process to modelling rather than a tool to generate inputs for the model. Relegating scenarios to the role of a benchmark is seen by some risk managers as too extreme a solution. Other alternatives that use scenarios in the modelling framework but do not use them as data inputs mixed with internal data are available but are still in early stages of development (Dutta and Babbel 2010); Ergashev

(2012) and Ergashev *et al* (2012) provide promising solutions along these lines).

As operational risk modelling evolves, a potential role for scenarios will be that of helping helping to identify which variables should be used as factors in models, similarly to what is regularly done in credit risk modelling. This is similar to what is routinely done in credit risk where workshops are held to identify variables that should be considered in models predicting probabilities of default. Such an approach would shift the focus from the estimation of a loss amount towards understanding and analysing the sources of the risk. It would also encourage the interaction between modelling teams and scenario participants.

2.2.4 BEICFs

In practice, banks have not used BEICFs extensively as a model component, often relegating them to the role of post-modelling adjustments even though they could be a key risk management tool. This is due to the lack of metrics that could be used to link controls to operational risk losses. Such metrics are common in other risks. For example, when modelling probabilities of default in credit risk, modellers use variables such as debt-to-asset ratios. Efforts undertaken by numerous institutions around key risk indicators (KRIs) are a step in the right direction in trying to identify such metrics, but a significant amount of work remains to be done, as successful KRIs are very rare.

The reason for this is the lack of consistent time series and the fact that, because of the confidentiality of the data, it is difficult to do cross-sectional validation of the metrics across banks. It is very likely that over a short time period at a single institution it is difficult to observe any statistical significance.

2.3 THE LOSS DISTRIBUTION APPROACH STANDARD

The LDA has become the modelling standard for operational risk quantification. Every institution that models operational risk uses some form of LDA. The LDA is an actuarial model that models separately the frequency and the severity of operational losses and generates a total loss distribution for a given time horizon, usually a year, by convoluting those two components. The LDA was borrowed from the insurance industry, where it has been used successfully since the mid 20th-century. It is a natural choice given the many similarities between operational risk and the risks that insurers are exposed to. However, despite the similarities between the modelling needs in the insurance industry and those in operational risk, characteristics unique to operational risk have made the implementation of LDA models challenging. Data in operational risk is not as abundant as it is in the insurance industry and the types of losses being modelled are far less homogeneous than in the insurance world. Insurance contracts tend to be very specific and significantly limit the types of losses that are covered, significantly simplifying the modelling effort. Furthermore, it is common for insurance contracts to be capped, limiting the severity of each individual loss. Such capping makes the quality of the fit of severity distributions at very high quantiles less relevant than in operational risk where it is the most significant modelling issue.

2.3.1   Frequency modelling

The most common distribution used to model frequency is the Poisson distribution, which is appealing because it only requires one parameter to be calibrated and because it is an infinitely divisible distribution. The Poisson distribution is typically calibrated by simply calculating the average frequency of losses in the sample. Of course, a number of factors need to be taken into account when calculating the Poisson parameter, such as mergers or acquisitions, potential trends in the data, organic growth, etc. All too often these factors are ignored or dealt with simplistically by using, for example, moving windows of x years. This is due to the fact that, historically, the focus in operational risk has been on the severity side and frequency has been perceived as an element of marginal importance. This might be true for low-frequency–high-severity units of measure but it is not true for all units of measure and, as the usefulness of models moves beyond simply calculating a capital number, the calibration of the frequency will become increasingly important. As we will see in the next section, on factor modelling, frequency is where the link between risk factors and operational risk is the most obvious and the easiest to model.

2.3.2   Severity modelling

The modelling of the severity distribution is considered to be the cornerstone of operational risk modelling. Large catastrophic losses, such as the fraudulent trading loss at Société Générale, that could potentially single-handedly break the bank have focused the industry's attention on severity modelling. The nature of operational risk losses is such that only distributions with fat tails are considered when modelling severity. The workhorse distribution is the lognormal, which generally provides a relatively good fit. Other distributions, such as the gamma–lognormal, the Weibull and the generalised Pareto distribution are popular alternatives. Another technique used to model severity is extreme value theory (EVT), which has the advantage of being "distribution agnostic". The objective of EVT is not to infer the distribution that generated the data but to provide an asymptotic estimate of the behaviour of the tail of the data-generating distribution. The use of EVT in operational risk is one of the reasons people in the field often differentiate the body distribution from the tail distribution. While this differentiation is natural in an EVT setting, it is less so when using standard inference techniques to fit a distribution to data that is assumed to have been generated by a single, homogeneous distribution.

2.3.3 LDA limitations

One of the main drawbacks of the LDA, at least for operational risk, is that it does not address the risk factors driving losses. The LDA tries to model losses regardless of their causes by assuming that the data-generating process never changes. In other words, the assumption is that the risk profile of an institution is unchanging, with the implication that neither risk management changes nor environmental changes will affect the loss process. In credit risk, this would be analogous to assuming that losses on a portfolio will always be the same independent of, say, the economic environment, and independently of how much a bank changes the composition and quality of the portfolio. Insensitivity to factors such as the economic environment is a realistic assumption for certain event types (damage to physical assets (DPA), for example). However, even in the case of DPA, the assumption that the loss process is immutable over time is questionable. Take a bank that has a certain number of buildings in an earthquake-prone area. If this institution decides to sell some of these assets or invest in upgrades to the buildings to make them more earthquake resistant, it is reasonable to assume that its risk exposure should decrease. When using an LDA model, this would not be the case. Losses suffered in the past, when it owned more buildings or less resistant buildings, will be used for the projection of losses in the future under the assumption that the exposure is unchanged.

The perception that operational risk is exclusively characterised by low-frequency–high-severity losses, or that these are the losses that matter, is one of the reasons behind the limited interaction between modelling and risk management referred to earlier. Risk managers focus as much on the improvement of processes and controls to limit these recurrent smaller losses as they do on trying to avoid exposure to the multi-billion-dollar catastrophic losses. If models are ever to be used for risk management purposes, similar emphasis needs to be put on understanding the risk drivers of UoMs with low-frequency–high-severity events and of those with high frequency and low severity. Both can result in material losses to an institution.

2.4 FACTOR MODELLING

The concept of factor modelling is not new in operational risk. The interest in KRIs, which goes back to the early days of modelling, was driven by the desire to understand the drivers of operational risk and to potentially incorporate this information in models. Unfortunately, the development of models based on KRIs or other types of factors has been a bumpy road. These models are still in the very early stages of development at the time of writing. There are two main reasons for the difficulty in successfully integrating factors in operational risk models. First, the data availability issues that have plagued LDA models are even more severe when trying to incorporate risk factors, because long time series are needed to establish a statistical link between the risk and the factor driving it. Most institutions have fairly short data sets, making it very challenging to identify factors. Second, operational risk refers to very different types of risk, ranging from trader fraud to damage to physical assets resulting from natural disasters, which have very different drivers. A consequence of this heterogeneity is that no standardised set of factors can be considered for modelling purposes. Models have to be tailored by unit of measure. Because of the sensitivity of operational risk data, there are no publicly available quality data sets that would allow researchers outside of the banking world to experiment with new modelling techniques.

Operational risk modelling is about to enter a new stage of development. The techniques developed since the early 2000s have helped to introduce the necessary rigour to the field and helped modellers to better understand the risk. It seems, however, that we have reached the limits of what these simple techniques can yield and that a new generation of models needs to be developed. This is particularly important to eliminate the perception of operational risk models as "black boxes". This lack of understanding by non-modellers of the functioning of operational risk models has slowed down the adoption of the information generated by these models for business and risk management purposes. Factor models that link operational risk losses to firm-specific and environmental factors can resolve this problem.

2.4.1 Frequency and severity modelling

In principle, the introduction of factors in operational risk modelling can be done at both the frequency and severity levels. Thus far, all attempts to introduce factors in operational risk modelling have focused on linking changes in the frequency of events to underlying risk drivers. Chernobai *et al* (2011) is the most comprehensive study of factor modelling through the frequency distribution. Chernobai *et al* (2011) showed that changes in frequency can be explained by factors for a number of UoMs. Another interesting paper exploring the drivers of frequency is Cagan and Lantsman (2007), in which it is established that the frequency of certain risk types tracks market volatility as measured by the Volatility Index (VIX) from the Chicago Board of Exchange (CBOE).

The focus on the link between frequency and factors, as opposed to the link between severity and factors, is due to the availability of tools such as the Poisson regression but also to the fact that the variability of frequency is more easily identifiable in the data. The fat-tailed nature of the severity distributions makes it challenging to distinguish between changes that are due to randomness and those due to changes in the underlying distribution. For example, if a tail event is observed, is it the result of sampling (ie, the bank just got unlucky and drew a large event) or is it the result of some underlying risk factors that made it much more likely to draw such an event?

From a practical point of view, introducing factors that drive frequency is fairly straightforward. To illustrate the approach we use the most commonly used distribution for frequency, the Poisson distribution. The current standard approach is to assume that the Poisson parameter is constant over time. The frequency Y

$$\Pr(Y = y) = \frac{e^{-\lambda}\lambda^y}{y!}$$

where λ is the Poisson parameter.

When the frequency is assumed to depend on factors, the Poisson parameter has to change over time as the factors vary. Consequently, the frequency can now be described by

$$\Pr(Y_t = y_t) = \frac{e^{-\lambda_t}\lambda_t^{y_t}}{y_t!}$$

where here the subscript "t" indicates that the Poisson parameter, and by extension the variable itself, now changes over time. The Poisson parameter is a function of certain factors and can itself be modelled using the following regression

$$\ln(\lambda_t) = \alpha + X_t\beta + \varepsilon_t$$

where X is a vector of factors driving frequency and ε_t is the error term.

The biggest challenge facing institutions attempting to use this framework is that of finding statistically significant results. Most institutions have data sets covering fairly short time periods during which the bank's characteristics that could be used as factors, such as asset size, number of employees, etc, have typically not changed in any meaningful way. Furthermore, the data sets often cover one business cycle, making them too short for identifying macroeconomic drivers. Despite these limitations, there are still subsets of operational risk where techniques like this one can be successfully implemented as long as the right factors are identified.

2.4.2 Stress-testing

An interesting application of factor modelling in operational risk is stress-testing. Stress-testing in operational risk has been widely assumed to be either impossible or redundant. This view is a direct result of the non-factor-driven AMA approaches used in the industry and of the general perception of operational risk as a risk linked

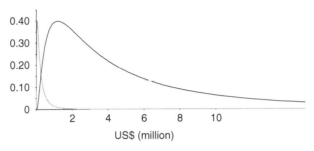

Figure 2.1 Stress-testing operational risk

US$ (million)

The two loss distributions are constructed using the same severity distribution with identical parametrisation, but with a different parameter for the Poisson distribution due to changes in the economic environment.

to the risk profile of an institution, which is assumed to be stable over time and independent of external factors. Consequently, operational risk stress-testing has historically been conducted by simply looking at higher percentiles of the loss distribution. The 2008 crisis brought renewed attention to stress-testing, with regulators around the world requiring institutions to subject their systems to some form of stress-testing. At the onset of the crisis, stress-testing referred to a variety of exercises ranging from reverse stress-testing, when the break point of an institution is identified, to understanding the impact of changing the parameters used in a particular model to macroeconomic stress-testing. The commonly agreed upon definition of stress-testing has converged to that of estimating the impact of an economic downturn on losses. This type of macroeconomic stress-testing consists in estimating the expected loss (or, alternatively, the capital requirements) conditional on a downturn as shown in Figure 2.1. In other words, the intent is to understand how the loss distribution itself shifts because of changes in the macroeconomic environment instead of assuming a constant loss distribution and looking at how the environment results in losses at higher quantiles of the distribution as was often done in operational risk.

This type of thinking is natural in credit or market risk, but such an analysis is pretty much impossible with existing LDA models, which have no factors (see discussion on LDA models in Section 2.3) and is at odds with many people's perception of operational risk as a non-cyclical risk. The introduction of factor models makes it possible to start thinking of stress-testing in operational risk along those

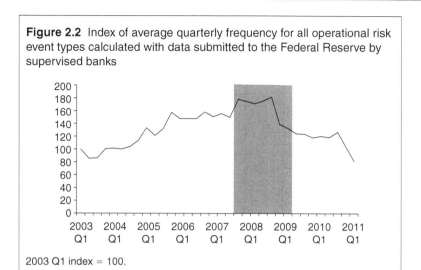

Figure 2.2 Index of average quarterly frequency for all operational risk event types calculated with data submitted to the Federal Reserve by supervised banks

2003 Q1 index = 100.

lines. The key to the success of the approach is the ability to identify macroeconomic factors that affect frequency in a statistically significant manner. Identifying macroeconomic factors that are statistically significant is even more challenging than identifying firm-specific factors because of the indirect nature of their relationship with operational risk and of the large time lags. The short time series available to individual firms often cover only one business cycle, making macroeconomic factor modelling nearly impossible until they collect samples covering longer periods. However, the fact that, at the time of writing, individual datasets are insufficient for most institutions to establish the link between operational risk and the business cycle does not mean that the link does not exist. A study of data from 19 US banks by the Federal Reserve confirms that certain operational risk event types seem to be related to the business cycle.

Figures 2.2–2.5 contain the plots of the index of the average frequency of events for all event types and for clients, products and business practices (CPBP), external fraud (EF) and damage to physical assets (DPA) for the 19 US institutions used in the Federal Reserve's study. This is a quarterly dataset covering the start of the first quarter of 2003 up to the second quarter of 2011. To our knowledge, this is the first comprehensive dataset with individual firm identifiers covering such a large number of institutions over an extended period. Figure 2.2 shows that the frequency of all operational risk events clearly exhibits cyclicality. Interestingly, the increase in the

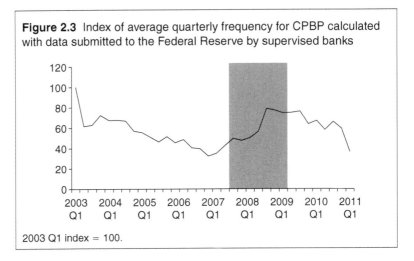

Figure 2.3 Index of average quarterly frequency for CPBP calculated with data submitted to the Federal Reserve by supervised banks

2003 Q1 index = 100.

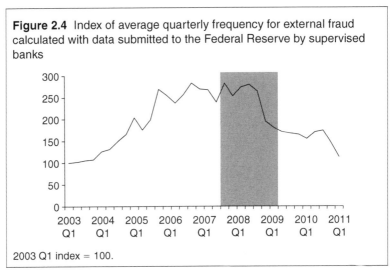

Figure 2.4 Index of average quarterly frequency for external fraud calculated with data submitted to the Federal Reserve by supervised banks

2003 Q1 index = 100.

frequency seems to have started in late 2005, with a second spike starting in 2008 Q4 at the beginning of the recession. This is due to the fact that the 2008 recession was triggered by a banking crisis, and that problems in the banking industry started to materialise before the crisis hit its climax and triggered an economy-wide recession. The increase in frequency prior to the crisis also raised the potential for some operational risk losses to increase in frequency towards the peak of the bubble, probably as a result of the increased activity. This pattern underscores the significant amount of research that

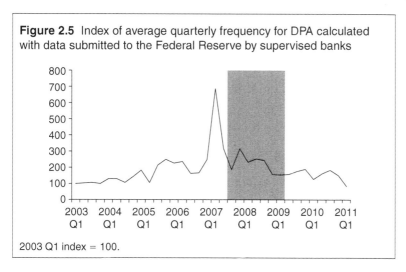

Figure 2.5 Index of average quarterly frequency for DPA calculated with data submitted to the Federal Reserve by supervised banks

2003 Q1 index = 100.

still needs to be done in order to better understand the relationship between operational risk and the business cycle. Figures 2.3–2.5 look at the behaviour of the frequency of specific event types and show that event types have different cyclical patterns. As expected, DPA (Figure 2.5) exhibits no cyclicality, confirming the "act of God" nature of those losses. Spikes in this series are purely random and not linked to any economic factor. CPBP (Figure 2.3) and EF (Figure 2.4) both exhibit cyclical patterns, but with some stark differences. The frequency of CPBP started trending up slowly in late 2007, spiked in 2008 Q4 and started decreasing well after the end of the recession, whereas EF reached its peak frequency levels as early as 2006 Q1 and maintained high levels for a number of quarters, but started to decrease in the middle of the recession in 2008 Q4. The changes in frequency are also non-trivial, dispelling another common misconception that the frequencies for both CPBP and EF more than double (nearly triple) from trough to peak. The lag in CPBP's reaction to the crisis is explained by the fact that a number of CPBP losses were legal losses, and that it took some time for plaintiffs to build a case and sue. The early increase in EF is most likely due to the fact that fraud is affected by both business volume and the economic downturn; fraud was rampant at the height of the mortgage bubble.

Figures 2.2–2.5 not only confirm the existence of cyclical patterns in the frequency of certain operational risk event types but also highlight the amount of research that still remains to be done on this topic. US regulators state that they have been able to find statistically significant relationships between macroeconomic variables and frequency (Federal Reserve Board of Governors 2012). However, they also indicate that direct links were difficult to establish and that most statistically significant results where indirect ones where the factors used to model frequency are firm-specific factors that are themselves correlated with the macroeconomic factors. Stress-testing in operational risk is still in its infancy. The lack of maturity of the AMA models used at the time of writing leads most institutions to conduct stress-testing as a separate exercise. As factor models evolve and are incorporated in the AMA frameworks, stress-testing and AMA will converge.

2.5 CONCLUSION

Operational risk has significantly matured and is now a fully fledged risk discipline to which risk managers pay as much attention as they do other more traditional risks such as credit and market risk. This evolution is the result of the Basel II Accord, which, for the first time, established a regulatory capital requirement for operational risk. While the discipline as we know it today owes its very existence to regulatory requirements, the main weakness of current AMA frameworks is also attributable to regulatory requirements. Most AMA frameworks in place at institutions have been primarily developed to calculate regulatory capital and not for risk management purposes. This has led to the creation of modelling teams that often operate in a silo, disconnected from the management of the risk. Not surprisingly, these models are viewed suspiciously by risk managers, who do not understand the technicalities of the models and tend to see them as black boxes that spew out capital numbers with no explanations as to why these numbers are what they are. The fact that actions taken by risk managers typically have no impact on the capital number aggravates the mistrust in the models.

The next step for operational risk is to bridge this gap between modelling and risk management. In order for this to be achieved, existing modelling techniques will have to evolve and become more risk sensitive. Models will have to become more responsive to actions taken by risk managers and to changes in the business environment. This is only achievable through the development of factor-driven models that link operational risk losses to underlying risk factors. A number of operational risk modellers are researching such models but these efforts are still in their infancy. Stress-testing requirements, such as those required by the Dodd–Frank Act, also require the development of effective factor models linking (directly or indirectly) the realisation of operational risk losses to underlying macroeconomic factors.

1 Power (2003) provides an excellent account of how operational risk came to be as a discipline.

2 See http://www.federalreserve.gov/bankinforeg/srletters/sr1108a1.pdf.

The views expressed herein are the author's and do not necessarily represent those of the Federal Reserve Bank of Richmond or the Federal Reserve System.

REFERENCES

Basel Committee on Banking Supervision, 2006, "Basel II: International Convergence of Capital Measurement and Capital Standards: A Revised Framework", Bank for International Settlements, June, URL: http://www.bis.org/publ/bcbs128.pdf.

Baud, N., A. Frachot and T. Roncalli, 2002, "Internal Data, External Data, and Consortium Data for Operational Risk Measurement: How to Pool Data Properly?", Technical Report, Groupe de Recherche Operationnelle, Credit Lyonnais, France.

Blunden, T., and J. Thirlwell, 2010, *Mastering Operational Risk* (Englewood Cliffs, NJ: Prentice Hall).

Cagan, P., and Y. Lantsman, 2007, "The Cyclicality of Operational Risk: The Tracking Phenomenon", Working Paper, Algorithmics.

Chernobai, A., S. T. Rachev and F. J. Fabozi, 2007, *Operational Risk, a Guide to Basel II Capital Requirements, Models and Analysis* (Wiley Finance).

Chernobai, A., P. Jorion and F. Yu, 2011, "The Determinants of Operational Risk in US Financial Institutions", *Journal of Financial and Quantitative Analysis* 46(6), pp. 1683–1725.

Coles, S. G., and J. A. Tawn, 1996, "A Bayesian Analysis of Extreme Rainfall Data", *Journal of the Royal Statistical Society. Series C (Applied Statistics)* 45(4) pp. 463–78.

Cruz, M. G., 2002, *Modeling, Measuring and Hedging Operational Risk* (New York: John Wiley & Sons).

Dahen, H., and G. Dionne, 2010, "Scaling Models for the Severity and Frequency of External Operational Loss Data", *Journal of Banking and Finance* 34(7), pp. 1484–96.

Dutta, K. K., and D. F. Babbel, 2010, "Scenario Analysis in the Measurement of Operational Risk Capital: A Change of Measure Approach", Working Paper, Wharton Business School, University of Pennsylvania, September.

Ergashev, B., 2012, "A Theoretical Framework for Incorporating Scenarios into Operational Risk Modeling", *Journal of Financial Services Research* 41(3), pp. 145–161.

Ergashev, B., S. Mittnik and E. Sekeris, 2012, "The Bayesian Approach to Extreme Value Estimation in Operational Risk", Mimeo.

Federal Reserve Board of Governors, 2012, "Comprehensive Capital Analysis and Review 2012: Methodology and Results for Stress Scenarios Projections", Federal Reserve Board of Governors, p. 54.

Meek, J., 2012, "Dexia Rejected AMA over Uncertain Capital Relief", URL: http://www.risk.net/operational-risk-and-regulation/news/2165075/dexia-rejected-ama-uncertain-capital-relief.

Power, M., 2003, "The Invention of Operational Risk", Working Paper, ESRC Centre for Analysis of Risk and Regulation.

Rebonato, R., 2010, *Coherent Stress Testing, a Bayesian Approach to the Analysis of Financial Stress* (Chichester: John Wiley & Sons).

Rozenfeld, I., 2010, "Using Shifted Distributions in Computing Operational Risk Capital", Working Paper.

Salmon, F., 2009, "Recipe for Disaster: The Formula that Killed Wall Street", *Wired* 17(3), URL: http://www.wired.com/techbiz/it/magazine/17-03/wp_quant?currentPage=all.

3

The Regulatory Treatment of Operational Risk in Insurance

Andreas A. Jobst

Bermuda Monetary Authority

The credit crisis illustrated that many sources of systemic risk were triggered, or at least propagated, by vulnerabilities in operational risk management. At the same time, many institutions were (and still are) at different stages of systems development and show considerable dispersion in operational risk management practices. This chapter explains the importance of operational risk in insurance and assesses existing regulatory approaches to the standardised treatment of operational risk for capital assessment purposes. It provides an overview of two prominent regulatory regimes for globally active insurance companies that include an explicit operational risk capital charge, Solvency II and the Bermuda Solvency Capital Requirement, and concludes with a comparative empirical analysis of both approaches.

3.1 OVERVIEW

The scale of the credit crisis revealed major shortcomings in risk management in the financial sector, which underscored the apparent failure of the past regulatory framework – predicated on combining capital market discipline, principles-informed prudential oversight, and risk-based capital guidelines – to safeguard financial stability. It also illustrated that many sources of macro-financial shocks were triggered, or at least propagated, by vulnerabilities in operational risk management, which had not kept pace with financial innovation, and an insufficient recognition of infrastructural resilience to operational risk as an essential element of financial stability. At the same time, many financial institutions were (and continue to be) at different stages of systems development and showed considerable dispersion in operational risk management practices, while growing complexity in the insurance industry, large-scale mergers and acquisitions, as well as greater use of outsourcing arrangements, raised the susceptibility to operational risk (Jobst 2010).

Against the background of rising concerns about system-wide vulnerabilities and greater focus on macroprudential surveillance, it is hardly surprising that operational risk is becoming a salient feature of risk management in financial institutions, including insurance companies. The increase in scope of operational risk is largely explained by two important characteristics:

(i) operational risk amplifies system-wide risk levels and has a greater potential to transpire in greater and more harmful ways than many other sources of risk, given the increased size, interconnectedness and complexity of financial institutions (which increase the possibility of errors and fraud); and

(ii) techniques aimed at identifying worst-case scenarios associated with the inherently elusive nature of extreme events, as the hallmark of early-warning and financial stability analysis, fall naturally within the domain of operational risk management.

This development has translated into new emerging practices of strategic and integrated operational risk management based on a centralised taxonomy of risk drivers and a risk-based assessment of vulnerabilities (Table 3.1).

This chapter explains the importance of operational risk in insurance and assesses existing regulatory approaches to the standardised treatment of operational risk for capital assessment purposes. After defining the scope of operational risk in general and, more specifically, in the context of insurance activities, we give an overview of two selected regulatory regimes for globally active insurance companies that include an explicit operational risk capital charge: the "standard formula" for operational risk under Solvency II and the Bermuda Solvency Capital Requirement (BSCR). Finally, the chapter concludes with a comparative empirical analysis of both approaches and offers some suggestions on the future development operational

Table 3.1 Traditional and emerging practice of operational risk management

	Traditional practice	Emerging (modern) practice
Definition	Undesirable incident/event, such as fraud/system failure ("what/where are the risks?").	Measure of exposure to loss from undesirable event/incident ("how much risk do I have?").
Objective/ implementation	Tactical and isolated: "silo approach" of risk management by individual business units; day-to-day management of current threats from imminent operational errors.	Strategic and integrated: comprehensive OR management framework of policies and guidelines; management of key risks, especially the optimisation of cost-benefit trade-off (with largest scope possible) under consideration of risk-reward/risk-control and risk transfer possibilities.
Risk identification process	BL managers identify their major risks (risk factors, controllable factors, events and effects; no restriction on overlaps; generally no differentiation made between risks and controls); results in voluminous performance indicators.	Centralised OR management supplements and reinforces BL risk ownership by defining "risk universe", consisting of a finite (comprehensive) set of mutually exclusive (non-overlapping) "risk classes"; use hard and soft data to identify sources of (largest) risks; results in defined common data standards and risk tolerance levels.

OR, operational risk; BL, business line.
Sources: Ranson and Samad-Khan (2008) and author's own data.

risk management, from both an organisational and an industry perspective.

Table 3.1 Continued.

	Traditional practice	Emerging (modern) practice
Risk assessment	Reliance on qualitative processes to improve risk management.	Extension of measurement to defined quantitative methods to capture potential operational risk exposure, identify sources of risk and improve existing risk management practices.
Risk measurement	Calculate risk by multiplying likelihood and impact for each risk type (conditional on one event) and one risk at a time; assume discrete nature of risk.	Estimate distribution (closed form/simulation) based on frequency and severity to derive cumulative loss potential from multiple events and across all risk classes simultaneously; assumes stochastic nature of risk.
Aggregation	Results based on likelihood cannot be aggregated.	Results based on frequency may be aggregated (but assume independence of units of measure).
Measurement metric	Probability-weighted loss from one specific incident/event.	Cumulative loss from one or more "risk classes" at different degrees of statistical confidence and time horizon.
Risk reporting	Inconsistent BL reporting; availability and quality of data on operational risk events.	Concise, standardised reporting in a structured and formal OR management process to senior management.

Sources: Ranson and Samad-Khan (2008) and author's own data.

3.2 OPERATIONAL RISK MANAGEMENT PRACTICES

The measurement and regulation of operational risk are quite distinct from that of other types of risk. Moreover, given that operational risk is not priced, incentives underlying operational risk management are different from those determining the hedging of credit and market risk, and remedies are process driven rather than mathematical. Operational risk is difficult to conceptualise, especially as the demarcation line between this and other types of risk (eg, market and credit risks) has become increasingly blurred.

Operational risk deals mainly with tail events rather than central projections or tendencies, reflecting aberrant rather than normal behaviour and situations. Thus, the exposure to operational risk is less predictable and even harder to model, because extreme losses are one-off events of large economic impact without historical precedent. While some high-frequency operational risk events follow from very predictable stochastic patterns, whose high frequency caters to quantitative measures, there are many other types of operational risk for which there is not, and never can be, data to support anything but an exercise requiring subjective judgment and estimation. In addition, the diverse nature of operational risk from internal or external disruptions to business activities and the unpredictability of their overall financial impact complicate systematic measurement and consistent regulation.

Thus, the historical experience of operational risk events suggests a heavy-tailed loss distribution, ie, there is a higher chance of an extreme loss event (with high loss severity) than the shape of the standard limit distributions would suggest. While firms should generate enough expected revenues to support a net margin to absorb expected losses from predictable internal failures, they also need to provision sufficient economic capital as risk reserves to cover the unexpected losses from large, one-off internal and external shocks.

There are three major concepts of operational risk measurement:

1. the volume-based approach, which assumes that the operational risk exposure is a function of the type and complexity of business activity, especially in cases when notoriously low margins (such as in transaction processing and payments-system related activities in banking) have the potential to magnify the impact of operational risk losses;

2. the comprehensive qualitative self-assessment of operational risk with a view to evaluating the likelihood and severity of financial losses based on subjective judgment rather than historical precedent; and

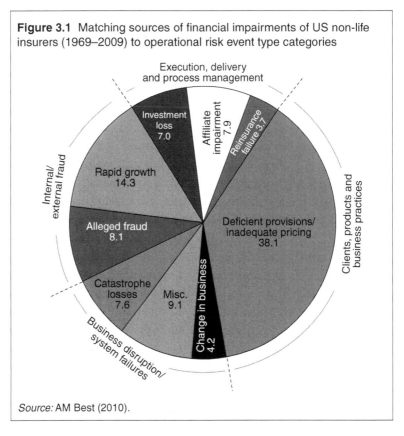

Figure 3.1 Matching sources of financial impairments of US non-life insurers (1969–2009) to operational risk event type categories

Execution, delivery
and process management

Investment loss 7.0

Affiliate impairment 7.9

Reinsurance failure 3.7

Internal/ external fraud

Rapid growth 14.3

Alleged fraud 8.1

Deficient provisions/ inadequate pricing 38.1

Clients, products and business practices

Catastrophe losses 7.6

Misc. 9.1

Change in business 4.2

Business disruption/ system failures

Source: AM Best (2010).

3. quantitative techniques, which have been developed as part of "internal models" for the purpose of assigning economic capital to operational risk exposures in compliance with regulatory capital requirements.

Despite considerable variation of economic capital measurement techniques ranging from qualitative managerial judgments to comprehensive statistical analysis, capital allocation for operational risk tends to be mainly driven by the quantification of losses relative to explicit exposure indicators (or volume-based measures) of business activity.

3.3 OPERATIONAL RISK IN INSURANCE

Given this apparent overlap of operational risk with other risk areas in insurance, the inherent operational risk element in the insurance/underwriting cycle makes it conceptually difficult to dislodge operational risk from other sources of risk. Operational risk is frequently considered the largest threat to insurers, primarily due to the complex interactions between the variability of business processes and their implications for the subsequent losses incurred. Operational risk can occur in claims management, underwriting, renewals, invoice handling and process inefficiencies, to name just a few (Figure 3.1). Since operational risk is intertwined with other risks affecting insurance activities, without adequate processes and controls in place, capital adequacy could be adversely affected by operational risk events. However, unlike banks, insurers' business is not transactional and removed from financial services, which tend to be susceptible to high operational risk.

While this explains the greater attention paid to operational risk management in insurance, its regulatory treatment and the practical implementation have followed a different path to the banking sector. A consistent regulatory treatment of operational risk across different jurisdictions has gained traction only since 2007 as simple ratio-based models have given way to risk-based models via standardised approaches and internal model approval process. Unlike in the banking sector, where the revision of the Basel Accord has led to the adoption of standardised supervisory approaches (for firms with less sophisticated risk management systems) and specific guidelines for internal models, similar efforts in the insurance sector have been protracted and less comprehensive in scope (Table 3.2).

Thus, operational risk in insurance has not achieved the same prominence, in terms of quantitative measures, as operational risk in banking.[1] In addition, the measurement and disclosure of operational risk exposures in insurance is complicated by the absence of such activities in the past.[2] There is often limited available data covering operational risk losses for individual firms and, more widely, the insurance industry as a whole. Insufficient internal data on operational losses represents a significant challenge to the development and calibration of internal models for operational risk, which are closely aligned with economic capital considerations.

Insurance regulations that impose an explicit operational risk capital charge tend to do so with a focus on standardised approaches, while capital assessments based on internal models imply an integrated treatment of operational risk. Among the most relevant regulatory regimes that affect global insurance activities, only the

Table 3.2 Overview of operational risk measures in banking regulation under Basel II

Method	Computation	Definition
Basic indicator approach (BIA)	A fixed percentage of average annual gross income over the previous three years; any non-profit year to be excluded from calculation.	Capital charge $(K_{BIA}) = [\sum_{\text{years }(1-n)} \sum (GI_{1...n}, \alpha)]/N$, where GI is annual (positive) gross income[1] over the previous three years ("exposure factor"), n is number of the previous three years (N) for which gross income is positive, and $\alpha = 15\%$, which is set by the Basel Committee, relating the industry wide level of required capital to the industry wide level of the indicator ("multiplier").
(Traditional) standardised approach (TSA)	The three-year average of the summation of the regulatory capital charges across each of the BLs in each year.	Capital charge $(K_{TSA}) = \{\sum_{\text{years}(1-3)} \max[\sum (GI_{1-8}\beta_{1-8}),]\}/3$, where GI_{1-8} is GI for each of the eight BLs ("exposure factor"), β_{1-8} is fixed percentage relating the level of required capital to the level of the gross income for each of eight BLs defined by the Basel Committee; β equals 18% for the BLs corporate finance (β_1), trading & sales (β_2), payment & settlement (β_5); 15% for commercial banking (β_4) and agency services (β_6); and 12% for retail banking (β_3), asset management (β_7), and retail brokerage (β_8).

[1] Gross income (GI) is defined as net interest and non-interest income. This measure should: (i) be gross of any provisions (eg, for unpaid interest), (ii) be gross of operating expenses, including fees paid to outsourcing service providers, (iii) exclude realised profits/losses from the sale of securities in the banking book, and (iv) exclude extraordinary or irregular items as well as income derived from insurance.
Sources: Basel Committee on Banking Supervision (2004, 2005, 2006).

Table 3.2 Continued

Method	Computation	Definition
Alternative standardised approach (ASA)	Same as TSA, but applies different exposure factor to retail banking and commercial banking.	Capital charge $(K_{ASA}K) = \{\sum_{years(1-3)} \max[\sum (GI_{1-2,5-8}\beta_{1-2,5-8}), 0]\}/3$ $+ \{\sum_{years1-3} \max[\sum (LA_{3-4}m\beta_{3-4}), 0]\}/3$, where $GI_{1-2,5-8}$ is the GI for each of the eight six BLs other than retail/commercial banking ("exposure factor"), $\beta_{1-2,5-8}$ is fixed percentage relating the level of required capital to the level of the gross income for each of six BLs other than retail/commercial banking defined by the Basel Committee, LA_{3-4} is the total outstanding loans and advances (non-risk weighted and gross of provisions)[2] for each retail banking and commercial banking ("exposure factor"), β_{3-4} is the fixed percentage relating the level of required capital to the level of the gross income for retail banking and commercial banking, and $m = 0.035$ is the fixed factor that replaces GI as exposure indicator.

[2] For ASA, total loans and advances in retail banking consist of the total drawn amounts in the following credit portfolios: retail, SMEs treated as retail, and purchased retail receivables. For commercial banking, total loans and advances consists of the drawn amounts in the following credit portfolios: corporate, sovereign, bank, specialised lending, SMEs treated as corporate and purchased corporate receivables. The book value of securities held in the banking book should also be included.

Table 3.2 Continued

Method	Computation	Definition
Advanced measurement approaches (AMA)	Generated by the bank's internal operational risk measurement system.	AMA includes quantitative and qualitative criteria for the self-assessment of operational risk, which must be satisfied to ensure adequate risk management and oversight. The qualitative criteria[3] centre on the administration and regular review of a sound internal operational risk measurement system. The quantitative[4] aspects include: (i) the use of internal data, (ii) external data, (iii) scenario analysis, and (iv) business environment and internal control factors. Under the AMA soundness standard, a bank must be able to demonstrate that its operational risk measure is comparable to that of the internal ratings-based approach for credit risk, ie, a one-year holding period and a 99.9th percentile confidence interval. Banks are also allowed to adjust their capital charge for operational risk exposure under AMA by (i) the amount of expected losses (ELs) ("EL breakout"), (ii) diversification benefits from loss correlation between operational loss ETs both across and within BLs, (iii) and the risk mitigating impact of insurance on measures of operational risk used for regulatory minimum capital requirements. Capital adjustment is limited to 20% of the total operational risk capital charge calculated under AMA.

[3]The qualitative criteria include (i) an ORM function, (ii) a well-documented and well-integrated, internal operational risk measurement system, (iii) regular reporting of operational risk exposures and loss experience to business unit management, senior management, and to the board of directors, as well as (iv) regular reviews and validation of the ORM processes and measurement systems by external auditors. [4]The quantitative criteria include (i) internal data requirements (ie, internal loss data must be clearly linked to a bank's current business activities, technological processes and risk management procedures and must cover a minimum five-year observation period (though a three-year historical data window is acceptable when AMA is applied for the first time)), (ii) the use of external data (on actual loss amounts, information on the scale of business operations where the event occurred, information on the causes and circumstances of the loss events or other information) when there is reason to believe that the bank is exposed to infrequent, yet potentially severe, losses, (iii) scenario analysis, and (iv) business environment and internal control factors.

forthcoming Solvency II standard in Europe and the national regulations in Bermuda contain explicit (standard) provisions for an operational risk capital charge.[3] Both regimes include a standard formula for the explicit treatment of operational risk: although each motivated by a different rationale, internal (ie, firm-specific) estimates of operational risk under either regime are not treated in a distinct model approval process like in banking (unless warranted by the supervisor). In general, internal models for operational risk in insurance have not been subjected to a separate set of principles and guidelines that define supervisory expectations of the approval process under the advanced measurement approach (AMA). Advanced methods for operational risk measurement tend to vary significantly and are commonly found as inherent elements of economic capital frameworks.

3.4 REVIEW OF EXISTING REGULATORY APPROACHES

3.4.1 Operational risk under Solvency II

The Solvency II framework represents a risk-based regulatory framework for insurance companies in the European Union, which aims at facilitating the development of a single market for insurance activities by harmonizing solvency regulation of insurance companies that conduct business in EU member states. The Solvency II directive was adopted by the European Parliament and Council in 2009, which set out the key principles ("Level 1 principles") promoting confidence in the financial stability of the insurance sector and securing adequate consumer protection by reducing the probability of institutional failure. In accordance with the so-called Lamfalussy Process within the European Union, the Level 1 Framework Directive of Solvency II was followed by the drafting of Level 2 implementing measures and consultations of the Level 3 committee, consisting of representatives from the various insurance supervisory authorities across Europe, which gave advice to the Commission on the implementation of the Solvency II Directive. Like the Basel II framework (Basel Committee on Banking Supervision 2006), Solvency II covers different aspects of the economic risk faced by insurance companies within a three pillar structure:

1. the first pillar ("Pillar 1"): risk-weighted measures of capital requirements;

Table 3.3 Solvency II pillar structure

	Main elements
Pillar 1: capital adequacy (quantitative standards)	Solvency capital requirement (SCR) and minimum capital requirement (MCR), representing different levels of supervisory intervention: • SCR (via standard formula or internal model): risk-based target level of capital; covers all quantifiable risks an insurer or reinsurer faces and takes into account any risk mitigation technique; breach triggers corrective action to restore health of firm • MCR: lower requirement; breach triggers ultimate supervisory intervention, the revocation of the insurer's license (withdrawal of authorisation).
Pillar 2: supervisory review (qualitative standards)	Contains qualitative requirements on undertakings such as risk management and supervisory activities; in particular, capital planning and "structural" explanation for Pillar 1 results (and definition of mitigants, if applicable).
Pillar 3: market discipline (reporting and disclosure)	Firms need to disclose certain information publicly to support market discipline and help ensure stability of (re)insurer (disclosure and transparency); also reporting of more information to supervisors.

2. second pillar ("Pillar 2"): management and control of these risks; and

3. the third pillar ("Pillar 3"): requirements for disclosure and transparency of information to both supervisors and the public (Table 3.3).

The capital assessment under the Solvency II (European Commission 2011) comprises a bottom-up calculation of different risks affecting the value of the economic balance sheet of insurers with respect to both new and old business (ie, changes in asset and liability risk factors). Based on the Level 2 implementation measures, the Solvency II framework establishes total balance sheet economic capital approach, which allows insurers to determine their own statutory capital needs using internal models, subject to supervisory approval, or prescribed approaches for various risks based a standard formula (European Commission 2008). The minimum capital adequacy (ie, the solvency capital requirement (SCR)) is calibrated to satisfy 99.5% VaR-based change in economic capital and surplus over one-year time horizon.[4] The standardised approach under Solvency II is divided into five risk modules (life underwriting risk, non-life underwriting risk, market risk, counterparty default risk, and operational risk), which themselves are further divided into component sub-risks (eg, premium/reserve risk and catastrophe risk in the non-life underwriting risk module). As part of the bottom-up calculation of the SCR, the standardised approach applies a combination of stress tests, scenarios and factor-based capital charges to determine capital charges for each risk (ie, risk modules and sub-risk components) and incorporates a diversification benefit from correlation across risk modules (and reduction for reinsurance and capital market hedging programs). Thus, the generic definition of the SCR for a particular risk (based on net impact of a given change in the risk factor on the economic balance sheet after hedging) is defined as

$$\text{SCR} = \sqrt{\sum_i \sum_j \rho(i,j) \times \text{SCR}_i \times \text{SCR}_j} \qquad (3.1)$$

where $\rho(i,j)$ denotes the overall correlation between sub-risk components i and j, which is applied to the sum of the individual risk exposures of each risk category.

The operational risk module ("standard formula for operational risk") within the Solvency II framework relates to "risk of loss arising from inadequate or failed internal processes, or from personnel and systems, or from external events" (Article 13(33) of Level 1 text) if it has not been explicitly covered in other risk modules.[5] In contrast to other risk modules, it does not include sub-risk components but specifies a direct, "volume-based" capital charge.[6] The calculation method and the calibration of parameters underling an explicit charge for operational risk under the "standard formula" has evolved significantly over time in response to industry consultations. In its original definitions prior to the finalisation of Level 2 implementation in October 2011, the SCR of the operational risk module was defined as

$$\mathrm{SCR}_{\mathrm{Op}} = \min\{\mathrm{Basic\ SCR}_{\mathrm{cap}_{\{\mathrm{life,\ non\text{-}life}\}}} \times \mathrm{Basic\ SCR}; \mathrm{Op}_{\ln\ \mathrm{ul}}\}$$
$$+ \mathrm{UL\ factor} \times \mathrm{Exp}_{\mathrm{ul}} \qquad (3.2)$$

with $\mathrm{Op}_{\ln\ \mathrm{ul}}$ as the basic operational risk charge for all business other than unit-linked business (and gross of reinsurance) derived as the maximum

$$\mathrm{Op}_{\ln\ \mathrm{ul}} = \max\{\mathrm{Op}_{\mathrm{prem}}; \mathrm{Op}_{\mathrm{prov}}\} \qquad (3.3)$$

based on

$$\mathrm{Op}_{\mathrm{prem}}$$
$$= f(\mathrm{Op}_{\mathrm{prem\ life}}) \times (\mathrm{Prem}_{\mathrm{life}} + \mathrm{Prem}_{\mathrm{SLT\ health}} - \mathrm{Prem}_{\mathrm{life\ ul}})$$
$$+ f(\mathrm{Op}_{\mathrm{prem\ non\text{-}life}}) \times (\mathrm{Prem}_{\mathrm{non\text{-}life}} + \mathrm{Prem}_{\mathrm{non\text{-}SLT\ health}})$$
$$+ \max\{0; f(\mathrm{Op}_{\mathrm{prem\ life}}) \times (\Delta\mathrm{Prem\ life} - \Delta\mathrm{Prem}_{\mathrm{life\ ul}})|_{\Delta>10\%}\}$$
$$+ \max\{0; f(\mathrm{Op}_{\mathrm{prem\ non\text{-}life}}) \times \Delta\mathrm{Prem}_{\mathrm{non\text{-}life}}|_{\Delta>10\%}\} \qquad (3.4)$$

and

$$\mathrm{Op}_{\mathrm{prov}}$$
$$= f(\mathrm{Op}_{\mathrm{prov\ life}}) \times (\mathrm{Prov}_{\mathrm{life}} + \mathrm{Prov}_{\mathrm{SLT\ health}} - \mathrm{Prov}_{\mathrm{life\ ul}})$$
$$+ f(\mathrm{Op}_{\mathrm{prov\ non\text{-}life}}) \times (\mathrm{Prov}_{\mathrm{non\text{-}life}} + \mathrm{Prov}_{\mathrm{non\text{-}SLT\ health}})$$
$$+ \max\{0; f(\mathrm{Op}_{\mathrm{prov\ life}}) \times (\Delta\mathrm{Prov}_{\mathrm{life}} - \Delta\mathrm{Prov}_{\mathrm{life\ ul}})|_{\Delta>10\%}\}$$
$$+ \max\{0; f(\mathrm{Op}_{\mathrm{prov\ non\text{-}life}}) \times \Delta\mathrm{Prov}_{\mathrm{non\text{-}life}}|_{\Delta>10\%}\} \qquad (3.5)$$

for a given level of earned premium income ("Prem") and technical provisioning ("Prov"), respectively, with pre-specified scaling factors $\mathrm{Op}_{\mathrm{prem\ life}}$, $\mathrm{Op}_{\mathrm{prem\ non\text{-}life}}$, $\mathrm{Op}_{\mathrm{prov\ life}}$, and $\mathrm{Op}_{\mathrm{prov\ non\text{-}life}}$, and subject to an upper limit based on a fixed percentage, $\mathrm{Basic\ SCR}_{\mathrm{cap}_{\{\mathrm{life,\ non\text{-}life}\}}}$, of the total capital charge under the standard formula for life and non-life insurance activities (without an operational risk element).

Moreover, the capital charge was augmented by an additional charge commensurate to the amount of annual (administrative) expenses $\mathrm{Exp}_{\mathrm{ul}}$ (gross of reinsurance and excluding acquisition expenses) incurred with respect to unit-linked (UL) business during the last available reporting period (not based on future projected expenses) but scaled by a "UL factor". The last two terms of Equations 3.4 and 3.5 also applied the scaling factors to the first order change Δ in premium income and technical provisioning between periods $t-1$ and t (without any possibility of offsetting life and non-life Δ) if the periodic change was 10% or higher. The individual input variables (based on prudential returns) were defined as follows.

- $Prov_{life}$: total life insurance technical provisions (gross of reinsurance), with a floor equal to zero (including unit-linked business and life-like obligations on non-life contracts such as annuities).

- $Prov_{SLT\ health}$: technical provisions for health insurance (gross of reinsurance) that qualifies as SLT, with a floor equal to zero.

- $Prov_{life\ ul}$: total life insurance technical provisions for unit-linked business (gross of reinsurance), with a floor equal to zero.

- $Prov_{non-life}$: total non-life insurance technical provisions (gross of reinsurance), with a floor equal to zero (excluding life-like obligations on non-life contracts such as annuities).

- $Prov_{non-SLT\ health}$: technical provisions for health insurance that do not qualify as SLT (gross of reinsurance), with a floor equal to zero.

- $Prem_{life}$: total earned life premium (gross of reinsurance), including unit-linked business.

- $Prem_{SLT\ health}$: total earned premiums for health insurance (gross of reinsurance) that qualifies as SLT.

- $Prem_{life\ ul}$: total earned life premium for unit-linked business (gross of reinsurance).

- $Prem_{non-life}$: total earned non-life premium (gross of reinsurance).

- $Prem_{non-SLT\ health}$: total earned premiums for health insurance that do not qualify as SLT (gross of reinsurance).

After consultation with the CRO Forum (Chief Risk Officers Forum 2008) and the completion of two quantitative impact studies on the implementation of Solvency II (QIS 4 and QIS 5), the original specification of the standard formula (and its parameterisation as of March 2008; see Table 3.4) was enhanced to establish the greatest possible consistency with internal (undiversified) models that estimate capital requirements at the 99.5% VaR of (unexpected) operational risk losses over a one-year risk horizon (European Commission 2008,

Table 3.4 Parameters for the standard formula for operational risk under Solvency II (in percent)

	Solvency II (10/2011)	QIS 5 factors (10/2009)	"Undiversified" QIS 4 factors (CRO forum)	QIS 4 factors (03/2008)
UL factor	25.0	25.0	N/A	25.0
$BSCR_{cap}$ (life/non-life)	30.0	30.0	n.a.	30.0
$f(Prem_{life})$	4.0	5.5	6.0	3.0
$f(Prem_{non\text{-}life})$	3.0	3.8	4.0	2.0
$f(Prov_{life})$	0.45	0.6	0.6	0.3
$f(Prov_{non\text{-}life})$	3.0	3.6	4.0	2.0

2010). In 2009, the CRO Forum found that the QIS 4 requirements for operational risk in the standard approach were significantly lower than the pre-diversification allowance in internal models.

In particular, empirical analyses of the previous standard formula under QIS 4 suggested that the parameters were "undercalibrated", ie, they did not provide incentives for internal model development due to favorable regulatory treatment under a simple standardised approach. As a result, for the final version of the standard formula (European Commission 2011) several parameter values (Table 3.4) were updated for the QIS 5 exercise (and subsequently for the adoption of the final Level 2 text of Solvency II), and the standard formula (see Equation 3.2) was simplified to

$$SCR_{Op} = \min\{\text{Basic } SCR_{cap_{\{life, non-life\}}} \times \text{Basic } SCR; Op_{ln\ ul}\} \quad (3.6)$$

$$Op_{prem}$$

$$= f(Op_{prem\ life}) \times (Prem_{life} - Prem_{life\ ul})$$

$$+ f(Op_{prem\ non\text{-}life}) \times (Prem_{non\text{-}life})$$

$$+ \max\left\{0; f(Op_{prem\ life}) \times \left(\begin{array}{c}(Prem_{life_t} - 1.2Prem_{life_{t-1}}) \\ -(Prem_{life\ ul_t} - 1.2Prem_{life\ ul_{t-1}})\end{array}\right)\right\}$$

$$+ \max\{0; f(Op_{prem\ non\text{-}life}) \times (Prem_{non\text{-}life_t} - 1.2Prem_{non\text{-}life_{t-1}})\}$$

$$(3.7)$$

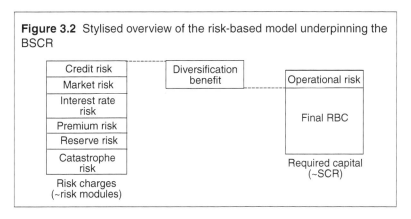

Figure 3.2 Stylised overview of the risk-based model underpinning the BSCR

and

$$Op_{prov} = f(Op_{prov\ life}) \times \max(0; Prov_{life} - Prov_{life\ ul})$$
$$+ f(Op_{prov\ non\text{-}life}) \times \max(0; Prov_{non\text{-}life}) \quad (3.8)$$

Note, however, that even after the re-calibration of the various input parameters after QIS 4, many European insurers reported lower capital charges under the standard formula, which led many firms to exclude operational risk from their internal models ("partial internal models").

3.4.2 Operational risk under the BSCR

The BSCR represents a principles-based regulatory regime for insurance companies, which is geared towards understanding the risk profile or characteristics of the Bermuda (re)insurers within a risk-based approach consistent with similar approaches in other jurisdictions. It was established under the Insurance (Prudential Standards) (Class 4 and 3B Solvency Requirement) Rules 2008 (the "Rules") by the Bermuda Monetary Authority (BMA) in combination with the Guidance Note No. 17 on Commercial Insurer Risk Assessment. Together with the Insurance Act 1978, Insurance Returns and Solvency Regulations 1980, Insurance Accounts Regulations 1980 and the Insurance Code of Conduct 2010, it forms the regulatory regime for the (re)insurance sector in Bermuda.[7]

Much like the Solvency II framework, the capital assessment comprises a bottom-up calculation, which is informed by primarily applying risk factors to capital and solvency return elements, including investments and other assets, premiums and reserves, operational

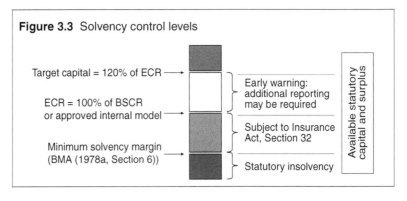

Figure 3.3 Solvency control levels

Target capital = 120% of ECR →

ECR = 100% of BSCR
or approved internal model →

Minimum solvency margin
(BMA (1978a, Section 6)) →

Early warning:
additional reporting
may be required

Subject to Insurance
Act, Section 32

Statutory insolvency

Available statutory
capital and surplus

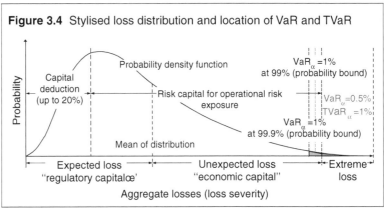

Figure 3.4 Stylised loss distribution and location of VaR and TVaR

Probability

Capital
deduction
(up to 20%)

Probability density function

Risk capital for operational risk
exposure

Mean of distribution

$VaR_\alpha = 1\%$
at 99% (probability bound)

$VaR_\alpha = 0.5\%$
$TVaR_\alpha = 1\%$

$VaR_\alpha = 1\%$
at 99.9% (probability bound)

Expected loss
"regulatory capitaloe'

Unexpected loss
"economic capital"

Extreme
loss

Aggregate losses (loss severity)

risk, and insurer-specific catastrophe exposure in order to establish an overall measure of capital and surplus for statutory solvency purposes. However, some elements within the BSCR are designed with characteristics of Bermuda market in mind (such as a catastrophe capital charge). Insurers are required to maintain a solvency level that satisfies the target capital level (TCL), which represents 120% of the enhanced capital requirement (ECR) as a risk-based capital measure (Figure 3.3). This solvency capital requirement is calibrated to satisfy a 99.0% TVaR-based (Figure 3.4) change in economic capital and surplus over one-year time horizon (with full run-off insurance liabilities),[8] and (as under the Solvency II regime) may be calculated using prescribed approaches for various risks or the firm's internal model, subject to supervisory approval.[9]

The operational risk component within the BSCR framework comprises a qualitative assessment of operational risk, rather than a volume-based performance metric like in the standard formula for operational risk under Solvency II, for which a quantitative capital charge is determined. In recognition of the empirical constraints (of data scarcity and model robustness at higher percentile levels of empirical calibration), the analytical focus is placed on the governance process (in keeping with the spirit of Pillar 2 of the Solvency II framework) as critical input to understanding risk profile, recognising that capital is not always the best (i) deterrent to excessive risk-taking and (ii) mitigant for unexpected losses arising from capital events. More specifically, it is defined as add-on capital charge

$$C_{op} = \rho \times \text{Acov} \tag{3.9}$$

which is mapped to an aggregate risk score ρ (ranging between 1 and 10%) based upon the quality of operational risk management (ORM) systems and procedures via qualitative self-assessment (see Tables 3.5–3.8 and Figure 3.9), and Acov is the basic risk-based capital (RBC) (Figure 3.2) (after covariance adjustment)

$$\underbrace{\sqrt{C_{fi}^2 + C_{eq}^2 + C_{int}^2 + C_{prem}^2 + (\tfrac{1}{2}C_{cred} + C_{rsvs})^2 + (\tfrac{1}{2}C_{cred})^2 + C_{cat}^2}}_{\text{Final RBC}} + C_{op}$$

$$\tag{3.10}$$

or an amount approved by the Bermuda Monetary Authority (BMA). In Equation 3.10, C_{fi} is the fixed income investment risk charge, C_{eq} is the equity investment risk charge, C_{int} is interest rate/liquidity risk charge, C_{prem} is the premium risk charge, C_{cred} is the credit risk charge, C_{rsvs} is the reserve risk charge, and C_{cat} is the catastrophic risk charge. Although this specification does not imply a claim to the unique identification of scope/scale of operational risk, capital add-ons are applied where unmitigated material risks are not captured by the model.

The operational risk charge within the BSCR is the result of applying a "maturity model approach" under Commercial Insurer Risk Assessment (CIRA), which specifies a qualitative assessment of operational risk (but without defining a structural model) (Figure 3.5).[10] The capital charge is determined by an overall risk score that is composed of six individual scores corresponding to the stage of the insurer's self-assessment of the effectiveness corporate governance, risk management policies and practices, as well as control procedures for operational risk.[11] At its core, the CIRA emphasises the interrelationships between the risk management and corporate governance functions and rewards firms' graduated implementation of

Table 3.5 BSCR: aggregate risk score for the operational risk under CIRA

Overall score	OpRisk charge ρ (%)
$\leqslant 5{,}200$	10
$> 5{,}200$ and $\leqslant 6{,}000$	9
$> 6{,}000$ and $\leqslant 6{,}650$	8
$> 6{,}650$ and $\leqslant 7{,}250$	7
$> 7{,}250$ and $\leqslant 7{,}650$	6
$> 7{,}650$ and $\leqslant 7{,}850$	5
$> 7{,}850$ and $\leqslant 8{,}050$	4
$> 8{,}050$ and $\leqslant 8{,}250$	3
$> 8{,}250$ and $\leqslant 8{,}450$	2
$> 8{,}450$	1

Table 3.6 BSCR: risk categories for the operational risk under CIRA

Sub-category	Sub-score
Corporate governance	0–1,200
Risk management function	0–1,050
Risk identification process	0–1,600
Risk measurement process	0–1,600
Risk response process	0–1,600
Risk monitoring and reporting process	0–1,600
Total	1,600–8,650

policies and practices in achieving progress in each risk management area. In particular, it assesses the quality of the insurer's risk management function surrounding its operational risk exposures and serves as a critical tool to furnish the Board with the necessary information to make appropriate decisions and assist the insurer's management in steering the organisation forwards based on the following.[12]

- **The self-assessment of the quality of corporate governance and risk management functions** on four broad dimensions, which are defined separately in individual maturity modules – risk identification, risk measurement, risk response and risk monitoring and reporting (Tables 3.7 and 3.8).

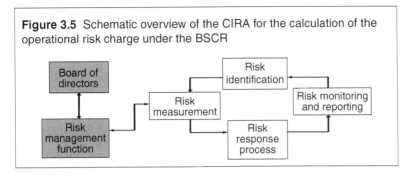

Figure 3.5 Schematic overview of the CIRA for the calculation of the operational risk charge under the BSCR

- The application of a maturity model approach to identify an insurer's developmental stage (ie, the effectiveness of policies and procedures) in each dimension with respect to a specific operational risk area (Figure 3.9). The following eight operational risk exposures (which are comparable to "event types" in the implementation of operational risk frameworks in banking) are examined: fraud, human resources, outsourcing, distribution channels, business processes, information systems and regulatory and legal compliance (Table 3.9). On-site inspections confirm or overturn self-assessment scores leading to a capital add-on.

3.4.3 Empirical analysis

While the inherent differences between these two standardised approaches for the treatment of operational risk prevent a direct empirical comparison, it is still possible to quantify relative differences in their impact on the capital assessment for a sample of insurance companies for which both regulatory regimes could be applied. We review prudential information on operational risk obtained from the annual BSCR filings of 34 registered Class 4 and 3B commercial (re)insurers in Bermuda as of end-2010 and replicate the theoretical capital charge for operational risk under in comparison.

For the standard formula of the Solvency II framework, we adjust Equations 3.2, 3.4 and 3.5 to

$$SCR_{Op} = \min\{Basic\ SCR_{cap_{non\text{-}life}} \times Basic\ SCR; Op_{ln\ ul}\} \qquad (3.11)$$

$$Op_{prem} = f(Op_{prem\ non\text{-}life}) \times (Prem_{non\text{-}life})$$
$$+ \max\{0; f(Op_{prem\ non\text{-}life})$$
$$\times (Prem_{non\text{-}life_t} - 1.2Prem_{non\text{-}life_{t-1}})\} \qquad (3.12)$$

Table 3.7 BSCR: corporate governance risk score for the operational risk under CIRA

Criterion	Implementation	Score
Board sets risk policies, practices and tolerance limits for all material foreseeable operational risk at least annually and ensures they are communicated to relevant business units	Y/N	200
Board monitors adherence to operational risk tolerance limits more regularly than annually	Y/N	200
Board receives, at least annually, reports on the effectiveness of material operational risk internal controls as well as management's plans to address related weaknesses	Y/N	200
Board ensures that systems or procedures, or both, are in place to identify, report and promptly address internal control deficiencies related to operational risks	Y/N	200
Board promotes full, open and timely disclosure from senior management on all significant issues related to operational risk	Y/N	200
Board ensures that periodic independent reviews of the risk management function are performed and receives the findings of the review	Y/N	200

and

$$\mathrm{Op_{prov}} = f(\mathrm{Op_{prov\ non\text{-}life}}) \times \max(0; \mathrm{Prov_{non\text{-}life}}) \qquad (3.13)$$

recognising that all large commercial (re)insurers that make up the above sample do not report significant long-term business. Moreover, the calculations are also performed for previous specification of the standard formula (prior to the finalisation of the Level 2 text of the Solvency II framework), which, given the exclusion of non-SLT health insurance business in the calculation of the maximisation term for $\mathrm{Op_{prem}}$ and $\mathrm{Op_{prov}}$ (see Equations 3.7 and 3.8), necessitated a mapping routine for some statutory business lines under the Bermuda regime.[13] Under Option 1, only the "health" business line is excluded from the general non-life component for

Table 3.8 BSCR: risk management risk score for the operational risk under CIRA

Criterion	Implementation	Score
Risk management function (RMF) is independent of other operational units and has direct access to the Board of Directors	Y/N	150
RMF is entrenched in strategic planning, decision making and the budgeting process	Y/N	150
RMF ensures that the risk management procedures and policies are well documented and approved by the Board of Directors	Y/N	150
RMF ensures that the risk management policies and procedures are communicated throughout the organisation	Y/N	150
RMF ensures that operational risk management processes and procedures are reviewed at least annually	Y/N	150
RMF ensures that loss events arising from operational risks are documented and loss event data are integrated into the risk management strategy	Y/N	150
RMF ensures that risk management recommendations are documented for operational units, ensures that deficiencies have remedial plans and that progress on the execution of such plans are reported to the Board of Directors at least annually	Y/N	150

the calculation of the operational risk charge and attributed to non-SLT health insurance business. Alternatively, also "US casualty/speciality/professional" business lines are considered in the calculation of the non-SLT health insurance business non-life component of the standard formula (and, thus, are excluded from the non-life component; Figure 3.10). Since the scaling factors $f(\text{Op}_{\text{prem non-life}})$ and $f(\text{Op}_{\text{prem non-life}})$ remain unchanged irrespective of this categorisation, periodic increases in premiums/provisions must be material ($> 10\%$) relative to the previous year to be considered in the standard formula, and, thus, generate a difference in results between Options 1 and 2.

Table 3.9 Event type classification: banking (under Basel II) and BSCR–CIRA

Basel II: event-type category (Level 1)[1]	Definition	Categories (Level 2)[1]	BSCR–CIRA: event-type category
Internal fraud	Losses due to acts of a type intended to defraud, misappropriate property or circumvent regulations, the law or company policy, excluding diversity/discrimination events, which involves at least one internal party.	Unauthorised activity; theft and fraud	Fraud
External fraud	Losses due to acts of a type intended to defraud, misappropriate property or circumvent regulations the law by a third party.	Theft and fraud; system security	
Employment practices and workplace safety	Losses arising from acts inconsistent with employment, health or safety laws or agreements, from payment of personal injury claims, or from diversity/discrimination events.	Employee relations; safe environment; diversity and discrimination	Human resources

[1]The Level 1 and Level 2 categorisation of ETs conforms to the specification of ETs in Basel Committee on Banking Supervision (2003).
Sources: Jobst (2007a,b,c, 2010) and Bermuda Monetary Authority (2008a,b).

Table 3.9 Continued

Basel II: event-type category (Level 1)[1]	Definition	Categories (Level 2)[1]	BSCR–CIRA: event-type category
Clients, products and business practices	Losses arising from an unintentional or negligent failure to meet a professional obligation to specific clients (including fiduciary and suitability requirements), or from the nature or design of a product.	Suitability, disclosure and fiduciary; improper business and market practices; product flaws; advisory services.	Compliance
Damage to physical assets	Losses arising from loss or damage to physical assets from natural disaster or other events.	Disasters and other events	Business continuity, information technology
Business disruption and system failures	Losses arising from disruption of business or system failures.	Systems	
Execution, delivery and process management	Losses from failed transaction processing or process management, from relations with trade counterparties and vendors.	Transaction capture, execution and maintenance; monitoring and reporting; customer intake and documentation; customer/client account management; trade counterparties; vendors and suppliers	Business processes

[1]The Level 1 and Level 2 categorisation of ETs conforms to the specification of ETs in Basel Committee on Banking Supervision (2003).

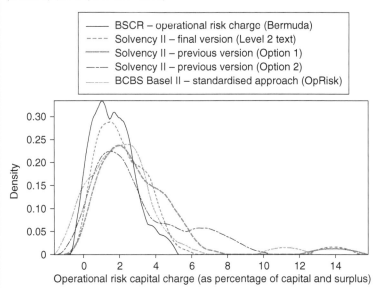

Figure 3.6 Bermuda Class 4 and 3B (re)insurance firms: kernel density function of the capital charge for operational risk under BSCR, the standard formula of Solvency II, and the quasi-basic indicator approach (Basel II) (as of year-end 2010)

If Bermuda (re)insurers were to apply the standardised approach for operational risk under Solvency II, they would exhibit capital levels that are very similar to the current capital add-on under the BSCR. The firm-by-firm results (Figures 3.7 and 3.8) and the corresponding kernel density function of the overall dispersion of the estimated operational risk charge (relative to capital and surplus as of the end of 2010) across firms (Figure 3.6) show a very close match of results obtained under both regulatory regimes. In addition, it is apparent that the last revision of the standard formula after the QIS 5 has helped reduce the incidence of large capital charges. Interestingly, both approaches yield results that are consistent with the basic indicator approach (BIA), which is one of two standardised approaches used in the banking sector in accordance with the revised regulatory regime under Basel II (Table 3.2).

3.4.4 Comparative assessment

Despite their shared technical characteristics and similar roles within each solvency regime, the standardised approaches under the BSCR and Solvency II differ in their regulatory incentives underpinning

Figure 3.7 Bermuda class 4 and 3B (re)insurance firms: capital charge for operational risk under BSCR and the standard formula of Solvency II (as of year-end 2010)

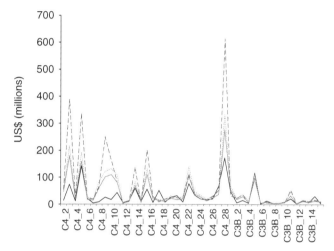

Note that for the definition of the operational risk module for the QIS 5 of the Solvency II framework, we distinguish between two possible options (Options 1 and 2) to accommodate health-related premiums and provisions. Under Option 1, only the BSCR health business line is excluded from the non-life component for the calculation of the operational risk charge. Under Option 2, health as well as US casualty/speciality/professional business lines are excluded from the calculation of the non-life component of the standard formula. The simplification of the standard approach under the final Solvency II directive no longer requires a separate treatment of health-related premiums/provisions.
Sources: BMA and author's own estimates.

the prescriptive capital guidance. Whereas the treatment of operational risk under the standard formula in the Solvency II framework encapsulates operational risk in a based measure (based on the current level of earned premium income and technical provisioning), the maturity model approach under the BSCR defines a process of periodic qualitative self-assessment of corporate governance and risk management functions to derive a capital charge that rewards the graduated implementation of desirable policies and practices (Figure 3.10).

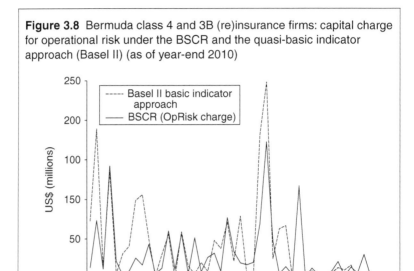

Figure 3.8 Bermuda class 4 and 3B (re)insurance firms: capital charge for operational risk under the BSCR and the quasi-basic indicator approach (Basel II) (as of year-end 2010)

Sources: BMA and author's own estimates.

Figure 3.9 BSCR: risk scores for risk management processes for operational risk under CIRA (risk identification processes/risk measurement processes/risk response processes/risk monitoring and reporting processes)

Operational risk areas (~event type)

Criterion	Stage	Score	Fraud	HR	Compliance	Business continuity	IT	Business processes
... are ad hoc	1	50						
... have been implemented but not standardised across the organisation	2	100						
... have been implemented, well documented and understood by relevant staff and standardised across the entire organisation	3	150						
... are also reviewed at least annually with a view to assessing effectiveness and introducing improvements (in addition to Stage 3)	4	200						

Table 3.10 Comparison of standardised regulatory approaches to operational risk: Solvency II and BSCR

	Solvency II: operational risk module (standard formula)	BSCR: operational risk charge (standardised approach)
Empirical approach (~Pillar 1)	Quantitative assessment (high-level prudential data on earned premiums and technical provisioning/reserves); calibrated to 99.5% VaR of changes in economic value of balance sheet over risk horizon, assuming that operational risk is not covered in other risk modules ("exclusive treatment of operational risk")	Qualitative assessment (scoring system), separate from the calibration of the other capital risk charges; does not directly measure the quantum of residual operational risk, ie, operational risk can also be covered in other risk modules ("non-exclusive treatment of operational risk"), for instance, in the capital charge for underwriting risk
Identification (~Pillar 2)	Focus on volume-dependence of operational risk	Focus on structural identification of sources of operational risk/potential mitigants ("risk drivers")
Incentives (~Pillar 2)	Provides no incentive to integrate operational risk management in governance structure/enterprisewide risk management	Considerable incentive to integrate operational risk management in governance structure/enterprise-wide risk management

While both approaches have their own merits in terms of practical implementation and methodological clarity, they also entail the

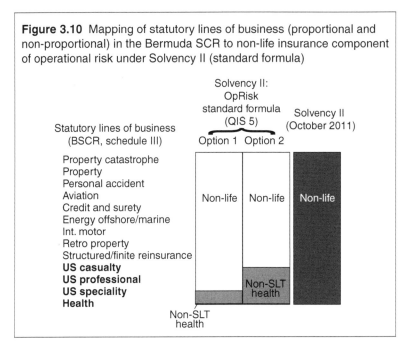

Figure 3.10 Mapping of statutory lines of business (proportional and non-proportional) in the Bermuda SCR to non-life insurance component of operational risk under Solvency II (standard formula)

following significant drawbacks associated with their underlying rationale.

- **The standardised treatment of operational risk under Solvency II does not relate the capital charge to actual risk drivers (and offers little discriminatory power across firms).** Relating capital requirements for operational risk exposures to some generic indicator of business activity fails to acknowledge that firms specialise in a wide-ranging set of activities and maintain very different measurement methods, risk-control procedures and corporate governance standards, which affect both the incidence and the level of events. The fixed capital charge should not be defined as a function of revenue but instead as a measure of the loss impact of operational risk events on the quality and stability of earnings, which can serve as a scaling factor of loss severity.[14] Thus, capital charges would in fact be inversely related to income generation in the absence of an identified causality between a volume indicator and the realisation of operational risk losses.[15] Even if quantitative standards for operational risk as a basis for the assessment of capital adequacy were satisfied, higher operating costs due to process inefficiencies (but also areas of operational risk that cannot be separated easily from other types of risk) could have an adverse impact of competitiveness (with attendant effects on solvency over time).

- **The operational risk capital charge as part of the BSCR establishes clear incentives for the adoption of policies and practices aimed at mitigating operational risk in lieu of a hardwired reference to some measure of business activity.** However, it neither distinguishes between the severities of operational risk exposures based on actual causes nor attempts to quantify any residual operational risk (ie, that not reflected in the other risk types). Instead, it implicitly relies on the assumption that the implementation of sound governance and appropriate risk management processes will invariably lower operational risk exposures. While it is acknowledged that the approach is driven by changes in overall risk-based capital for other sources of risk (which may also contain some elements of operational risk), the maturity model approach is still connected to financial performance (albeit weaker than the operational risk charge under Solvency II) as business activity would likely be the largest contributor to overall capital given the design of a risk-based capital model, with the lion's share stemming from activity in volume related to premiums and provisions. In addition, the BSCR allows for company variation in the application of the maturity model (ie, the model is insensitive to non-applicable areas in the calculation of the qualitative scores of the four areas of the risk management function) and provides uniform incentive across all scoring criteria. However, this may not reflect the relative importance of some of the dimensions that may be larger contributors to operational risk than others (if analysed in greater detail).

Under both the BSCR and the Solvency II regimes, insurers have an economic incentive to switch to internal models for the capital assessment of operational risk as they expand their activities (and arguably increase their risk management capabilities). The comparison of the two approaches, which include the use of arbitrary caps on the magnitude of operational risk, illustrates that operational risk regulation (even in standardised approaches) would need to be geared towards exploring options for (and greater flexibility in the administration of) measures that strike a balance between prescriptive and principle-based guidelines, which better reflects the economic reality of operational risk across firms and over time. The one-off nature of large operational risk events frequently eludes purely quantitative models and warrants a qualitative overlay that explains the causality of operational risk events and the sensitivity of their financial impact. Thus, structural (predictive factor) models based on key risk indicators (KRIs) have become commonplace as a way of blending both quantitative and qualitative approaches in internal models, which provide clues of possible enhancements to standardised approaches.

In fact, the identification problem of operational risk in the insurance sector challenges the exclusive regulatory treatment via a separate capital charge.[16] Given the pervasiveness of operational risk in insurance, it can be reasonably argued that potential areas of overlap with other sources of risk are significant, suggesting that an integrated (and possibly more qualitative) approach would be more suitable for many business models in the insurance sector. Since many areas of insurance business are operational by nature, the design and implementation of the operational risk management process is mostly aligned to meet regulatory requirements and does not entirely fit with a firm's actual operational risk profile. Thus, capital adequacy for operational risk appears incidental to the importance of corporate governance paired with suitable risk management and control procedures, especially if an operational risk management regime should not only enable timely and proactive decision-making to reduce capital requirements but also identify process inefficiencies and vulnerabilities outside the capital assessment.

3.5 CONCLUSION

Going forward, the diverse treatment of operational risk in regulatory frameworks requires effectiveness and relevance of supervisory principles that establish suitable incentives for the mitigation of operational risk (in the case of existing standardised approaches) and the development of internal models for operational risk that are consistent with similar demands and objectives implied by AMA in the banking sector.

In particular, the straightforward implementation of standardised approaches, such as the ones included in the Solvency II framework and the BSCR, does not remove insurance companies from the obligation of institutionalising operational risk as an end-to-end process with delegated authorities that escalate remedies to identified vulnerabilities and influence risk-taking (even if operational risk is perceived as less consequential than market and credit risk), while recognising control limitations (as basis for the assessment of effectiveness).

Since operational risk represents a high-dimensional problem that requires a holistic and comprehensive assessment of the interrelationships between the risk management and corporate governance functions. Operational risk management cannot progress without considering the subjectivity associated with the identification of operational risk exposures, which depends on the individual insurer's overall risk philosophy, business model, and corporate strategy to achieve its business objectives (Acharyya 2012). Understanding the causality of operational risk events and their time-varying dynamics also requires negotiating successfully a balance between qualitative and quantitative information so that:

- Operational risk management can identify vulnerabilities and map out risk scenarios sufficiently in advance so that corrective policies can be implemented ("flag raising"). It has a poor record of predicting the timing of large losses because precise triggers differ across events and are notoriously unpredictable. Operational risk management is much more successful in identifying the underlying vulnerabilities, ie, the predisposition to shocks, whether they are caused by failed internal process, human error or external disasters;

- Operational risk management needs to warn of imminent risk that suggests tail events are about to materialise; and

- Operational risk management needs to help prioritise policy recommendations and formulation of contingency plans based on probability and potential impact while recognising that vulnerabilities are still relevant even in benign times.

Despite the impressive evolution of operational risk management practices in the insurance sector over the recent past, from a measurement perspective, the explicit regulatory treatment of operational risk in insurance remains very diverse, integrated operational risk management still has some way to go in combining heuristic and quantitative approaches. The greater emphasis on management and internal control of operational risk requires insurance supervisors to explore enhanced measures that strike a balance between prescriptive and principle-based guidelines, which better reflects the economic reality of operational risk. Thus, we are likely to see a convergence of standardised approaches, a greater focus on supervisory review (such as under Pillar 2 of the Solvency II framework), and a more inclusive definition of operational risk.

The author would like to thank conference participants at OpRisk NorthAmerica (in New York on March 20, 2012) and OpRisk Europe (in London on 12 June 2012) where most of the content was presented as part of a seminar on operational risk quantification and measurement for insurance companies. The views expressed in this chapter are those of the author and should not be attributed to the Bermuda Monetary Authority, its Board of Directors or its management. Any errors and omissions are the sole responsibility of the author.

1   Some of the papers covering operational risk in insurance companies are Verrall (2007) and Tripp et al (2004), as well as Cummins et al (2006), which examined both banking and insurance models.

2   Some of these data challenges have been overcome by external sources of loss information that provide evidence for the robust assessment of capital requirements for operational risk. For instance, the Association of British Insurers founded the Operational Risk Industry Consortium to provide thought leadership and enhance quantitative and qualitative understanding of operational risk, which included industry-wide initiative to improve completeness of firm data through external loss data collection (Financial Services Authority 2008). Consortium data also offer an adequate benchmark against which individual loss profiles can be compared.

3   Note that, while the BSCR was implemented in 2008, at the time of publication of this book in 2012, the Solvency II framework has not come into force, which means that country-specific rules are currently in place for respective EU member states. For instance, in the case of the UK, the Financial Services Authority's Individual Capital Adequacy Standards (ICAS) regime for insurers (Financial Services Authority 2005) also requires operational risk to be explicitly reflected within the capital assessment. The ICAS was the UK's attempt to forestall Solvency II, but will be replaced once Solvency II becomes effective. In contrast, other regimes with "globally active insurance companies", such as in the US or Canada, for instance, do not mandate a separate operational risk charge. However, in the case of the former, regulators are now considering explicit inclusion of operational risk.

4   For instance, most notably, the estimation of the discount factor for assets and liabilities over long time horizon has focused on actuarial methods of determining the interest rate term structure for valuation purposes.

5   Like in the operational risk regime in banking, the definition of operational risk "…shall include legal risks, and exclude risks arising from strategic decisions, as well as reputation risks" (Article 101(4)(f) of Level 1 text).

6   This contrasts with other important regulatory regimes, such as the Canadian and US approaches, which do not include a separate treatment of operational risk.

7   Commercial (re)insurance companies in Bermuda are licensed in one of three categories, Class 4, Class 3B and 3A insurers: (i) Class 4: insurers and reinsurers capitalised at a minimum of US$100 million underwriting direct excess liability and/or property catastrophe reinsurance risk; (ii) Class 3B: percentage of unrelated business represents 50% or more of net premiums written or loss and loss expense provisions (and/or where the unrelated business net premiums are more than US$50 million); and (iii) Class 3A: small commercial insurers whose percentage of unrelated business represents 50% or more of net premiums written or loss and loss expense provisions and where the unrelated business net premiums are less than US$50 million. Since only Class 4 and 3B insurance companies were subject to the standardised solvency assessment under the BSCR framework as of end-2010, the empirical section of this chapter excludes Class 3A insurers, and, thus, covers only large commercial (re)insurers.

8   The TVaR (or "Tail VaR") is as frequently referred to as the expected shortfall (ES), ie, the average density of extreme losses beyond VaR at a selected percentile level.

9   For instance, most notably, the estimation of the discount factor for assets and liabilities over long time horizon has focused on actuarial methods of determining the interest rate term structure for valuation purposes.

10   Note that this approach is similar to the assessment methodology for enterprise risk management (ERM) used by Standard & Poor's (Ingram *et al* 2005).

11   If the assessment of operational risk area shows a quality of implementation of policies and practices between the different stages of evaluation, the lower stage must be used for determining the appropriate risk score. Non-applicable areas are deemed to have met the criterion of the highest stage (ie, no capital effect).

12   Supervisory guidance on best practices in the area of operational risk is provided in the Insurance Code of Conduct (Bermuda Monetary Authority 2011b, 14f), which stipulated that "systems and operations risk (operational risk) component of the risk management framework should include: (i) defining the systems and operations risk and establishing tolerance limits for each material risk area, which may include business process risk, business continuity risk, compliance risk, information systems risk, distribution channels risk, fraud risk, human resources risk, and outsourcing risk; (ii) establishing a system to identify systems and operations exposures, and to capture and track systems and operations near-miss data; (iii) establishing a system of effective internal reporting and operating controls (including IT infrastructure) to manage and appropriately mitigate the systems and operations risk; (iv) establishing measurement techniques, such as stress and scenario testing, to assess the vulnerability of the insurer; and (v) establishing frequent reviews to ensure mitigation strategies, such as an early warning system, has been effectively deployed and the systems and operations risk is within a tolerable limit."

13   These proportional and non-proportional lines of business include:

1.   US casualty

   (a) US casualty motor: coverage of US risks arising from injuries to persons or damage of the property of others and/or legal liability imposed upon the insured for motor related activities/actions, including auto liability;

   (b) US casualty (general): coverage of US risks arising from injuries to persons or damage of the property of others and/or legal liability imposed upon the insured for non-motor related activities including theft, fraud, negligence and workers' compensation;

   (c) Terrorism: coverage of risks arising from acts of both certified and uncertified acts of terrorism (the calculated use or threat of violence against civilians to achieve an objective(s)) and related losses associated with act of terrorism;

   (d) Other: business that does not fit in any other category;

2. US professional: coverage of US risks arising from injuries to persons and/or legal liability imposed upon the insured as a professional (eg, Director of a Board, etc.) for negligent or fraudulent activities;

3. US speciality, medical malpractice: coverage of US risks arising from injuries to persons and/or legal liability imposed upon the insured as a medical professional for negligent (or other) medical-related activities; and

4. Health: coverage of care, curative or preventive medical treatment (or financial compensation) arising from illness, accident, disability or frailty, including hospital, physician, dental, vision and extended benefits.

14 For instance, Financial Services Authority (2006) suggests that "a firm should relate its operational risk capital to its own business, systems and controls and management and not rely on applying a loading to other elements of its risk capital, premium income or provisions."

15 Normative assumptions, such as gross income as a volume-based metric in standardised approaches, avoid measurement bias from model risk and parameter instability in favor of greater reliability, but they do so at the expense of less discriminatory power and, quite possibly, higher capital charges.

16 However, greater supervisory sensitivity and regulatory attention to operational risk could entail additional administrative demands under a more rigorous regime, which carries the potential of undermining the focus on simplicity in standardised approaches, especially if operational risk elements in other areas of insurance risk are taken into account (Tyron 2011).

REFERENCES

Acharyya, M., 2012, "Why the Current Practice of Operational Risk Management in Insurance is Fundamentally Flawed – Evidence from the Field", Mimeo, Bournemouth University, January 16, URL: http://www.ermsymposium.org/2012/OtherPapers/Acharyya-Paper-01-16-12.pdf.

AM Best, 2010, "Best's Impairment Rate and Rating Transition Study: 1977 to 2009", AM Best Methodology, Criteria – Insurance, May 19, URL: http://www.ambest.com/ratings/methodology/Impairment-Rate-Transition-Methodology.pdf.

Basel Committee on Banking Supervision, 2003, "Sound Practices for the Management and Supervision of Operational Risk: Final Document", Bank for International Settlements, February, URL: http://www.bis.org/publ/bcbs96.pdf.

Basel Committee on Banking Supervision, 2004, "International Convergence of Capital Measurement and Capital Standards: A Revised Framework", Bank for International Settlements, June, URL: http://www.bis.org/publ/bcbs107.htm.

Basel Committee on Banking Supervision, 2005, "Basel II: International Convergence of Capital Measurement and Capital Standards: A Revised Framework", Bank for International Settlements, November, URL: http://www.bis.org/publ/bcbs118.htm.

Basel Committee on Banking Supervision, 2006, "Basel II: International Convergence of Capital Measurement and Capital Standards: A Revised Framework, Comprehensive Version", Bank for International Settlements, June, URL: http://www.bis.org/publ/bcbs128.htm.

Bermuda Monetary Authority (BMA), 1978a, "Insurance Act 1978", URL: http://www.bma.bm/uploaded/657-120117_Insurance_Act_1978.pdf.

Bermuda Monetary Authority (BMA), 1978b, "Insurance Returns and Solvency Regulations 1980", BR 16/1980, URL: http://www.bma.bm/uploaded/702-Insurance_Returns_and_Solvency_Regulations_1980.pdf.

Bermuda Monetary Authority (BMA), 1980, "Insurance Accounts Regulations 1980", BR 18/1980, URL: http://www.bma.bm/uploaded/604-110411_Insurance_Accounts_Regulations_1980.pdf.

Bermuda Monetary Authority (BMA), 2008a, "Insurance (Prudential Standards) (Class 4 and Class 3B Solvency Requirement) Rules 2008 (Consolidated, excluding Schedules VII, VIII, IX and X)", BR 83/2008, URL: http://www.bma.bm/uploaded/855-120223_Ins _(Prudential_Standards)_(Class_4_and_Class_3B_Solvency_Req)_Rules_2008.pdf.

Bermuda Monetary Authority (BMA), 2008b, "Insurer Risk Assessment", Guidance Note No. 17, 23 December, URL: http://www.bma.bm/uploaded/417-Guidance_Note_No._17 _Commercial_Insurer_Risk_Assessment.pdf.

Bermuda Monetary Authority (BMA), 2011a, "Commercial Insurer's Solvency Self-Assessment (CISSA): Instruction Handbook", 21 January, URL: http://www.bma.bm/ uploaded/637-110121_CISSA_2011_Instructions_Handbook_-_Final.pdf.

Bermuda Monetary Authority (BMA), 2011b, "Insurance Code of Conduct, Notice and Appendices", 30 November, URL: http://www.bma.bm/uploaded/814-111130_BMA _Insurance_Code_of_Conduct_Notice_and_Appendices_-_May_2011.pdf.

Bermuda Monetary Authority (BMA), 2012, "Enhancements to the Regulatory and Supervisory Regime for Commercial Insurers", Consultation Paper, 27 January, URL: http://www.bma.bm/uploaded/854-120127_CP_Enhanced_Limited_Purpose _Insurer_Reporting_(FINAL).pdf.

Chief Risk Officers Forum, 2008, "QIS4 Benchmarking Study", 30 October, URL: http:// www.thecroforum.org/assets/files/publications/croforumqis4_benchmarkstudy _oct2008.pdf.

Cummins, J. D., L. M. Christopher and R. Wei, 2006, "Market Value Impact of Operational Loss Events for US Banks and Insurers", *Journal of Banking and Finance* 30(10), pp. 2605–34.

European Commission, 2008, "QIS4 Technical Specifications (MARKT/2505/08) and Operational Risk Questionnaire (MARKT 2506/08)", Internal Market and Services DG, Financial Institutions: Insurance and Pensions (31 March), URL: https://eiopa.europa.eu/ consultations/qis/quantitative-impact-study-4/index.html.

European Commission, 2010, "QIS5 Technical Specifications (Annex to Call for Advice from CEIOPS on QIS5)", Internal Market and Services DG, Financial Institutions – Insurance and Pensions (July 5), URL: http://ec.europa.eu/internal_market/insurance/docs/ solvency/qis5/draft-technical-specifications_en.pdf.

European Commission, 2011, "Draft Implementing Measures Solvency II", Internal Market and Services DG, Financial Institutions: Insurance and Pensions (October 31).

European Parliament/European Council, 2009, "Directive 2009/138/EC of 25 November 2009 on the Taking-up and Pursuit of the Business of Insurance and Reinsurance (Solvency II)", *Official Journal of the European Union* 335/1, 17 December (Brussels).

Financial Services Authority (FSA), 2005, "Insurance Sector Briefing: ICAS – One Year On", November (London: Financial Services Authority), URL: http://www.fsa.gov.uk/ pubs/other/isb_icas.pdf.

Financial Services Authority (FSA), 2006, "Financial Services Authority ISG Expert Groups: Draft ICA Principles and Guidance", 5 June (London: Financial Services Authority), URL: http://www.fsa.gov.uk/pubs/international/isgdraftica.pdf.

Financial Services Authority (FSA), 2008, "The Path to Solvency II", Discussion Paper 08/4, September (London: Financial Services Authority), URL: http://www.fsa.gov.uk/ pubs/discussion/dp08_04.pdf.

Ingram, D., L. Santori and M. Puccia, 2005, "Evaluating the Enterprise Risk Management Practices of Insurance Companies", Standard & Poor's Ratings Direct, Criteria-Insurance-General, October 17 (New York).

Jobst, A. A., 2007a, "Operational Risk – The Sting Is Still in the Tail but the Poison Depends on the Dose", *Journal of Operational Risk* 2(2), pp. 1–56.

Jobst, A. A., 2007b, "It's All in the Data: Consistent Operational Risk Measurement and Regulation", *Journal of Financial Regulation and Compliance* 15(4), pp. 423–49.

Jobst, A. A., 2007c, "The Regulatory Treatment of Operational Risk under the New Advanced Capital Adequacy Framework", *Journal of Banking Regulation* 8(4), pp. 316–52.

Jobst, A. A., 2007d, "The Regulation of Operational Risk under the New Basel Capital Accord: Critical Issues", *International Journal of Banking Law and Regulation* 21(5), pp. 249–73.

Jobst, A. A., "The Credit Crisis and Operational Risk: Implications for Practitioners andRegulators", *The Journal of Operational Risk* 5(2), pp. 43–62.

Ranson, N. J., and A. Samad-Khan, 2008, "An Actuarial Perspective on Measuring Operational Risk", Society of Actuaries Annual Meeting & Exhibit, Session 82, October 21, URL: http://www.soa.org/files/pd/annual-mtg/2008-orlando-annual-82.pdf.

Tripp M. H., H. K. Bradley, R. Devitt, G. C.Orros, G. L. Overton, L. M. Pryor and R. A. Shaw, 2004, "Quantifying Operational Risk in General Insurance Companies", *British Actuarial Journal* 10(5), pp. 919–1012.

Tryon, D., 2011, "Will Your Process Efficiency Impact Your Operational Viability in a Solvency II World?", White paper, DST Global Solutions Ltd., 29 June (Surbiton, UK), URL: http://www.dstglobalsolutions.com/_db/_documents/SII_AWD_WP_Web _201107115032.pdf.

Verrall, R. J., R. Cowell and Y. Y. Khoon, 2007, "Modelling Operational Risk with Bayesian Networks", *Journal of Risk and Insurance* 74(4), pp. 795–827.

4

The Future of Operational Risk as a Discipline

Andrew Sheen
Financial Services Authority

In this chapter we investigate what the future may hold for operational risk. In order to do so we first review the various factors that gave rise to the existing regulatory framework. We then consider the impact of the global financial crisis, the danger that operational risk may become marginalised and the issues that are likely to influence the future direction of the discipline. We then discuss whether the advanced measurement approach (AMA) has a role to play in the future development of operational risk. We conclude that operational risk must focus on generating benefits for the business, thereby stimulating senior management support and buy-in. We will see that the future development of operational risk is heavily dependant on contributions from all members of the operational risk community.

4.1 BACKGROUND

While banks have been managing operational risk since the inception of the banking industry, operational risk did not emerge as a distinct discipline until the 1990s. This owes much to the various concerns that arose following a number of high-profile operational risk loss events, including the collapse of Barings Bank (Davis 2009). The response by the Basel Committee on Banking Supervision (BCBS) to those events, and the European Union's subsequent application of the Basel requirements to all banks and investment firms, provided the catalyst for the emergence of an industry-wide operational risk capability. A review of the role of regulators in the development of

139

operational risk shows how far the discipline has come in such a short period.

In 1999 the BCBS issued a consultative paper (Basel Committee on Banking Supervision 1999) acknowledging the importance of risks other than credit and market risks for banks, and noting that most banks had only recently begun to develop a framework for explicitly measuring and monitoring operational risk. Operational risk was seen as sufficiently important for banks to devote the necessary resources to quantifying the level of such risks and to incorporate them into their assessment of their overall capital adequacy.

Two years later the BCBS detailed their proposal to encompass operational risk in the New Basel Capital Accord (Basel Committee on Banking Supervision 2001a). At that time the Committee's goal was to develop the following three operational risk methodologies, which increasingly reflect a bank's risk profile:

1. the basic indicator approach (BIA), predetermined by regulators and linking the capital charge for operational risk to a single risk indicator (gross income) for the whole bank;

2. the standardised approach (TSA), predetermined by regulators and using a combination of financial indicators and institutional business lines to determine the capital charge;

3. the internal measurement approach, with the capital charge driven by banks' own operational loss experience.

The methodology used by a bank would be determined by its ability to meet specific criteria.

At that time it was estimated that operational risk accounts for an average of 20% of economic capital and this figure was used to set a provisional multiplication factor (α) for BIA of 30% and the following multiplication factors (β) for the then seven TSA business lines (Table 4.1).

Later that year the BCBS issued a working paper (Basel Committee on Banking Supervision 2001b) outlining their latest thinking. The paper showed a willingness to incentivise banks to develop further loss data collection and analysis. In light of the responses from industry to the previous paper, and with information from a quantitative impact study, the target for the average of economic capital was reduced from 20% to 12%. As a consequence it was proposed that the BIA α be reduced from 30% of gross income to 17–20% with

Table 4.1 Original BCBS βs

Business line	Range (%)
Corporate finance	8–12
Trading and sales	15–23
Retail banking	17–25
Commercial banking	13–20
Payment and settlement	12–18
Retail brokerage	6–9
Asset management	8–12

Table 4.2 Revised βs

Business line	Range (%)
Corporate finance	18
Trading and sales	18
Retail banking	12
Commercial banking	15
Payment and settlement	18
Agency services	15
Retail brokerage	12
Asset management	12

the betas in a range around this level. An additional business line, "agency services and custody", was proposed.

A new regulatory capital approach was introduced which was based on banks' internal risk estimates (the advanced measurement approach). The level of capital required under the AMA would be lower than under the simpler approaches in order to encourage banks to make the improvements in risk management and measurement needed to move towards the AMA. At that time it was suggested that a floor be set for AMA at 75% of the TSA capital requirement. Under AMA the regulatory capital requirement would equal the risk measure generated by the bank's internal operational risk measurement system using qualitative and quantitative criteria.

By 2003 the Basel Committee's proposals for the treatment of operational risk had adopted their current structure (Basel Committee on Banking Supervision 2003). The BIA α had been reduced to 15% and the TSA βs comprised 12%, 15% or 18% (Table 4.2).

In many parts of the industry, banks began to strive to achieve their preferred methodology in advance of the introduction of the New Basel Accord and the European Capital Requirements Directive. Banks seeking to adopt AMA were required to obtain supervisory approval to employ this methodology and, in most countries, those seeking to use either of the simpler approaches were able to do so without the prior consent of their regulatory authority. It seems likely that, despite the differences in qualifying criteria, many of the banks adopting one of the simpler approaches based their final choice of methodology solely on capital impact, electing to adopt the methodology generating the lowest operational risk capital charge.

Much of the focus during the implementation of the Basel Accord was on AMA and the modelling component in particular. Nevertheless, a disappointingly low number of banks have adopted AMA. While it is impossible to obtain a detailed list of the membership of this elite group, as most national supervisors choose not to disclose the names of AMA firms, the 2008 Loss Data Collection Exercise for operational risk (Basel Committee on Banking Supervision 2009) received responses from 42 banks that were considered to be AMA or equivalent (some of these were US banks that had yet to receive regulatory approval to use AMA).

4.2 THE WAY FORWARD

Basel II has been severely tested by the 2008 financial crisis and in many ways operational risk as a discipline has failed to meet its first major challenge. Although operational risk failures were an important factor in many of the events affecting banks, these events and their impact are generally considered to have constituted a credit crisis. This may in part reflect the failure of the operational risk community to become fully embedded within banks and of those banks to accurately assess the factors that gave rise to the global financial crisis. For example, model error and selling unsuitable products are both operational risks that went unchecked during the years leading up to the crisis.

It may follow that a failure to fully understand the operational risk implications of the financial crisis will result in a failure to implement robust and effective measures to prevent a reoccurrence. While not many members of the operational risk community would have welcomed being at the centre of the global financial storm, it is likely that the development of operational risk will have been impeded by remaining on the periphery. Although banks and global standard setters have subsequently taken active steps to strengthen capital and improve liquidity, only minimal attention has been focused on operational risk.

As a consequence, operational risk is at a crossroads and in danger of becoming marginalised. The board and senior management in many firms have simply failed to understand either operational risk or the contribution that it can make to their business, and many operational risk functions have failed to demonstrate their value, often as a result of implementing flawed operational risk frameworks. Events over the next year or so will determine whether the discipline can emerge as a true equal to credit and market risk or whether it will become a somewhat distant and impoverished relative.

Much will depend on the interplay between a variety of conflicting factors. There are a large number of issues that have the potential to devalue operational risk and these could lead to the effective marginalisation of the discipline. We expect the key issues to include the following.

- **The contribution of operational risk to a bank's total capital requirement:** the original intention had been for operational risk to contribute about 20% of capital, although this "target" was subsequently reduced to 12%. Analysis undertaken as a result of the BCBS 2008 Loss Data Collection Exercise (Basel Committee on Banking Supervision 2009) suggests that for the firms participating in the exercise the median figure was less than 8% of Tier 1 capital. Post-crisis increases in credit and market risk capital requirements will have further reduced the contribution of operational risk to the overall capital requirement. It is therefore possible to envisage a situation where individual banks elect to focus attention and resources on risks that attract a larger capital burden.

- **Operational risk as a compliance exercise:** many firms fail to recognise the contribution that an effective and robust operational risk framework can make, instead viewing operational risk as a compliance exercise that must be completed, albeit at minimal cost and effort, to avoid censure by their supervisory authority. The failure to embed the operational risk framework into the day-to-day risk management processes of the bank is one of the most consistent weaknesses in banks' operational risk frameworks and, as a result, many firms fail to obtain real benefit.

- **Inconsistencies in the existing approach:** some elements of the existing methodologies are flawed and it is unlikely that operational risk will achieve its true role until these deficiencies are addressed. The Basel Accord effectively recognises that gross income serves as a proxy for the likely scale of operational risk exposure and introduces the erroneous concept of "negative" operational risk, further compounding the problem by allowing negative operational risk in one business line to offset positive operational risk in another. This implies, for example, that a trading and sales activity can become loss making without generating any operational risk and, furthermore, that any "negative" operational risk generated can somehow offset operational risk generated in another business line, eg, corporate finance.

- **Continuing operational risk events:** banking history is littered with a number of high-profile events that have proved extremely damaging, and in some cases terminal, to the banks involved. While it is impossible to envision a world where these events could not reoccur, we should strive to reduce their frequency and impact. Continued operational risk events that reflect common risk management and control failures will make it difficult for operational risk functions to gain traction or board and senior management support in some banks.

- **Inconsistent application across firms:** there is considerable diversity in the standard and content of operational risk frameworks that cannot be accounted for solely in terms of size, nature, scale and complexity. In some cases the poor quality of the operational risk framework reflects a desire to minimise the resources devoted to operational risk. The BCBS have taken the following steps to ensure appropriate operational risk frameworks.

  - The Basel Accord (Basel Committee on Banking Supervision 2006) requires TSA banks' operational risk management processes and assessment systems to be subject to validation and regular independent review.

– Basel Committee on Banking Supervision (2011) requires the bank to undertake an independent review and challenge of the bank's operational risk management controls, processes and systems. This review may be undertaken either by audit or by staff independent of the process or system under review, but may also involve suitably qualified external parties.

Unfortunately, a number of banks have not yet subjected their operational risk framework to a robust review process. In addition, the parties undertaking the review do not always understand the standards required and in many cases review the benchmark bank against "peers" who have themselves failed to implement an appropriate operational risk framework.

- **Impact of boundary issues:** there has always been tension over the classification of events involving operational risk and credit or market risk. Some commentators have expressed concern that banks may arbitrage the impact on capital between classifying an event as operational, credit or market risk. It is often argued that banks obtain a more favourable capital treatment by classifying events as credit or market risk rather than operational risk.

- **Lack of board and senior management buy-in:** board and senior management support is crucial to a successful and effective operational risk framework and it is generally the case that banks with a good risk management culture and strong board and senior management support have the most effective operational risk frameworks.

- **Resourcing and training:** there is a shortage of good operational risk staff globally and this is even more acute for staff with operational risk modelling experience. It is difficult to see how this issue can be resolved in the short term without firms providing focused training for staff in operational risk functions.

While these issues are likely to impede, and even threaten, the development of operational risk as a discipline, there are also a number of factors, listed below, that could enhance operational risk and create the potential for the development of a vibrant and effective discipline that provides tangible benefit to firms.

- **Operational risk guidance:** the BCBS, EBA/CEBS and a number of regulatory authorities have provided guidance that will prove beneficial to firms' operational risk frameworks if implemented effectively. Some examples include the following.

  - The BCBS have published a number of papers that provide firms with an understanding of supervisory expectations and an insight into the processes and procedures being adopted by banks globally. Several of these papers are listed in the references at the end of this chapter.

  - Committee of European Banking Supervisors (CEBS, now the European Banking Authority or EBA) has published a range of guidance on operational risk issues. Committee of European Banking Supervisors (2010) was specifically aimed at helping firms prevent the occurrence of operational risk events in market-related activities and mitigate their impact on the institution. It contains 17 overarching principles and a large number of paragraphs containing supporting guidance.

  - The FSA published guidance (Financial Services Authority 2011) aimed at firms using the TSA approach, although much of this guidance is also applicable to firms using other approaches. The guidance was published to counter the lack of any guidance on the appropriate components and form of an acceptable TSA framework.

  Despite the range of operational risk documents produced by supervisory bodies and regulators, it is not always clear that firms have robustly assessed themselves against the resultant guidelines. There is an understandable, but nonetheless concerning, tendency for firms undertaking self-assessments against published guidance to paint an unduly rosy picture of their operational risk frameworks. The failure to undertake a robust self-assessment results in a failure to implement measures that will develop and improve existing operational risk frameworks and therefore represents a missed opportunity to enhance current frameworks and practices.

- **Increase focus on qualitative issues:** the early years of the development of operational risk frameworks were dominated by a misplaced focus on operational risk quantification and modelling. Events since 2007 have clearly demonstrated the importance of good risk management and, generally speaking, during the global financial crisis, firms with effective risk management structures and practices performed better than those without. While capital has provided a defence against operational risk events, once utilised, either capital must be replaced or firms must scale down their activities to the level determined by the remaining capital. Risk management, on the other hand, has no finite limit and can continue to help protect firms from the likelihood or impact of risk events.

- **Senior management and board support and buy-in:** operational risk functions that are best able to provide benefits for the firm and its business units are most likely to gain traction and receive the support of the board and senior management. Conversely, operational risk functions that receive tangible support from the board and senior management are most likely to establish effective operational risk management frameworks. Unfortunately it is often difficult to tangibly demonstrate the extent of the benefit generated. A fully effective and successful operational risk function will result in failures being identified and rectified as part of business as usual and will make it difficult to demonstrate the contribution it has made to the firm. Nevertheless, this benefit will manifest itself as reductions in the frequency and impact of operational risk losses over time.

- **Resourcing:** one reason for the problems experienced in securing resources for the operational risk function is the difficulty in demonstrating that the function adds value. This is in stark contrast to credit and market risk, where the personality, profile and competence of the head of credit or market risk management has a direct and traceable impact on the quality of the underlying portfolio. In operational risk, unfortunately, it is difficult to demonstrate that a relationship exists between the effectiveness of the head of operational risk and the speed and effectiveness of improvements to operational risk controls at grass-roots level. Perhaps, in the future, heads of operational risk will need to become more closely involved in the day-to-day risk management of the firm.

- **Training and education:** 2011 saw the publication of a number of good quality, informative operational risk books and articles. In addition, some academic institutions now include risk management on their course syllabuses, and these courses provide an excellent foundation for students looking to move into risk management in financial institutions. Operational risk functions should ensure that they have clear learning and development targets for all operational risk staff and that staff development is seen as an important consideration.

- **Operational risk "holy grails":** as a developing discipline, operational risk still has a number of areas in which further progress is required to enable operational risk tools or components to fulfil their potential. Examples of such components include risk appetite, key risk indicators, business environment and internal control factors and management reporting. The development of clear, effective and well-understood solutions and methodologies for these tools and components will greatly assist the development of operational risk.

- **Capital:** increasing the proportion of total capital attributable to operational risk is one potential mechanism for raising the profile of operational risk. Operational risk may be suffering as a result of the relatively small contribution made by operational risk capital to a firm's overall capital requirement.

4.3 DOES AMA HAVE A ROLE?

No discussion of the future of operational risk would be complete without addressing whether we should abandon the Advanced Measurement Approach. Critics of the AMA point to the limited number of firms that have adopted this methodology. We have already seen that only 42 of the banks responding to the BCBS 2008 Loss Data Collection Exercise (Basel Committee on Banking Supervision 2009) were shown to be AMA institutions, although at least 10 of these had not yet received formal AMA approval. While it is likely that not all AMA firms participated in the exercise, the number of firms globally with formal AMA approval is unlikely to be significantly larger.

In addition, it is argued that a disproportionate level of resources has been devoted to these AMA institutions, both internally and by supervisors, and that AMA is expensive and resource intensive to implement.

Modelling operational risk is widely seen as a black art with too many poorly defined and understood components. Techniques for providing a value for some key components are imprecise and lack mathematical rigour, making it possible to reverse engineer the model's output to generate the desired level of operational risk capital. This enables AMA firms to generate an operational risk capital requirement below the level required by the simpler approaches. AMA firms may, for example, use internally determined correlations on operational risk losses across individual operational risk estimates, provided they can demonstrate to the satisfaction of the national supervisor that the systems for determining correlations are sound, implemented with integrity, and take into account the uncertainty surrounding any such correlation estimates. The bank must validate its correlation assumptions using appropriate quantitative and qualitative techniques, although there is room for disagreement between supervisors and firms about the techniques employed, particularly where expert judgement is used to estimate dependence.

Models that rely on scenarios are subject to additional cynicism. The process for generating scenarios is often seen as being subject to a great deal of uncertainty and many firms appear to have ignored the biases that their approach may embody (Watchorn 2007). The approach is further discredited in cases where firms ignore internal and external events when using scenarios to generate modelling inputs.

The BCBS results from the "2008 Loss Data Collection Exercise for Operational Risk" show that, on average, the AMA respondents' operational risk capital equated to 11% of gross income, compared with 15% for BIA firms. However, the Basel Committee on Banking Supervision (2009) also notes that the amount of capital relative to the frequency of large losses is generally higher at non-AMA banks than at AMA banks and that AMA banks have a higher frequency and severity of large losses than non-AMA banks, even when data is scaled by exposure indicators.

Nevertheless, AMA offers a number of potential benefits for firms adopting this approach, including the qualitative standards associated with this methodology. It is recognised that modelling operational risk has some way to go before we can have total confidence in the outcome, but it would seem a backwards step to abandon the AMA approach. Operational risk will truly have come of age once we can accurately assess the potential impact of operational risk events, and it is difficult to see how this can be achieved in the absence of an AMA model. Abandoning AMA would also force firms to adopt one of the simpler approaches, using gross income as a proxy for the scale of business operations and thus the likely scale of operational risk exposure. This would seem akin to a sailor abandoning a functional but under-inflated life vest in favour of a tyre inner tube.

Industry and regulators' understanding of operational risk modelling has developed since the first models were approved in 2007. A number of lessons have been learnt by all participants and it is possible that some of the firms with AMA accreditation would not now receive approval for their operational risk model. It was always understood that AMA firms would continue to develop their models, and it is only through development and enhancements that we can expect operational risk models to evolve.

Scenarios provide a key source of model inputs and a forward-looking mechanism for capturing the frequency and impact of potential risks. It is difficult to see how some AMA firms would be able to continue to use this methodology if models were to be solely based on loss data. There are a number of ways in which assessment biases can be mitigated and these should become an integral element of the scenario process. Challenges should also be well documented to ensure the accuracy and reliability of the scenario process.

The role of operational risk modelling in determining the Pillar 2 operational risk capital charge is often overlooked when this topic is discussed. It is possible for a non-AMA firm to use an operational risk model to estimate their Pillar 2 charge, and this would seem to offer an acceptable route to developing modelling capability and experience that paves the way for a fully fledged AMA model in due course. It also appears reasonable to expect major non-AMA firms to use an operational risk model to calculate their Pillar 2 operational risk capital charge.

The evolution of operational risk modelling requires firms to devote valuable resources to resolving current modelling deficiencies and to providing transparent solutions to identified areas of weakness. Operational risk would be badly damaged by a decision to abandon AMA, and such a decision could contribute to the demise of this discipline.

At the time of writing, many firms feel there is little incentive to adopt AMA. The simpler approaches impose relatively low operational risk capital requirements, and as a result the overall benefit to a firm from moving to AMA, with its significant resourcing implications, may be minimal. For example, consider a hypothetical bank whose operational risk capital requirement might fall from 13% of gross income under the TSA approach to the equivalent of 10% using the AMA. Nevertheless, in our hypothetical example, operational risk's contribution to the bank's total Pillar 1 capital requirement might only fall from 8% to 6%. In these circumstances many banks would elect to devote valuable resources to reducing the capital impact of credit or market risk. An increase in the operational risk capital required under the simpler approaches would increase the potential differential and should result in an increase in interest in AMA, with an improvement in operational risk frameworks as a consequence.

4.4 CONCLUSION

In conclusion, operational risk is at a crossroads and currently faces some of its most important challenges. A failure by firms to develop effective operational risk frameworks, and to resolve the outstanding issues associated with this discipline, could well signal the marginalisation of operational risk. There is already anecdotal evidence that some firms have reduced their operational risk capability and allocated valuable resources elsewhere.

By focusing time and attention on generating benefits for the business, operational risk functions can ensure that the discipline continues to develop and establishes itself as a key component of any firm's risk management capability. This will help generate senior management and board support and buy-in. The operational risk community must also devote time and energy to resolving the key issues facing the discipline, most notably risk appetite, key risk indicators, business environment and internal control factors and management reporting.

Full advantage must be taken of all available guidance, and firms should be much more realistic, and therefore self-critical, when assessing themselves against new guidance. Training and education also have an important role to play in the development of operational risk.

Achieving these objectives will require considerable effort from all members of the operational risk community; firms, supervisors, consultants, operational risk groups and all members of the operational risk community have an important role to play in this process.

The views expressed in this chapter are entirely those of the author and cannot, in any way, be attributed to the author's current employer or any future employers.

REFERENCES

Basel Committee on Banking Supervision, 1999, "A New Capital Adequacy Framework", Bank for International Settlements, June, URL: http://www.bis.org/publ/bcbs50.pdf.

Basel Committee on Banking Supervision, 2001a, "Operational Risk Consultative Document", Bank for International Settlements, January, URL: http://www.bis.org/publ/bcbsca07.pdf.

Basel Committee on Banking Supervision, 2001b, "Working Paper on the Regulatory Treatment of Operational Risk", Bank for International Settlements, September, URL: http://www.bis.org/publ/bcbs_wp8.pdf.

Basel Committee on Banking Supervision, 2003, "Basel II: The New Basel Capital Accord", April, URL: http://www.bis.org/bcbs/bcbscp3.pdf.

Basel Committee on Banking Supervision, 2006, "Basel II: International Convergence of Capital Measurement and Capital Standards: A Revised Framework", Bank for International Settlements, June, URL: http://www.bis.org/publ/bcbs128.pdf.

Basel Committee on Banking Supervision, 2009, "Results from the 2008 Loss Data Collection Exercise for Operational risk", Bank for International Settlements, July, URL: http://www.bis.org/publ/bcbs160a.pdf.

Basel Committee on Banking Supervision, 2011, "Principles for the Sound Management of Operational Risk", Bank for International Settlements, June, URL: http://www.bis.org/publ/bcbs195.pdf.

Committee of European Banking Supervisors, 2010, "Guidelines on the Management of Operational Risks in Market-Related Activities", October.

Davis, E., 2009, "The History of Op Risk: The Unsung Hero", *Operational Risk & Regulation*, March 1.

Financial Services Authority, 2011, "Enhancing Frameworks in the Standardised Approach to Operational Risk", January, URL: http://www.fsa.gov.uk/pubs/guidance/guidance11.pdf.

Watchorn, E., 2007, "Applying a Structured Approach to Operational Risk Scenario Analysis in Australia", Working Paper, September, Australian Prudential Regulatory Authority.

5

The Value at Risk of Data Pools: The Experience of German Savings Banks

Johannes Voit

Deutscher Sparkassen- und Giroverband

There is, at the time of writing, an increased interest in the calculation of operational value-at-risk (OpVaR) in banks. It provides an important and generally accepted compression of detailed loss information in one number. This number makes feasible the evaluation of bank-wide risk, and can be used in the internal capital adequacy assessment process (ICAAP) on par with market or credit risk. Moreover, the new capital rules (Basel III) have reopened the discussion on capital savings from an advanced measurement approach (AMA) in many banks.

The value-at-risk (VaR) of a data pool, on the contrary, is usually considered quite an irrelevant quantity, or just a calculation exercise. There is no financial institution for which this quantity would indicate the amount it could lose over a certain holding period and with a certain confidence level. In this chapter, we discuss how the scaling relations that have been uncovered for many operational loss data pools allow us to define VaR benchmarks from data pools. These benchmarks are useful for understanding operational risk and its underlying data both within a bank and across banks. The dependence of the benchmarks on proxies for bank size provides valuable information for the calibration of functions that must be applicable to all banks, such as the regulatory capital requirements for the basic indicator and the standardised approaches.

These points are illustrated by comparing risk estimates for two entities: a case savings bank (CSB) is a typical individual mid-sized bank whose actual data has been slightly altered here to ensure confidentiality. A synthetic benchmark bank (SBB) is a constructed benchmark using all of the information contained in a group- or industry-wide loss data pool, and the scaling relations established for this pool. The SBB is designed so as to provide the benchmark information appropriate for the CSB so that meaningful comparisons can be performed. The reader may imagine the CSB to be their own bank, and the SBB to be a benchmark constructed from the data pool into which their bank feeds its operational losses, following rules given below. The SBB represents a banking group at large or, in a more global view, "the industry".

5.1 MEASUREMENT OF OPERATIONAL RISK IN GERMAN SAVINGS BANKS

The German Savings Banks Association (Deutscher Sparkassen- und Giroverband) is the central hub of a network of, among others, 430 independent savings banks in Germany. These banks[1] operate under a full banking licence but do business only within the region of their (public) owner, typically a city or county. Typically, they are retail banks without significant investment bank activities. In terms of balance sheet, the size of savings banks varies from about €100 million to about €40 billion. Risk management instruments are developed by the German Savings Banks Association and rolled out to the member banks.

The instruments for operational risk management in the savings banks have been built as a modular system with a loss database, various tools for scenario analysis, a risk and control self-assessment and data pools (Voit 2006). The Association operates two operational risk data pools, one for losses (Voit 2007) and one for scenarios. In the loss data pool, scaling relationships have been identified successfully for frequency of losses versus various indicators of bank size, but no such relationship could be found for loss severity. Finally, the organisation has developed a quantification engine for calculating an OpVaR.

This chapter is based on the organisation's experience from implementing the VaR engine in the first 20 banks. The following important questions were asked at that stage.

- Can the results of the calculation, ie, the OpVaR, be classified as high or low?

- What are suitable benchmarks upon which such a classification can be based?

- What are the causes of the unavoidable deviations between the specific OpVaR of the bank and the benchmark?

- How can the results be interpreted, and what is their relevance for management?

- What are specific toeholds for management action?

Before coming to this stage, many savings banks enquired about a prediction of the results in terms of risk figures. Is it worth the effort at all?

Since 2009, savings banks in Germany have been using a statistical model for the quantification of operational risk. This model has been designed to make the treatment of operational risk consistent with the long-standing practice in market and credit risk management. Target quantities of this model are expected and unexpected losses. The unexpected loss is the OpVaR at a certain confidence level, eg, 99.9% (denoted OpVaR(99.9%)).

The confidence level must be set by the individual bank. Consistency in the integration of operational risk in the calculation of the risk-bearing capacity (the German equivalent of the ICAAP) requires us to use the same confidence level (and time scale, ie, "holding period") as for the other risk types (market and credit risk). For capital calculations under an AMA, the regulatory texts are interpreted as requiring a confidence level of 99.9% (or higher). In this chapter, the OpVaR is calculated at a 99.9% confidence level and presented after subtracting the expected loss.

The model implements a generalised loss distribution approach (LDA), a standard procedure of actuarial science (Aue and Kalkbrenner 2006; Voit *et al* 2009). Basically, the loss distribution of a bank is derived from a convolution of a frequency distribution (modelling the number of losses per year) and a severity distribution (modelling the loss given event).

In the savings bank implementation of this method, the frequency distribution is determined by the internal losses of the bank, and is assumed to be Poissonian. The severity distribution is parametrised based on "external" losses, ie, the loss data pool of the savings

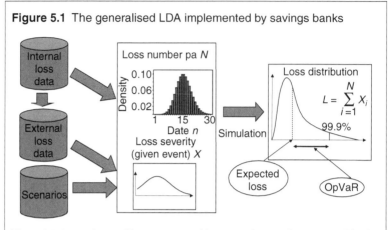

Figure 5.1 The generalised LDA implemented by savings banks

Three data types, internal losses, external losses and scenarios, are used for the capital calculation. The convolution of the distributions of loss frequencies and loss severities produces the loss distribution. Expected and unexpected losses (OpVaR) can be read off the loss distribution.

banks' finance group, and on scenario estimates from a variety of self-assessment instruments used by the savings banks (the inclusion of the scenarios explains the label "generalised" LDA). Severity distributions are selected from the lognormal, generalised Pareto, Weibull and log-Gamma distributions, and are used as either single or composite distributions, depending on the loss data. Frequency and severity distributions are convoluted by Monte Carlo simulation to yield the loss distribution. Expected and unexpected losses can be read off this loss distribution (Figure 5.1).

5.2 THE RISK OF A CASE SAVINGS BANK

Assume that a case savings bank has a sufficiently long data history, and that its expected loss frequency is 50.15 pa. Its OpVaR(99.9%) has been calculated at €14.2 million. Table 5.1 summarises the risk estimates and the observed loss frequencies as well as their distributions on the various cells of the matrix built from the risk categories and functions. Savings banks use a classification of loss and scenario data based on causal categories (instead of/in addition to Basel II event types) and functions (a kind of coarse-grained process, used instead of business lines). A "cell" is an element of the risk matrix generated from risk categories and functions, and is represented in the text as [category/function].

Table 5.1 Case savings bank (expected loss frequency 50.15 per year)

Loss frequencies pa	External impact	Infrastructure	Internal processes	Human resources
Loan processes	0.71	—	0.18	3.75
Service processes	20.00	0.18	0.36	13.39
Investment processes	0.36	0.16	0.18	2.32
Support processes	3.75	0.36	0.36	3.57
Business for commission	0.16	—	—	0.36

OpVaR(99.9%) in million euros	External impact	Infrastructure	Internal processes	Human resources
Loan processes	1.27	—	0.44	2.64
Service processes	2.97	0.07	0.09	2.00
Investment processes	0.18	0.09	2.55	1.06
Support processes	3.08	0.06	1.77	0.73
Business for commission	0.12	—	—	0.26

OpVaR(99.9%) in million euros	14.2			
Expected loss in million euros	0.395			

Loss frequencies and risk estimates of the case savings bank. The dashes (—) indicate that the loss data pool did not contain a sufficient number (10–20) of losses for an independent risk quantification. The loss data in these cells has been added to the cell of the respective risk category in the function service processes.

In eight cells, the OpVaR exceeds €1 million; in five cells, it exceeds €2 million; and in the two cells [external impact/service processes] and [external impact/support processes] the OpVaR is approximately €3 million. Typical loss events in the support processes are related to facility management (eg, also by outsourcing) and vandalism and damage to property. Typical loss events in the cell [external impact/service processes] concern fraud involving credit cards, money transfers and ATMs, as well as bank robbery. However, a cell-by-cell comparison of the OpVaR with the loss frequencies demonstrates that the risk cannot be deduced in a simple manner from the loss frequencies. The key to understanding the results of the statistical quantification is the interplay of loss frequency and severity distributions (Figure 5.1).

An OpVaR of almost €3 million in the cell [external impact/ service processes] is generated from 20 loss events per year, while only 3.75 events per year suffice to generate a comparable risk in the cell [external impact/support processes]. Apparently, the various cells contain very different severity distributions that translate the risk of the underlying processes.

Are the risk estimates of this case savings bank high or low? There are two lines of thought to answer this question.

1. We can use the regulatory capital requirement, eg, under a basic indicator approach (BIA). Assume that the bank earns a gross income, as defined by Basel II, of €154 million, and thus carries a BIA capital charge of €23.1 million. This figure is almost twice the OpVaR calculated. This might suggest that the bank is "low risk". The disadvantage of this line of reasoning is that the BIA capital charge has been calibrated on an unknown sample, which may not be representative of the group of savings banks. Deviations may be due either to the situation of the specific institution or to the particularities of the savings banks group in general. Moreover, this figure (and to a lesser extent the capital requirement of the standardised approach) cannot be disaggregated into contributions of the individual cells of the risk matrix. It is thus unsuitable for a more in-depth analysis.

2. The OpVaR of a comparable bank that is similar in size to the CSB, and is representative both for the business model and the processes of the CSB. Such a savings bank can be constructed from the loss data pool of the German Savings Banks Association. We call it a "synthetic benchmark bank".

During the implementation of the model in a series of savings banks, the following thought pattern was elaborated.

5.3 THE LOSS DATA POOL ALLOWS THE DEFINITION OF BENCHMARKS

The loss data pool of the German Savings Banks Association collects the complete loss histories of the participating savings banks, and makes them available, in an anonymised data set, to all participating banks. The underlying proposition is that it is representative for every savings bank. In the OpVaR calculation, this basic proposition is modified in two elements.

1. The loss frequencies are determined from the actual internal losses of the bank (and not, eg, by rescaling the data pool).

2. Every bank can modify the parametrisation of the severity distributions by including the loss estimates of its specific scenario estimates.

The SBB are generated exclusively from the loss data pool with the following assumptions.

- The loss frequency is obtained by dividing the loss frequencies of the data pool by a global factor X. Specifically, the relations between the loss frequencies of the various cells [risk category/function] remain unchanged, ie, we have $\text{FREQ}_{\text{SBB}} = X \times \text{FREQ}_{\text{pool}}$ both for the entire SBB and for each cell. In 2008, the average loss frequency of the loss data pool was $\text{FREQ}_{\text{pool}} = 5015.43$, ie, a multiplier $X = 1/100$ implies a $\text{FREQ}_{\text{SBB}} = 50.15$.

- The loss frequency FREQ_{SBD} of the SBB and thus the multiplier X are determined from the operating expenditures of the banks through the rescaling of the data pool. This is based on the observation that the data pool displays a well-defined correlation between the loss frequency of the participating banks and various indicators of their size. We have consistently found that the best indicator is operating expenditures, followed by second-ranked gross income, as defined by Basel II. The best scaling function relating those size indicators to the loss frequency has been a second-order polynomial with coefficients that vary only slightly from year to year. It is derived from a regression of the data pool cumulated since its inception. In 2008, the scaling function relating the annual loss frequency and operating expenditures (OE, in euros) was

$$\text{FREQ} = 4.902 \times 10^{-15}(\text{OE})^2 + 1.312 \times 10^{-6}\text{OE} - 1.415$$

A loss frequency of 50.15 pa (ie, a multiplier of $X = 0.01$) corresponds to operating expenditures of €34.8 million.

- The severity distributions are identical to those of the loss data pool, ie, no scenarios are included in the VaR calculation of the SBB.

The loss frequencies and risk estimates of an SBB with a multiplier of 0.01 are displayed in Table 5.2. Loss frequencies and risk estimates derive from the data pool alone using rescaling. The SBB is thus representative of the group of pool contributors and thereby of a large part of the banking sector. The CSB (Table 5.1), on the other hand, is an actual bank that has been selected for the purpose of discussion. Since the frequency multipliers (and thus the scaling parameters) are the same for both banks, the SBB is an appropriate benchmark for the CSB.

The biggest risks are found in the cells [external impact/service processes] and [external impact/support processes], by analogy to the CSB shown in Table 5.1. However, a more detailed investigation shows marked differences. The OpVaR of the SBB is only €12.3 million, ie, €1.9 million or 15% inferior to the CSB. The SBB expected loss is €41,000 below that of the CSB. Only six cells have an OpVaR exceeding €1 million; three cells have more than €2 million and two cells more than €3 million. As with the CSB, in the SBB there is only a loose correlation between loss frequencies and OpVaR across the cells.

To better understand the severity distributions, we can perform an OpVaR calculation in a modified setting where all loss frequencies are fixed to 1 pa (Table 5.3). In this way, the risk contained in the severity distributions can be made transparent without interference from the frequency distributions.

Indeed, the biggest risk given an event is related to loans, and is contained specifically in the cells [external impact/loan processes] and [human ressources/loan processes]. This is followed by the cell [internal processes/investment processes]. These cells are not prominent in Table 5.2. Efficient controls are likely to keep the frequency of loss events rather low. The pro forma OpVaR of this calculation is €8.55 million, only 30% below the SBB shown in Table 5.2, although the loss frequency was less than a third of that of the SBB.

Table 5.2 Synthetic benchmark bank (SBB)

Loss frequencies pa	External impact	Infrastructure	Internal processes	Human resources
Loan processes	0.29	—	0.20	1.58
Service processes	19.65	0.46	1.01	10.78
Investment processes	0.28	0.07	0.17	3.56
Support processes	5.71	2.44	0.12	3.56
Business for commission	—	—	—	0.26

OpVaR(99.9%) in million euros	External impact	Infrastructure	Internal processes	Human resources
Loan processes	1.5	—	0.359	1.69
Service processes	3.02	0.0796	0.0879	0.868
Investment processes	1.64	0.0174	0.46	2.06
Support processes	3.64	0.148	0.208	0.891
Business for commission	—	—	—	0.325

OpVaR(99.9%) in million euros	12.3			
Expected loss in million euros	0.354			

A synthetic benchmark bank with $X = 1/100$. The calculations have been performed using the loss data pool of the German Savings Banks Association of 2008. Multiplier $X = 1/100$. Expected loss frequency 50.15 pa. Operating expenditures €34.8 million.

5.4 BENCHMARKS SUPPORT A BETTER UNDERSTANDING OF DATA AND RISK

Comparing individual bank data with an equivalent SBB is useful to better understand the bank's loss data and the risk estimates calculated from this data. Deviations between the risk estimates of a bank and those of an equivalent SBB can be due to one or more of three causes: data quality, risk profile and parametrisation.

Table 5.3 Risk contained in severity distributions (pro forma expected loss frequency 16 pa)

Loss frequencies pa	External impact	Infrastructure	Internal processes	Human resources
Loan processes	1.00	—	1.00	1.00
Service processes	1.00	1.00	1.00	1.00
Investment processes	1.00	1.00	1.00	1.00
Support processes	1.00	1.00	1.00	1.00
Business for commission	—	—	—	1.00

OpVaR(99.9%) in million euros	External impact	Infrastructure	Internal processes	Human resources
Loan processes	2.99	—	0.761	1.25
Service processes	0.4	0.124	0.911	0.219
Investment processes	0.345	0.0444	2.04	0.751
Support processes	0.695	0.103	0.682	0.356
Business for commission	—	—	—	0.893

OpVaR(99.9%) in million euros	8.55			
Expected loss in million euros	0.196			

Pro forma OpVaR when frequency is fixed at 1 pa in every cell (German Savings Banks Association loss data pool 2008). The calculation demonstrates that the biggest potential losses occur in the cells [external impact/loan processes], [human resources/loan processes], and [internal processes/investment processes].

- Deviations between the average loss frequencies are irrelevant for the CSB, which has the same loss frequency as its equivalent SBB. However, we often observed this situation during the implementation of our VaR engine in the savings banks: the rescaled loss frequency of the data pool, ie, of the SBB, was either higher or lower than the loss frequency of the bank under consideration.

- The distribution of the loss frequencies of a bank across the cells may differ from that of the data pool, ie, of its equivalent SBB. This is the case of the CSB of Table 5.1, and was observed regularly while we implemented the VaR engine. For example, the loss frequency of the cell [human resources/loan processes] of the CSB, which has a high-risk-severity distribution, is more than twice the loss frequency of its equivalent SBB. Other cells, too, exhibit major discrepancies between CSB and SBB.

Our experience shows that, at this point, an in-depth investigation can produce valuable insights for the bank. At the same time, it is important to understand both the data quality and the risk profile as the possible origins of the discrepancies, in two steps.

The first step concerns the data capture in the bank. Is the loss data collection complete, and are losses categorised correctly? Were collective losses identified correctly? Were flags for borderline cases overlapping with other risk types set correctly? Only when the loss collection is flawless do discrepancies between a data pool, ie, the SBB, and the internal loss experience, ie, the CSB, become significant and meaningful.

The second step is to understand precisely these differences in risk profile between the two banks. Why did the CSB have about twice as many losses in the cell [human resources/loan processes] as the SBB, during the period 2005–8? Which are the specific cases in question, and what were their causes? The same questions are asked for the cell [internal processes/support processes]: the loss frequency of the CSB is about three times that of the SBB, the cell OpVaR amounts to €1.77 million. A better understanding of these events, and subsequent management action, will almost certainly reduce those figures in the future.

However, research should not be limited to anomalously high OpVaR. We should also understand exceptionally low estimates, eg, the loss frequency in [human resources/investment processes] in the CSB is about a third below that of the SBB. This translates into an OpVaR only half of the SBB's OpVaR in this cell. What is the origin of this exceptional performance? Can this be translated to the processes examined in other cells?

Differences in the parametrisation of the severity distributions and of the simulation runs may also be at the origin of discrepancies in the risk estimates between CSB and SBB.

- The treatment of zero-loss cells: when there are cells where no losses have been observed at all, we prefer to build our calculation upon a conservative assumption, namely that one loss will occur until the end of the modelling period. This gives a frequency estimate FREQ $= 1/T$, where T is the length of the data history including the current year. This conservative assumption is certainly sensible when there are only one or two void cells in a bank. However, in small banks that experience only very few losses each year, an uncritical acceptance of such a zero-frequency correction will yield a significant overestimation of risk.

- For example, small banks that are members of our group may suffer only 10 losses per year. Suppose that there are six void cells in the internal risk matrix. The zero-frequency correction would then amount to adding six "artificial" losses until year-end, ie, increase the total number of losses by 60%. This may not be appropriate in many cases, and should be eventually corrected by the bank. The influence of this setting in the OpVaR of the CSB is negligible.

- Scenario estimates may alter the severity distributions in our quantification model. Depending on specific circumstances, they may either just change the parameters of the severity distribution with their functional form left unchanged, or alter the distribution type altogether. The importance of this effect depends both on the specific scenario estimates and on the overall weighting of the scenarios in the calculation scheme. Indeed, the CSB did use severity distributions modified with respect to those of the SBB. They reduce the OpVaR in the cells [external impact/loan processes] and [external impact/ investment processes] but increase it in [human resources/ service processes].

- Including scenarios in the VaR model may increase or decrease the risk estimate. The direction depends on the severity estimates of the scenario, and how they compare with the losses contained in the cell of the loss data pool to which the scenario applies. In general, an *a priori* prediction is not feasible. The quantitative impact of the scenario on the risk estimate further depends on the frequency estimate, and on the global weight attached to the scenarios.

5.5 VARIATION OF THE BENCHMARK PROPERTIES

In theory, there is an infinite continuum of SBBs, generated from the properties of the loss data pool by varying the multiplier X. This fact may be used to investigate the systematic variation of risk with institution size conditioned on the loss data pool of the German savings banks. The insights gained from such a variation may help to address the question of how good, in fact, the Basel II calibration of the simpler approaches for the operational risk capital charges (BIA, the standardised approach (TSA)) is. Initially, though, it was set up to help German savings banks in their decision-making on introducing (or not introducing) an OpVaR calculation in their risk management. What is a good prediction for the operational risk estimate of a savings bank based only on the assumption that the data pool is representative?

The equivalent SBB with a suitably chosen multiplier X for the loss frequencies just provides the answer. Figure 5.2 displays the dependence of the OpVaR(99.9%) on X.

An institution can obtain a rough prediction of its OpVaR(99.9%) by the following three quick steps.

1. Determine the expected loss frequency, either based on the internal losses when a sufficiently long loss history is available, or on the scaling relation of the data pool.

2. Determine the multiplier X by dividing by 5015 (or by the loss frequency of the relevant data pool).

3. Read off the OpVaR(99.9%) of Figure 5.2.

The three steps can also be summarised in one formula. The rescaling of the data pool establishes a relation between the loss frequencies of the banks and various size indicators. We consistently obtained the best fits using operations expenditures as a size proxy. Combining the scaling relationship above with the regression of the simulation results, we obtain the following formula, which expresses the OpVaR(99.9%) as a function of operations expenditures (OE, in

Figure 5.2 OpVaR(99.9%) as a function of the average annual loss frequency, expressed as the ratio X by dividing with the pool loss frequency of 5015 (solid line)

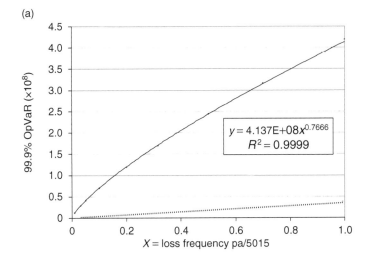

(a)

99.9% OpVaR ($\times 10^8$)

$y = 4.137\text{E}+08x^{0.7666}$
$R^2 = 0.9999$

X = loss frequency pa/5015

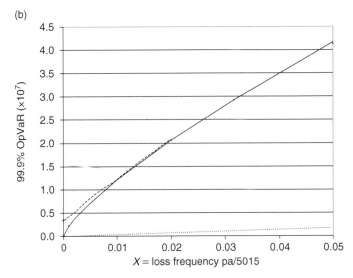

(b)

99.9% OpVaR ($\times 10^7$)

X = loss frequency pa/5015

The figures display the ranges of (a) high and (b) low frequencies. The regression in the top panel shows the dependence of the OpVaR on the loss frequency, and also applies to the solid line in (b). The dotted line indicates the expected loss. The dashed line shows the effect of the zero-frequency correction when the data history contains three full years, and the calculation is performed in year four. The longer the data history, the more the long-dashed line approaches the solid line, and the effect of the correction becomes negligible. All calculations are based on the 2008 loss data pool of the German savings banks.

euros)

OpVaR(99.9%)

$$= 4.137 \times 10^8 \left(\frac{4.902 \times 10^{-15} \text{OE}^2 + 1.312 \times 10^{-6} \text{OE} - 1.415}{5015} \right)^{0.7666}$$

The expression has been calibrated on our 2008 data pool. The numerator of the fraction is the scaling dependence of the expected loss frequency on the operations expenditures of the bank. The denominator is the aggregate pool loss frequency (5015 pa). The formula can be applied only to banks with operations expenditures in excess of approximately €1.4 million.

This expression neglects the zero-frequency correction for cells where no losses have been observed. When this correction is activated, the dependence of the OpVaR on loss frequency turns to linear below a crossover frequency, and follows the dashed blue line in Figure 5.2. The importance of this correction decreases when the loss frequency and/or the length of the time series increases. The crossover frequency decreases for longer time series. For the three-year history assumed in the calculations, in small SBBs with five to ten losses per year ($X = 0.001, \ldots, 0.002$), the frequency zero correction may easily double the OpVaR with respect to an infinite time series, and the effect becomes negligible only for loss frequencies around 50 pa ($X = 0.01$).

5.6 COMPARISON WITH REGULATORY CAPITAL REQUIREMENTS

When a financial institution has calculated its OpVaR(99.9%), it may wish to compare it with the BIA capital charge. This is justified because the capital requirement for an AMA is based essentially on the OpVaR(99.9%) although corrections may apply. The BIA capital charge is $0.15 \times \text{GI}$ where GI is gross income.

The construction of the SBB allows us to set up a general comparison of AMA and BIA in one central calculation. Such a calculation can provide a proxy for all savings banks. It is useful for decision-making and does not require us to implement the calculation methodology from the outset. It is feasible because our scaling investigations have demonstrated that gross income is consistently a good indicator for the loss frequencies observed in our loss data pool. The quality of the

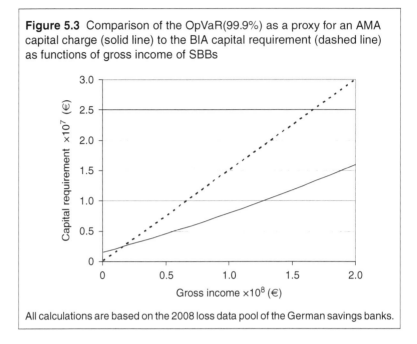

Figure 5.3 Comparison of the OpVaR(99.9%) as a proxy for an AMA capital charge (solid line) to the BIA capital requirement (dashed line) as functions of gross income of SBBs

All calculations are based on the 2008 loss data pool of the German savings banks.

scaling relationship is slightly inferior, though, to that of operations expenditures.

Injecting the scaling relation for loss frequency in terms of gross income (GI, in euros) into the regression of the OpVaR in terms of loss frequency (Figure 5.2), we obtain

OpVaR(99.9%)

$$= 4.137 \times 10^8 \left(\frac{8.456 \times 10^{-16} \text{GI}^2 + 1.737 \times 10^{-7} \text{GI} + 3.249}{5015} \right)^{0.7666}$$

Figure 5.3 compares the capital requirements of AMA and BIA as a function of gross income of the SBB assuming that the OpVaR(99.9%) is a valid proxy for the AMA. Of course, the comparison becomes both more accurate and more significant when the OpVaR is calculated individually instead of using that of an equivalent SBB.

The capital charges for BIA and AMA differ both in their functional dependences on gross income and in their numerical values. In general, the AMA capital charge, ie, the OpVaR(99.9%) is inferior to the BIA figures. However, this does not apply to the banks with the smallest gross incomes. Below a threshold gross income of about €20 million (corresponding to 7–8 losses per year), the

OpVaR(99.9%) is higher than the BIA capital charge. Based on capital considerations alone, an AMA would not be advantageous for such small institutions.

The different functional form of the dependences of AMA and BIA charges on gross income can be made plausible from two simple arguments:

(i) risk and return in general depend differently on the size of an institution;

(ii) an institution with zero gross income is still expected to have a non-zero risk, and thus capital charge.

Figure 5.3 shows that savings banks not only run their well-known risk-poor business model, but also their organisation and processes carry very limited risk. This is not adequately reflected in the BIA capital charge, which has been calibrated based on data from banks with rather different sizes and business models.

5.7 DETECTING RISK CONCENTRATIONS

Savings banks can use the quantification of operational risk to quickly identify risk concentrations,[2] an important new topic in the German implementation of Pillar-2 regulations (MaRisk – minimal requirements on risk management). Both in the CSB of Table 5.1 and in the equivalent SBB of Table 5.2, the biggest risks are contained in the category "external impact", in the two cells discussed in more detail above.

The minimal requirements document does not provide a quantitative definition of risk concentrations. In an institution, the following could be identified as a risk concentration or be used for a qualitative discussion of risk concentrations:

- those two cells;
- the cells with the N biggest OpVaR (eg, $N = 3$ or 5);
- the cells whose OpVaR exceeds a certain fraction Y of the total OpVaR (eg, $Y = 20\%$ or 30%); or
- a rank-ordered list of the cells, based on the value of the OpVaR

Next, we can ask if these concentrations are primarily driven by loss frequency (high values in the upper panels of Tables 5.1 and 5.2) or by loss severity (high values in a cell in the upper panel of Tables 5.1

and 5.2 correspond to high values in the same cells of the lower panels). This information is important when a bank wants to alter its risk concentrations by management action. In particular, severity-driven risk concentrations produce high losses when one additional event occurs. Whenever a search for risk concentrations based on OpVaR identifies important concentrations, a more detailed investigation is recommended in order to understand its underlying causes.

5.8 STRESS TESTS USING THE QUANTIFICATION ENGINE

"Stress test" is a generic term for methods that (financial) institutions use to evaluate their vulnerability to exceptionally severe but plausible events. Stress tests include, eg, sensitivity and scenario analyses.

In an LDA generalised by scenarios, specific stress scenarios can, in principle, be included in the parametrisation of the model when the necessary parameters have been estimated for the stress scenarios. However, such an approach is not required by the minimal requirements, which target exceptional but plausible events. An estimate of the probability of a stress event is not required by the regulators (at least in Germany). This would also imply a quantitative definition of the term "exceptional".

Savings banks have already performed simple sensitivity analyses using the quantification engine. One bank assumed that a new big loss occurred. This would double the amount of the biggest loss in the data pool, and would occur in the same cell. This cell then must be reparametrised, and the consequences for the OpVaR are calculated in a new simulation. Other savings banks used global changes in loss frequencies and severities. Loss frequencies can be changed manually cell by cell in our tool, and then require just an additional simulation. For an SBB, the effect can be directly read off Figure 5.2, eg, on doubling the loss frequency from 50 to 100 pa (ie, changing the multiplier X from 0.01 to 0.02), the OpVaR(99.9%) increases from €12.3 million to €21 million. When loss severities are increased by a certain percentage, the OpVaR changes by the same percentage. For more granular variations, simulations are required, however.

5.9 REMARKS FOR CAUTION

All quantitative analyses are based on the German savings banks' loss data pool for 2008. The general procedure of analysis is independent of the vintage year; numbers may change from year to year. However, our experience shows that changes are usually moderate, eg, the OpVaR(99.9%) of a SBB with 250 losses per year increased by 5% from 2008 to 2009.

The distribution of losses in a bank in the cells of the risk matrix can deviate significantly from that of an equivalent SBB. This can be checked using the data pool alone. No OpVaR calculations are necessary for this check.

Model parameters have an important influence on the results. As well as the frequency zero correction discussed above, this also applies the weighting of the body and tail parts of composite severity distributions, and to the thresholds used for separating body and tail. We use such distributions, and this is general practice, when a given loss data set cannot be described accurately by a single severity distribution function.

Finally, the potential advantages of an AMA should not be evaluated based on Figure 5.3 alone. Institution-specific calculations should be performed, as well as estimates of eventual capital supplements for requirements that cannot be adequately captured by an LDA. Banks should also consider the efforts for implementing, validating and continuously updating the model, and the requirements for organisation and processes in risk management.

5.10 CONCLUSION

We have observed an increased demand for the quantification of operational risk, with the following good reasons.

- The quantification allows banks to compress the essential information on operational risk in two well-established numbers, namely expected losses and unexpected losses (OpVaR). The enormous amount of data available in banks is summarised in those two important figures.

- These figures allow us to systematically include operational risk in the aggregation of risk, in the evaluation of total bank risk and in the ICAAP.

- In some cases, this interest is related to the new Basel III capital requirements. How much could a bank lower its capital charge by introducing an AMA approach for operational risk?

In our practice, the benchmark calculations based on SBBs have been very useful for a better understanding of data and of risks in banks. They pave the return path from the highly compressed risk estimates of expected and unexpected losses back to the grass-roots data, and to an improved understanding of the risk-bearing processes in those areas where the OpVaR values are eye-catching. The calculations described in this chapter provide a systematic framework of various partial aspects that have been elaborated in various savings banks to improve the understanding of models, data and processes.

Our experience shows that it is the in-depth data analysis that generates the value of the benchmark calculations. Why are there so many/so few losses in a particular cell? Why is the severity of losses in a bank at the upper/lower end of the spectrum contained in the data pool? Ultimately, these questions must be answered before the operational risk profile of a bank can be altered by specific management actions.

1 We will use the terms "savings bank", "bank" and "financial institution" interchangeably. Unless indicated otherwise explicitly, all statements derive from our experience in implementing our quantification tool in about 20 savings banks, and from the use of the data pool in approx 250 savings banks, and are valid, strictly speaking, only for this group of banks.

2 We prefer the term "risk concentration" to "concentration risk" because the issues of concentration, diversification and correlation are intimately and inseparably linked to all types of risk, such as credit, market, operational and liquidity risk, and to their aggregation towards the total risk of a bank. In no way do they constitute a risk type of their own.

REFERENCES

Aue, F., and M. Kalkbrenner, 2006, "LDA at Work", *Journal of Operational Risk* 1, pp. 46–93.

Voit, J., 2006, "Management of Operational Risk in Small Financial Institutions: A Necessity for Survival", *Financial Engineering News*, November.

Voit, J., 2007, "How to Create Value from Data Pooling", in E. Davis (ed), *Operational Risk 2.0* (London: Risk Books).

Voit, J., F. Beekmann and F. Camphausen, 2009, "Quantifizierung operationeller Risiken unterstützt Strategie", *Betriebswirtschaftliche Blätter* 1, p. 36.

6

Insurance Mitigation in Operational Risk: Voyage to Relief

Bahram Mirzai

EVMTech

This chapter is concerned with an assessment of insurance policies in view of a hedge for operational risks and their impact on
operational risk capital within an advanced measurement approach
(AMA). Similar to market and credit risks, operational risks can be
hedged by means of financial transaction. Indeed, an insurance policy is nothing but an option on the underlying insured risk. The
insurer, the issuer of the option, reimburses the insured, the option
holder, in cases where the policy is triggered. A non-refundable premium is paid, as in the case of an option, to enter the hedge. Unlike
option contracts, insurance policies exhibit a low degree of standardisation and, as a result, lack an exchange-type marketplace and
tradability. Lack of sufficient standardisation and tradability are core
drivers that make insurance mitigation, in its current state, an imperfect hedge. As a result, regulation has devised a number of qualifying
criteria and haircuts to account for the imperfections. Nevertheless,
the fact that regulation recognises insurance mitigation as a hedge,
and hence as a substitute for capital, is a is a promising sign for
the evolution of insurance products over time into more efficient
hedging instruments. The safety nets introduced by regulation in the
form of haircuts or qualifying criteria can indeed be addressed by
developing tailored insurance products without materially exposing
liability portfolios of insurers to risks that are not within the traditional product domain. In fact, in light of the increased transparency
of operational risks, by aligning product design with regulatory

Table 6.1 Traditional insurance products for banks

Insurance policy	Abbreviation
Bankers' blanket bond (fidelity)	BBB
Property insurance	PI
Business interruption insurance	BI
Unauthorised trading	UT
Bankers' professional indemnity insurance	BPI
Directors' and officers' liability	D&O
Electronic and computer crime	ECC
Employment practices liability	EPL
General liability	GL

language, the insurance industry can benefit from the increased risk transparency and improved pricing.

This chapter is organised in four sections. First, we present an outline of insurance products and continue by mapping of the insurance policies to operational risk categories. We then consider the impact of insurance mitigation on capital under some idealised assumptions. Next, we relax these assumptions to model real-world scenarios by accounting for qualifying criteria and haircuts. Finally, we provide some remarks on the implementation aspects of the proposed models.

6.1 RISK TAXONOMY AND MAPPING

In terms of operational risk taxonomy, the definitions of Basel II and insurance products differ. The insurance industry's risk taxonomy evolved from the product development and the perils that are covered by those products, whereas the Basel II taxonomy results from an attempt to classify operational risks into homogeneous sets of loss events. Table 6.1 provides a list of the traditional insurance policies that are available for banks to protect them against operational risks. Due to the underlying risk definitions and the resulting boundary issues and overlaps, the mapping of the two risk taxonomies is not a one-to-one mapping. A successful mapping requires thorough understanding of the policy wordings. As the wordings are fairly rigid and only subject to marginal changes over time, the mapping exercise is typically a significant effort when performed for the first time but with low maintenance requirements thereafter.

Table 6.2 Mapping of Basel level II categories to insurance policies

Level 1	Level 2	Mapping
Internal fraud	Unauthorised activity	UT, BBB
	Theft and fraud	BBB
External fraud	Theft and fraud	BBB
	Systems security	ECC
Employment practices and workplace safety	Employee relations	EPL
	Safe environment	GL
	Diversity and discrimination	EPL
Clients, products and business practices	Suitability, disclosure and fiduciary	BPI
	Improper business or market practices	D&O
	Product flaws	BPI
	Selection, sponsorship and exposure	D&O
	Advisory activities	BPI
Damage to physical assets	Disasters and other events	PI
Business disruption and system failures	Systems	BI
Execution, delivery and process management	Transaction capture, execution and maintenance	BPI
	Monitoring and reporting	BPI, D&O
	Customer intake and documentation	BPI
	Customer/client account management	BPI, D&O
	Trade counterparties	
	Vendors and suppliers	

The mapping is then revised only when changes apply to the policy wordings.

Table 6.2 provides a mapping of Basel II Level 2 risk categories to the insurance policies (Basel Committee on Banking Supervision 2006). The mapping provided here is indicative and is based on a range of policy wordings observed throughout our experience. The actual mapping applied by a bank must take into account the specific policy wordings, and preferably map to the Level 3 risk categories. Note that the mapping in Table 6.2 does not specify the degree to which these policies cover the Level 2 risk categories. This is addressed as part of the coverage mismatch.

It proves constructive to first establish what objectives a bank pursues with the mapping exercise. If the primary purpose of the mapping is computation of the capital relief, then mapping should be restricted to only those policies that are most relevant for capital relief. Consequently, working layer policies, which essentially trade premium for losses and contribute little to tail risk mitigation, should be excluded from the scope. This can significantly reduce the number of policies relevant for achieving the objective and increase feasibility and quality of the mapping exercise.

Intuitively, most of the capital relief will result from excess of loss policies. These policies are characterised by high deductibles and provide coverage for an insured sum specified by the policy limit. Such policies are typically written at group or holding level, providing coverage for all legal entities. Limiting the mapping exercise to such policies has the most impact and results in an optimal cost-benefit ratio.

The traditional products listed in Table 6.1 are typically offered as mono-line covers insuring only one peril within the limits of the policy. Insurers may also offer multi-line covers, where several excess of loss policies, each corresponding to a different insurance product, are pooled together and insured within one aggregate limit. There is a wide range of possibilities to structure multi-lines including different deductibles and limits for individual policies, or aggregate limits for individual policies or all policies. An accurate modelling of the policy conditions will be crucial for the calculation of the capital relief.

The first non-traditional insurance policy for operational risks, Financial Institutions Operational Risk Insurance (FIORI), was developed by Swiss Re in 1999. It was a basket claims-made policy deviating from the traditional products by defining risks according to risk categories of relationship: people, physical assets, technology and external fraud. The policy was ahead of its time when introduced and failed to receive sufficient market attention in the midst of a soft market cycle. Similar basket policies conforming to Basel II risk categories can offer advantageous risk transfer products, from the point of view of both the insured and the insurer. The insured benefits from a comprehensive cover aligned with Basel II taxonomy and

Table 6.3 Qualifying criteria of insurance policies

Regulatory concern	Qualifying criteria
Claim-paying ability of insurer	Credit rating "A" or higher
Initial policy period	No less than one year
Cancellation notice period	No less than 90 days
Mapping	Insurance policy should be mapped to operational risk exposure
Insurance provider	Must be a third party. In case of captive only the reinsured risk is eligible for relief
Exclusion or limitations	No exclusions or limitations in the policy triggered by supervisory actions or bankruptcy

a more effective hedge for operational risks. The insurer can benefit from market potential and, in the meantime, due to the amount of data available in consortiums such as the Operational Riskdata Exchange Association (ORX), from a level of risk transparency as well as implied pricing accuracy that is not even given for some of the traditional products today. Openness and a visionary approach by regulators, insurers and banks is a prerequisite for such products. Basket products cannot be a sudden replacement for the traditional ones and should therefore be introduced in parallel with traditional products with small but gradually increasing limits, allowing the stakeholders to gain confidence and comfort over time.

6.2 QUALIFICATION CRITERIA OF INSURANCE MITIGATION

For insurance policies to be eligible for capital relief, Basel II has set a range of qualifying criteria. For a description of the qualifying criteria we refer the reader to Basel Committee on Banking Supervision (2010). In this section we discuss selected aspects. However, for completeness, we have summarised the qualifying criteria in Table 6.3.

6.2.1 Claims-paying ability

For the insurance policies to be eligible for capital relief, Basel II requires a minimum claims-paying ability rating of A. Assuming that the policy inherits the same rating, we compute the expected and unexpected loss due to a "default" on the policy. It is assumed that the expected loss will be reflected in the calculation of the premium by the insurer. The unexpected loss is considered a proxy by which the capital relief is reduced due to the A rating.

Assuming that there will be no recovery at default, in the case of an operational risk loss, the expected loss is $EL = PD_A L$, where PD_A is default probability associated with the A rating, and L is the insured limit. To calculate the unexpected loss UL, it is assumed that $UL = 3\sigma^1$. Hence, we obtain $UL = 3PD_A(1 - PD_A)L$. To illustrate the impact of UL, take, for example, a policy with a limit of US\$100 million and a default probability of $PD_A = 0.1\%$. The resulting expected and unexpected losses are $EL = US\$100,000$ and $UL \approx US\$300,000$ respectively.

The assumption of $UL = 3\sigma$ can be rightfully challenged. However, in light of the resulting numbers, the impact of more accurate calculations is expected to remain insignificant. Furthermore, it is noted that UL is calculated in isolation, without being subject to the effects of portfolio diversification. In reality, the insurance limit applies only to some risks and not to all that are then aggregated. As a result of the risk diversification, the impact of the default will be less than that calculated on a stand-alone basis.

6.2.2 Captive treatment

To the extent that operational risks reside on a captive balance sheet, they must be excluded from the relief calculation, as the captive's balance sheet is consolidated with that of the holding bank. However, captives may be used as a risk transfer optimisation vehicle, reinsuring more risks during soft market cycles and fewer during hard market cycles. Therefore, it can be desirable to model the captive to account for the risks that are reinsured by the captive, as these risks are transferred to third parties and no longer reside on the balance sheet of the captive, hence bank.

6.2.3 To pay or not to pay

There are many reasons why an insurer may or may not decide to reimburse the insured. Nevertheless, those precise reasons can also determine whether or not the insured insists on a reimbursement. As outlined in Basel Committee on Banking Supervision (2010) such causes may be due to coverage mismatch, dispute over cause, failure to report a claim in a timely fashion or improper disclosure.

To model the mechanics of the reimbursement uncertainties, we introduce a simple approach that also suggests a process for assessing such uncertainties. Our approach is a conditional one consisting of the following two events:

- bank assumes the claim is covered (BC);
- bank assumes the claim is not covered (BN).

BC and BN are disjoint events and exhaust the possible outcomes, hence $\Pr(BC) + \Pr(BN) = 1$. The interesting case to pursue is BC. In the case of BC, the insurer will also have an opinion:

- insurer assumes the claim is not covered, given that the bank assumes it is covered (IN | BC);
- insurer assumes the claim is covered, given that the bank assumes it is covered (IC | BC).

Again, IN | BC and IC | BC are disjoint events and exhaust the possible outcomes for the specified condition, hence $\Pr(IN \mid BC) + \Pr(IC \mid BC) = \Pr(BC)$.

The part that should be excluded from capital relief calculation is IN | BC. Causes such as mismatch, dispute over cause or failure to report a claim in a timely fashion can result in IN | BC.

In the case of IC | BC, it is assumed that the insurer will reimburse in full according to the coverage limits. A partial recovery would suggest a settlement between the parties requiring separate treatment within IC | BC. Furthermore, delays in payment expose a bank to the credit risk of the insurers, which, as seen in Section 6.2.1, is of little impact relative to the coverage limit. Such delays should be discouraged by appropriate penalties in the policy wording. The amount of the penalty should be noticeably higher than the amount of the return the insurer may receive from the capital markets.

6.3 SYSTEMIC RISK

In this section we provide a high-level assessment of whether insurance of operational risks can be a cause of a systemic risk. By insuring operational risks, risks are transferred from the portfolio of an insured bank to that of the insurer. The insurer will enter similar arrangements with several banks in an attempt to construct a diversified portfolio of risks. In addition, the banking portfolio of the insurer will diversify with portfolios of other non-correlated or weakly cor-related risks. It is through such risk diversification that an insurer achieves risk–return levels justifying the risk taking behaviour.

The transfer of the operational risks to an insurer's portfolio has, however, one caveat. As part of its portfolio management, the insurer will allocate only limited risk capital, hence capacity, to underwrite operational risks.[2] The typical capacities for operational risks based on traditional excess of loss covers[3] vary between US$500 million and US$5 billion per insurer. Assuming a portfolio of 20 insured banks, this implies insured sums ranging from US$25 million to US$250 million per bank. In light of these numbers and the fact that, unlike credit and market risks, large operational risk losses are due to specific risk rather than systematic risk, the likelihood of a systemic risk for the insurance industry due to operational risk insurance seems to be very remote.

6.4 CALCULATION OF CAPITAL RELIEF

This section considers the methodology to recognise insurance mit-igation for AMA models. Although the main focus will be on com-putation of the capital relief, the approach developed can be applied to align insurance covers with operations risk profile by optimising policy terms and conditions with respect to risk transfer and capital relief objectives.

The impact of insurance mitigation on operational risk capital is recognised, subject to several regulatory constraints set out in Basel Committee on Banking Supervision (2006, 2010). The constraints are expressed partly in terms of qualifying criteria and partly as haircuts. While qualifying criteria seek to identify polices that are eligible for recognition of insurance mitigation, haircuts are applied to reflect the extent to which qualified policies substitute capital. The quali-fying criteria were discussed in previous sections. The haircuts are summarised in Table 6.4 and their impact on capital relief calculation is discussed below.

6.4.1 Modelling insurance policies

Our approach to compute the impact of insurance mitigation is based on actuarial techniques commonly used in the insurance indus-try (Klugman et al 2004). These techniques take into account the

Table 6.4 Policy haircuts

Residual term of policy haircut, where policy term is less than
one year

Policy's cancellation haircut, where the cancellation term is less
than one year

Mismatches in coverage of insurance policies

Uncertainty of payment

Overall capital relief must not exceed 20% of the gross capital

---

impact of insurance mitigation by reflecting the coverage conditions,
likelihood and the impact of loss.

The most common types of policy encountered in practice are
excess of loss and quota share covers. Each of these policy types can
be with or without aggregate limits and installments. In the following we start first by considering simple excess of loss policies and
then increase the complexity by adding other policy conditions such
as aggregate limits, reinstatements and quota shares. Furthermore,
for clarity, we assume that the policies meet the qualifying criteria
and no haircuts apply. These idealised conditions will be relaxed
later.

Assume that X and N denote the severity and the frequency of a
risk, and $P_{d,c}$ represents an excess of loss insurance policy with d and
c as deductible and cover per loss event, respectively. The cover c is
the amount that is guaranteed by the insurer after the deductible is
exceeded. The risk X may correspond to scenarios or losses within a
risk category or unit of measure (UoM). The policy $P_{d,c}$ is assumed to
match the risk X perfectly, ie, there is a one-to-one mapping between
losses and policy. Again, this is an idealised assumption that will be
relaxed later.

Under these assumptions the impact of an excess of loss policy is
given by

$$S_{\text{net}} = \sum_{i=1}^{N} X_i - \sum_{i=1}^{N} \mathcal{L}_{d,c}(X_i)$$

where X_i is a random draw of X, $\mathcal{L}_{d,c}$ is an operator that reflects policy
conditions and S_{net} is the aggregate risk after the impact of insurance.
The first term in this equation describes the gross aggregate risk, and
the second term the reduction due to insurance mitigation, ie, part
of the risk that is transferred. The operator $\mathcal{L}_{d,c}$ computes portions

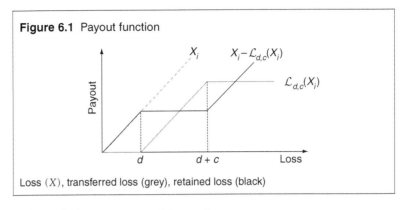

Figure 6.1 Payout function

Loss (X), transferred loss (grey), retained loss (black)

of the risk that are covered for each event

$$\mathcal{L}_{d,c}(X_i) = \min(\max(X_i - d, 0), c)$$

Figure 6.1 depicts the payout function of the operator $\mathcal{L}_{d,c}$.

Next, we consider an excess of loss policy $P_{d,c,L}$ with the additional feature of an aggregate limit L. As a result of the aggregate limit, S_{net} becomes

$$S_{\text{net}} = \sum_{i=1}^{N} X_i - \mathcal{L}_{0,L}\left(\sum_{i=1}^{N} \mathcal{L}_{d,c}(X_i)\right)$$

where the operator $\mathcal{L}_{0,L}$ is now also applied to the aggregate loss to account for the aggregate limit L. It is worth noting that some policies may even assume an aggregate deductible, also called an attachment point. In our approach, an attachment point A can be taken into account by replacing the operator $\mathcal{L}_{0,L}$ with $\mathcal{L}_{A,L}$, in the above equation.

A frequently encountered policy feature is a reinstatement, triggered when the aggregate limit of the policy is exhausted. As a result, the policy guarantees the same coverage terms and conditions as at inception, but now only for the residual period of the policy. Reinstatements can be conveniently modelled by adjusting aggregate limits. A policy with reinstatements may have one or many reinstatements. In the case where it has n reinstatements, S_{net} can be modelled by

$$S_{\text{net}} = \sum_{i=1}^{N} X_i - \mathcal{L}_{0,L+nL}\left(\sum_{i=1}^{N} \mathcal{L}_{d,c}(X_i)\right)$$

In other words, each reinstatement can be treated as an additional aggregate limit.

A further coverage possibility is given by quota shares. Quota shares are introduced for excess of loss policies to partially mitigate adverse selection by introducing co-insurance. The insured agrees to participate on losses in the insured layer, thereby stressing the willingness to avoid losses. The impact of a quota share $\alpha \in [0,1]$, where $(1 - \alpha)$ is the share of the insured, results in

$$S_{\text{net}} = \sum_{i=1}^{N} X_i - \mathcal{L}_{0,L+nL}\left(\sum_{i=1}^{N} \alpha \mathcal{L}_{d,c}(X_i) \right)$$

Quota shares are also offered as standalone policies in their own right, in which case we would ignore the operators $\mathcal{L}$ in the above equation to obtain the net risk S_{net}.

6.4.2 Modelling under realistic conditions

The methods in the previous section were developed by making several idealised assumptions, which are summarised here:

- one-to-one mapping between policies and risks;
- no coverage mismatch or uncertainty of payment;
- no residual policy term and cancellation period.

In the following subsection we relax these assumptions in order to make the developed methods applicable to more realistic situations. For a better overview, we will demonstrate it for excess of loss policies. The generalisation to other policy types is straightforward.

6.4.2.1 Mapping

In Table 6.2 we provide an indicative mapping of operational risk Level 2 categories to insurance policies. Operational risk categories may map to one or more insurance policies. However, those circumstances where operational risk categories map to two or more policies are far less frequent.

If a risk category maps to many policies, the simplest way to account for it is to split the frequency of losses between different policy types and then model each part separately. To illustrate this, assume for a risk category or UoM that λ_0, λ_{P_1}, and λ_{P_2} denote the portion of the loss frequency that maps to no policy, policy P_1 and policy P_2, respectively.[4] As a result, the equation for S_{net} becomes

$$S_{\text{net}} = \sum_{i=1}^{N} X_i - \sum_{i=1}^{\lambda_1 N} \mathcal{L}_{d_1,c_1}(X_i) - \sum_{i=1}^{\lambda_2 N} \mathcal{L}_{d_1,c_1}(X_i)$$

where d_1, c_1 and d_2, c_2 are the deductibles and covers of the policies P_1 and P_2, respectively. By the definitions in Section 6.2.3, λ_0 describes the subset BN, and λ_{P_1} and λ_{P_2} span the subset BC.

There are two challenges in applying the previous equation. First, the estimation of the parameters λ_0, λ_{P_1} and λ_{P_2}. This will be addressed in the next subsection. Second, we have implicitly assumed that the three parts follow the same severity distributions. Having risk categories or UoMs that consist of homogeneous sets of data would justify this assumption in general. However, we may need to analyse the losses with respect to the validity of this assumption.

6.4.2.2 *Coverage mismatch and uncertainty of payment*

In Section 6.2.3 we outlined a conditional approach to assess the coverage mismatch. In order to illustrate how this approach works, we consider the excess of loss policy from the previous section. The coverage mismatch must be analysed only for those losses that fall within the subset *BC*. In Section 6.2.3 we split *BC* into two disjoint and complementary subsets of IN | BC and IC | BC. For the excess of loss policy this means that we must split the fractions λ_1 and λ_2 in correspondence to IN | BC and IC | BC. This implies a split of each insured term in the previous equation, eg, for policy P_1 we obtain

$$\sum_{i=1}^{\lambda_1 N} \mathcal{L}_{d_1,c_1}(X_i) \;\rightarrow\; \sum_{i=1}^{\lambda_1(1-\alpha_{CM,P_1})N} X_i \;-\; \sum_{i=1}^{\lambda_1 \alpha_{CM,P_1} N} \mathcal{L}_{d_1,c_1}(X_i)$$

where $\alpha_{CM,P_1} \in [0,1]$ describes the fraction of losses that correspond to the subset IC | BC. Hence, the assessment of the mapping and coverage mismatch is a careful accounting task, requiring a good understanding of losses and policy wordings, rather than a modelling one.

We conclude this section with a remark on the uncertainty of payment. While the coverage mismatch assesses, in view of what is covered, the degree of discrepancy between insurer and insured, the uncertainty of payments addresses operational and compliance failures of the insured, such as timely reporting of the losses or proper disclosure to the insurer. In this chapter we will not consider additional discounts reflecting operational aspects of the insurance mitigation. Other causes of the uncertainty of payment overlap with other qualifying criteria or haircuts and are not treated separately.

6.4.2.3   Residual policy term and cancellation period

The residual policy term and cancellation period haircuts are accounted for by appropriate adjustments to the frequency of insured losses.

To achieve this, we assume the frequency at time τ to be given by $n(\tau)$. Hence the annual frequency can be expressed as

$$N = \int_0^1 n(\tau)\, d\tau$$

with 1 corresponding to a one-year period. In the presence of the two haircuts, the frequency of losses $N(t)$ for the annual period $[t, t+1]$, where t is the year for which the capital is computed, is given by

$$N(t) = \int_t^{t+1} \min(f_{\text{RPT}}(\tau), f_{\text{CP}}(\tau)) n(\tau)\, d\tau$$

where the functions f_{RPT} and f_{CP} model the haircuts for the residual policy term and cancellation period, respectively.

To compute $N(t)$ we assume that $n(t)$ is independent of time, ie, $n(t) = n$. This assumption implies, in particular, the absence of intra-year cyclical patterns in frequency. For all practical applications it provides a good approximation for the relevant frequency of excess of loss policy characterised by high deductibles.

As a result of the time independence assumption, $N(t)$ becomes a fraction of the annual frequency N, where the fraction α is determined by the following integral

$$\alpha = \int_t^{t+1} \min(f_{\text{RPT}}(\tau), f_{\text{CP}}(\tau))\, d\tau$$

Rather than developing a general scheme, we demonstrate through an example how to compute the integral. Assume that we would like to calculate the capital for the annual period starting at $t = 0$. Furthermore, assume a policy with an annual term that starts three months before the capital calculation period, ie, at time $t = -0.25$. Moreover, we assume a cancellation period of six months.

Figure 6.2 depicts the haircut functions under the assumption that we are calculating one year capital at time $= 0$. Moreover, it assumes that there has been no cancellation of the policy as of this date. From Figure 6.2, we obtain

$$\alpha = \int_0^1 \min(f_{\text{RPT}}(\tau), f_{\text{CP}}(\tau))\, d\tau = 1 \times 0.5 + (1 - p) \times 0.25$$

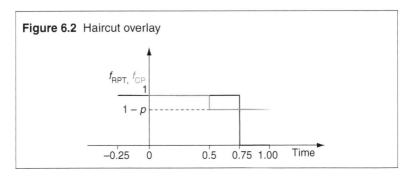

Figure 6.2 Haircut overlay

where p denotes the probability of cancellation.

Assuming $p = 5\%$, we obtain $N(0) \approx 74N\%$. To combine the impact of the residual policy term and cancellation period haircuts with other haircuts, we only need to replace the frequency N by $N(0)$ in the corresponding equations of the net aggregate loss S_{net}.

6.5 COMPUTATIONAL IMPLEMENTATION

So far we have considered one risk category or UoM that maps into one or many insurance policies. AMA models, in general, consist of many UoMs, where each UoM is modelled by a set of frequency and severity distributions.[5] The methods discussed in previous sections generalise easily to the case of many UoMs. The only point that deserves additional consideration is the interplay with dependency modelling.

UoMs are aggregated with an assumption of a dependence model. The dependence model considers the dependencies between different distributions: frequency and severity distributions, aggregate distributions or perhaps a mix of the two. When the dependence is modelled for frequency and severity distributions, corresponding losses are simulated for each UoM according to the copulas, and subsequently they are aggregated subject to the terms of the insurance policies.

However, when dependence is modelled at the aggregate level, the copula generates values in the range $[0, 1]$ for the gross aggregate losses of each UoM.[6] Therefore, we first need to identify the gross aggregate losses of each UoM with ranks corresponding to the generated copula values. The insurance impact is then modelled by applying the policy conditions to the losses that constitute the gross aggregate loss.

6.6 CONCLUSIONS

We have outlined a method of accounting for insurance mitigation by developing an approach that models insurance mitigation as realistically as possible. We do not find this a more complex task than some of the assumptions to be made when developing AMA models in the first place. In fact, it can be shown that the sensitivity of the results to the assumptions made, eg, to coverage mismatch, is orders of magnitude lower than those made for the tail severities. The market participants, including regulators, banks and insurers, should be encouraged to consider insurance mitigation as a viable mechanism to hedge operational risks. The existing insurance products provide a good starting point for this. Use of consortium data can be instrumental in developing products that are better tailored to operational risk language and needs. Indeed, consortium data can help us to design products with more robust pricing and risk transparency than is seen in some of the existing traditional products.

1 EL and σ are computed for the probability space consisting of the two events of a full limit loss and no loss with probabilities PD_A and $1 - PD_A$, respectively.

2 Capacity corresponds to the total liability of the insurer arising from underwriting risks. It is the sum of all insured limits. Risk capital is the amount of the capital required to support the written capacity after portfolio diversification.

3 In view risk transfer as well as capital relief, the excess of loss covers are the relevant covers.

4 Note that $\lambda_0, \lambda_{P_1}, \lambda_{P_2} \in [0,1]$, and $\lambda_0 + \lambda_{P_1} + \lambda_{P_2} = 1$. Moreover, a similar relation must hold for any number of policy mappings.

5 A UoM may be modelled based on a hybrid approach using LDA and scenarios. Nevertheless we can combine the corresponding distributions to obtain a set of frequency and severity distributions describing the respective UoM.

6 Note that the dependence is calibrated for gross losses.

REFERENCES

Basel Committee on Banking Supervision, 2006, "Basel II: International Convergence of Capital Measurement and Capital Standards: A Revised Framework", Bank for International Settlements, June, URL: http://www.bis.org/publ/bcbs128.pdf.

Basel Committee on Banking Supervision, 2010, "Recognising The Risk-Mitigating Impact of Insurance in Operational Risk Modelling", Bank for International Settlements, October, URL: http://www.bis.org/publ/bcbs181.pdf

Klugman, S. A., H. H. Panjer and G. E. Willmot, 2004, *Loss Models* (Wiley Interscience).

7

A Unified Approach to Dependency Calibration in Operational Risk Models

Mikhail Makarov
EVMTech

Paragraph 669(d) of the Basel II framework states:

> Risk measures for different operational risk estimates must be added for purposes of calculating the regulatory minimum capital requirement. However, the bank may be permitted to use internally determined correlations in operational risk losses across individual operational risk estimates, provided it can demonstrate to the satisfaction of the national supervisor that its systems for determining correlations are sound, implemented with integrity and take into account the uncertainty surrounding any such correlation estimates (particularly in periods of stress). The bank must validate its correlation assumptions using appropriate quantitative and qualitative techniques.

It follows from the above paragraph that, unless an internal model has a sound methodology for dependence estimates, it needs to assume full dependency between risks. For granular internal models, full dependency leads to unrealistically high capital numbers, thus defeating the purpose of building an advanced measurement approach (AMA) model.

The banks use the combination of expert judgement, internal loss data and external data to estimate dependence, but the problem is not a simple one to solve.

Operational risk models have to combine copula fitting, tail dependency estimation and analysis of simultaneous exceedances in order to measure dependencies (Cope and Antonini 2008).

Let us outline several issues arising from dependency estimates (Basel Committee on Banking Supervision 2011).

- Many methods require huge amounts of data to estimate dependencies. How can we hope to estimate joint cumulative distribution functions (CDFs) based on the data, which is barely sufficient to estimate marginal CDFs?

- Some of the methods make assumptions on the underlying copula (often a Gaussian copula). Copula assumptions are almost impossible to validate and are often very difficult to stress test.

- Standard frequency severity models lead to the assumption of no dependence within units of measure. However, we need to consider both dependence between units of measures and dependence within units of measure.

- Some of the sources of external data are incomplete, which makes them difficult to use for dependence estimates.

In this chapter we propose a method that will unify several approaches to model dependencies as well as addressing the issues mentioned above. The new statistic (volatility curve) provides a clear link between tail dependency, simultaneous exceedances and copula choice; it combines measurements of both severity and frequency dependencies, and it can be applied to incomplete data sets.

The chapter is organised as follows. In Section 7.1 we will introduce a statistic called a volatility curve that allows us to measure the concentration of large losses and analyse how the concentration of large losses is related to tail dependency. In Section 7.2 we will show how we can use the volatility curve to estimate capital diversification. In Section 7.3 we will look at the impact of copula selection. In Section 7.4 we will prove the main theoretical result of the paper: the connection between volatility curve and tail dependence. In Section 7.5 we will prove that volatility curve can also be used for incomplete data.

7.1 DEFINITION AND MAIN PROPERTIES OF VOLATILITY CURVE

Our approach to model dependence will be based on the following principle (Vapnik 1998):

> If you possess a restricted amount of information for solving some problem, try to solve the problem directly and never solve a more

general problem as an intermediate step. It is possible that the available information is sufficient for a direct solution but is insufficient for solving a more general intermediate problem.

In order to follow this principle, let us formulate the problem that we will try to solve. What is the impact of dependence on the tail of the aggregate distribution?

A standard approach, finding parameters of a copula, is an example of solving a much more general (and difficult) problem. Given a copula, we can of course find the impact of the dependence on the tail of the aggregate distribution, but using the copula we can, in addition, answer many other questions (many of which are of no interest to risk management, eg, finding the correlation between the last digits of the losses does not help to estimate the capital).

In order to introduce such a statistic, let us first discuss two notions: large loss clustering and tail dependence.

Let us select a threshold and count the number of losses in a bank above the threshold. If the outcome of the loss count is a sequence $\{1, 0, 2, 0, 1, 0, 0, 0, 1, 0\}$, we can conclude that large losses do not happen together often and dependence should not increase the capital number. If, on the other hand, the outcome of loss count is a sequence $\{0, 0, 0, 0, 5, 0, 0, 0, 0, 0\}$ we can conclude the opposite: large losses do happen together and dependence should increase the capital number.

In summary, we would expect a high concentration of large losses in one year if there are dependencies among losses and low concentration if there are no dependencies. In addition, a high concentration of large losses in one year should have a large impact on diversification and capital.

Let us introduce the following.

7.1.1 Notation

Let N_T denote a random variable equal to the number of losses exceeding threshold T in a year.

Then the volatility curve is defined as follows:

Definition 7.1. For a given threshold T, define volatility τ as

$$\tau_T = \frac{\text{var}[N_T]}{E[N_T]} - 1 + E[N_T]$$

For example, if the annual loss count of large losses is

$$\{1,0,2,0,1,0,0,0,1,0\}$$

then

$$E[N_T] \approx 0.5$$
$$\mathrm{var}[N_T] \approx 0.45$$
$$\tau_T \approx \frac{0.45}{0.5} - 1 + 0.5 = 0.4$$

If the annual loss count of large losses is

$$\{0,0,0,0,5,0,0,0,0,0\}$$

then

$$E[N_T] \approx 0.5$$
$$\mathrm{var}[N_T] \approx 2.25$$
$$\tau_T \approx \frac{2.25}{0.5} - 1 + 0.5 = 4$$

Let us explain the intuition behind the definition of tau.

1. Concentration of the large losses in one year does not have an impact on their expected frequency, but has an impact on $\mathrm{var}[N_T]$, so $\mathrm{var}[N_T]$ is a possible measure for the concentration.

2. If the timing of losses is independent, then the frequency of losses will be approximately Poisson. For Poisson process

$$\mathrm{var}[N_T]/E[N_T] = 1$$

so the term $(\mathrm{var}[N_T]/E[N_T] - 1)$ can be used to measure deviation of the frequency from the Poisson process and therefore capture dependency for the frequency.

Although the volatility curve captures clustering of large losses, it is not clear how it is connected to the standard statistical quantities used to measure dependence. As we will prove in Section 7.4, the volatility curve is closely related to the tail dependence statistics. Recall that, for two random variables X_1 and X_2, tail dependence is defined as $\theta_T = P[X_2 > T \mid X_1 > T]$. Then, for a typical frequency severity model, $\tau_T = \theta_T \tau_0$ (see Theorem 7.18). This relation allows us to analyse the volatility curve for different cases of frequency severity dependence.

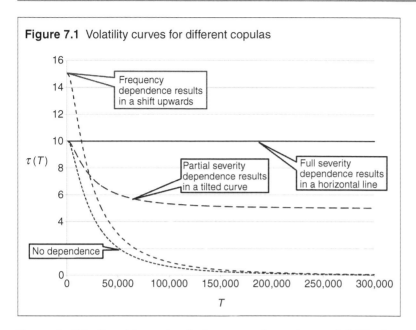

Figure 7.1 Volatility curves for different copulas

Example 7.2. Consider a simple frequency/severity model. The frequency N is a Poisson distribution and severities are independent and identically distributed with severity F. Then

$$\tau_T = E[N](1 - F(T))$$

In this case the volatility curve coincides with the expected loss frequency curve.

Example 7.3. Consider a frequency/severity model where the frequency N is a Poisson distribution and severities are fully dependent and identically distributed with severity F. Then

$$\tau_T = E[N]\Pr[X > T \mid X > T] = E[N]$$

In this case the volatility curve is a horizontal line.

Example 7.4. Consider a frequency/severity model where the frequency N is a Poisson distribution, severities are identically distributed and are dependent through a Gaussian copula. Then

$$\tau_T = E[N]\Pr[X_2 > T \mid X_1 > T]$$

The Gaussian copula induces zero tail dependence, ie

$$\lim_{T->\infty} \Pr[X_2 > T \mid X_1 > T] = 0$$

Therefore, τ_T is a decreasing curve with $\tau_0 = E[N]$ and $\tau_\infty = 0$.

Example 7.5. Consider a frequency/severity model with two units of measure. Assume that both units of measure have the same frequencies and severities, with frequencies fully dependent and severities fully independent. Then

$$\tau_T = \left(\frac{\text{var}[2N]}{E[2N]} - 1 + E[2N] \right)(1 - F(T)) = (E[2N] + 1)(1 - F(T))$$

Therefore, τ_T looks like a loss-expected loss-frequency function with additional multiplier.

We can summarise the above examples with the help of Figure 7.1.

7.2 CALIBRATION USING VOLATILITY CURVE

In this section we demonstrate how the volatility curve can be used to calibrate dependence model. The calibration process can be split into three steps:

1. volatility curve estimation;

2. model set up;

3. model calibration;

Step 1: volatility curve estimation
In the first step, we need to estimate the volatility coefficient τ_T for several values of the threshold T. If the data source is internal losses (at least ten years), then estimation is quite straightforward.

1. Scale loss sizes and loss frequencies in time to make sure that past loss history is representative for the model year (this step typically needs to be done anyway during frequency/severity analysis);

2. For several thresholds, for example $T(n) = n \times 10{,}000{,}000$ and $n = 1, \dots, 5$, estimate $\tau_{T(n)}$.

If the data source is based on external losses and the data source is complete, we need to add the additional step of scaling external data to match the exposure of the model bank. If the data source is based on the external losses, which are incomplete, we need to use the results of Section 7.5 to get an upper estimate on the volatility curve. More precisely, we can perform the following steps.

1. Select companies with sufficiently many years of loss history (at least ten years).

2. Scale loss sizes and loss frequencies in time.

3. Scale external loss sizes and loss frequencies to match exposure of the model bank.

4. Select same thresholds for the companies, for example $T(n) = n \times 10{,}000{,}000$ and $n = 1, \ldots, 5$.

5. For each company k and threshold $T(n)$, estimate

$$\frac{\tau^*_{T(n)}}{E[N^*_{T(n)}]}$$

6. The volatility τ for incomplete data can be used as an upper estimate for the volatility τ for the complete data (see Corollary 7.30). Thus, we can assume that, for banks similar to the selected ones

$$\frac{\tau_{T(n)}}{E[N_{T(n)}]} \leqslant \max_{k} \left\{ \frac{\tau^*_{T(n)}}{E[N^*_{T(n)}]} \right\}$$

7. A bank can estimate $E[N_{T(n)}]$ based on its internal data or based on its loss model and therefore obtain an upper bound on its $\tau_{T(n)}$.

Instead of scaling losses to match exposure of the model bank we can use different (scaled) thresholds for the banks.

Step 2: model set-up

Let us assume that a bank has a model that can generate single losses using Monte Carlo. Such models typically use copulas or shock models to induce dependency on losses. The user has to select one or two parameters in the dependence model that will be calibrated (for example, in the model that uses the Gaussian copula, we can assume that all non-diagonal values of the rank correlation matrix are equal and use that value as the parameter). Ideally we would be able to understand the impact of the parameters on the structure of dependence, eg, one parameter can control frequency dependence and the other severity dependence.

Given that the model can generate single losses, we can compute the volatility curve for the model: we can generate single losses for sufficiently many sample years and estimate τ_T for the losses using its definition.

Step 3: model calibration

As the internal model can generate single losses, it can be used to compute the volatility curve implied by the model. In order to do that, we perform the following steps.

1. Set initial values of dependency parameters.

2. Generate single losses for 10,000 sample years and compute the volatility coefficient τ_T based on the sample years for the same thresholds as in the volatility estimation.

3. Compare the empirical volatility curve and the model volatility curve. If the two curves are close, the dependency parameters have been found. If the two curves are different, adjust the dependency parameters in the model to increase or decrease frequency/severity dependency (we can use the chart from the end of Section 7.1 to help with the adjustment).

4. Repeat steps 2–3.

Let us summarise the main properties of the model calibration using the volatility curve.

- The method can be applied to both internal and external data sets.

- The method requires at least 10 years of loss history.

- The only information required is loss sizes and loss years.

- The method does not estimate dependency coefficients directly, but helps to select them in a way that captures clustering of large losses.

- The method estimates dependence both within and between units of measures.

7.3 VOLATILITY CURVE AND COPULA SELECTION

Let us recall that one of the main challenges in dependence modelling is uncertainty with respect to copula selection. In this section we will show that the volatility curve approach for dependence calibration is significantly less sensitive to copula selection than calibration based on dependence statistics such as rank correlation. In addition we will show that using volatility curve calibration together with a Gaussian copula leads to a conservative capital estimation.

Figure 7.2 Diversification benefit for right and left Clayton copulas as a function of rank correlation

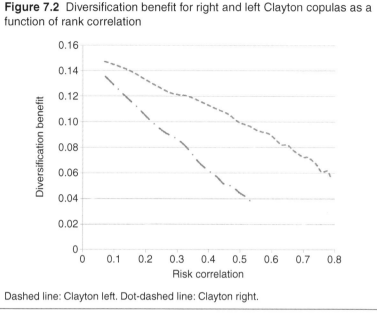

Dashed line: Clayton left. Dot-dashed line: Clayton right.

To simplify the computations, we will consider a risk model that generates two losses per year. Both severities X and Y are assumed to have lognormal distribution with $\mu = 1$ and $\sigma = 0.5$.

If risk estimates for X and Y are added, the capital is given by Quantile$(X; 0.95)$ + Quantile$(Y; 0.95)$. If dependence is modelled, the capital is given by Quantile$(X + Y; 0.95)$.

We will measure diversification benefit: the reduction in capital

$$\text{div}(X, Y) = 1 - \frac{\text{Quantile}(X + Y; 0.95)}{\text{Quantile}(X; 0.95) + \text{Quantile}(Y; 0.95)}$$

For the examples below we will recall the definitions of Clayton right and left copulas. The Clayton left copula is defined as

$$C_{\text{left}}(u_1, \ldots, u_d) = \psi(\psi^{-1}(u_1) + \cdots + \psi(u_d))$$

where

$$\psi(t) = (1 + t)^{-1/\theta}$$

It induces higher dependency on small quantiles and lower dependency on large quantiles. The Clayton right copula is defined as

$$C_{\text{right}}(u_1, \ldots, u_d) = C_{\text{left}}(1 - u_1, \ldots, 1 - u_d)$$

It induces higher dependency on large quantiles and lower dependency on small quantiles.

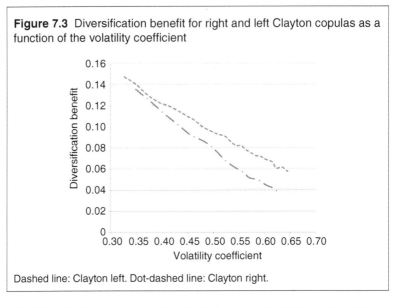

Figure 7.3 Diversification benefit for right and left Clayton copulas as a function of the volatility coefficient

Dashed line: Clayton left. Dot-dashed line: Clayton right.

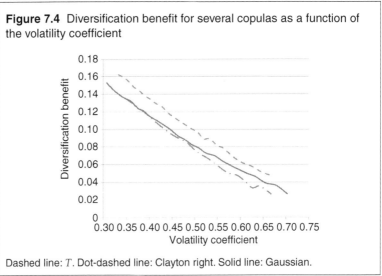

Figure 7.4 Diversification benefit for several copulas as a function of the volatility coefficient

Dashed line: T. Dot-dashed line: Clayton right. Solid line: Gaussian.

Example 7.6. Suppose that we make a mistake in choosing the joint copula: we choose the Clayton right copula while, in reality, the copula is Clayton left. If we use rank correlation to calibrate dependence (notice that rank correlation cannot help us distinguish between the copulas), then we may get substantially different diversification benefits for the two copulas for the same rank correlation (Figure 7.2).

Therefore, dependence calibration based on rank correlation is quite sensitive to the error in copula selection.

If we can compute just one value on the volatility curve, say at $T = 3.5$, to calibrate dependence then, depending on the level of dependence, we get the diversification shown in Figures 7.3 and 7.4.

Note that if we can compute values of the volatility curve at several thresholds then we can increase the precision substantially. Therefore, dependence calibration based on the volatility curve is less sensitive to the error in copula selection.

Example 7.7. Given the same severities as in Example 7.6, we can try to use several copulas. In the example below we will test three different copulas: Clayton right, Gaussian, and T copulas. We assume that the volatility curve is measured only at one threshold $T = 3.5$. Figure 7.4 compares the diversification benefit for the different copulas.

Looking at the figure we can make the following conclusions: if we use the volatility curve to calibrate the model, then copula selection has a limited impact on the diversification benefit, and the Gaussian copula leads to a conservative estimate of the diversification benefit.

7.4 CONNECTION BETWEEN VOLATILITY CURVE AND TAIL DEPENDENCE

In this section we will show how the volatility curve captures loss dependencies and, in particular, tail dependencies. Let us first consider the case where exactly two losses X_1 and X_2 with the same marginal distributions are generated each year.

Lemma 7.8. For two random variables X_1 and X_2 with the same marginal distributions

$$\tau_T = \Pr[X_1 > T \mid X_2 > T]$$

Proof

$$\tau_T = \frac{\text{var}[N_T]}{E[N_T]} - 1 + E[N_T]$$

$$= \frac{E[N_T^2] - E[N_T]^2}{E[N_T]} - 1 + E[N_T]$$

$$= \frac{E[N_T^2 - E[N_T]]}{E[N_T]}$$

To shorten the notation let us introduce

$$p_{0,0} = \Pr(X_1 \leqslant T, X_2 \leqslant T)$$
$$p_{0,1} = \Pr(X_1 \leqslant T, X_2 > T)$$
$$p_{1,0} = \Pr(X_1 > T, X_2 \leqslant T)$$
$$p_{1,1} = \Pr(X_1 > T, X_2 > T)$$

The excess loss count N_T can take values

$$N_T = \begin{cases} 0, & X_1 \leqslant T \text{ and } X_2 \leqslant T \\ 1, & X_1 \leqslant T \text{ or } X_2 \leqslant T \\ 2, & X_1 > T \text{ and } X_2 > T \end{cases}$$

Then

$$\begin{aligned} E[N_T] &= 0p_{0,0} + 1p_{0,1} + 1p_{1,0} + 2p_{1,1} \\ &= (p_{0,1} + p_{1,1}) + (p_{1,0} + p_{1,1}) \\ &= \Pr[X_1 > T] + \Pr[X_2 > T] \end{aligned}$$

Next

$$E[N_T^2] = 0p_{0,0} + 1p_{0,1} + 1p_{1,0} + 4p_{1,1}$$

Therefore

$$\begin{aligned} \tau_T &= \frac{E[N_T^2 - E[N_T]]}{E[N_T]} \\ &= \frac{(p_{0,1} + p_{1,0} + 4p_{1,1}) - (p_{0,1} + p_{1,0} + 2p_{1,1})}{\Pr[X_1 > T] + \Pr[X_2 > T]} \\ &= \frac{2p_{1,1}}{\Pr[X_1 > T] + \Pr[X_2 > T]} \\ &= \frac{2\Pr[X_1 > T, X_2 > T]}{2\Pr[X_1 > T]} \end{aligned}$$

$\square$

Lemma 7.8 shows that volatility τ measures tail dependency for two variables. In Theorem 7.18 we will generalise this result from two loss variables to any (including random) number of loss variables.

Consider a standard frequency/severity model. Denote by N the frequency of the losses, and by $X_1, \ldots, X_N$ the impacts of the losses. Similarly to the proof of Lemma 7.8, we are going to compute $E[N_T]$ and $E[N_T^2]$, which will lead to the formula for τ_T.

Definition 7.9. We say that two random variables X and Y are positively codependent if, for any constants a and b

$$\Pr[X > a \mid Y > b] \geqslant \mathbb{P}_{X>a}$$

or equivalently

$$\Pr[X > a \mid Y > b] \geqslant \mathbb{P}_{X>a}\mathbb{P}_{Y>b}$$

Definition 7.10. Define tail dependency coefficient theta for two random variables X and Y with the same marginal CDFs as the probability that Y is large given X is large

$$\theta_T = \Pr[Y > T \mid X > T]$$

In order to prove the results below we need to make the following assumptions:

1. independence of loss count N from the loss severities $(X_1,...,X_N)$;
2. identical distributions for loss impacts $X_1, \ldots, X_N$;
3. positive codependence between X_i and X_j for any i and j.

The above assumptions are not needed for the definition and computation of τ_T. However, some of the results below are much easier to prove under these assumptions. In other words, these assumptions are sufficient, but not necessary.

7.4.1 Notation

Denote by I the indicator function $\mathbf{1}_T(x) = 1$ for all $x > T$ and 0 for $x \leqslant T$.

Note that $N_T = \sum_{i=1}^{N} I_T(X_i)$. In order to compute the statistics of N_T, we shall compute different statistics of $I_T(X_i)$ and use them to estimate $E[N_T]$ and $E[N_T^2]$. Lemmas 7.11–7.16 together with Proposition 7.17 achieve this task.

Lemma 7.11. Let X be a random variable. Then

$$E[\mathbf{1}_T(X)] = \mathbb{P}_{X>T}$$
$$E[\mathbf{1}_T(X)^2] = \mathbb{P}_{X>T}$$

Proof Let $\Omega_{>T} = \{\omega \mid X(\omega) > T\}$. Then

$$E[\mathbf{1}_T(X)] = \int_{\Omega_{>T}} 1 \, d\mu = \Pr[\Omega_{>T}] = \mathbb{P}_{X>T}$$

The second equation in the lemma follows from the identity

$$\mathbf{1}_T(X)^2 = \mathbf{1}_T(X).$$

$\square$

Lemma 7.12. Let X and Y be two random variables with the same marginal distributions. Then

$$E[\mathbf{1}_T(X)\mathbf{1}_T(Y)] = \Pr[X > T, Y > T] = \theta_T \mathbb{P}_{X>T}$$

Lemma 7.13.
$$E[N_T \mid N = n] = n\mathbb{P}_{X>T}$$

Proof Using the definition of N_T and Lemma 7.11, we get

$$E[N_T \mid N = n] = E\left[\sum_{k=1}^{n} \mathbf{1}_T(X_k)\right] = nE[\mathbf{1}_T(X)] = n\mathbb{P}_{X>T}$$

$\square$

Lemma 7.14.
$$E[N_T^2 \mid N = n] = (n + n(n-1)\theta_T)\mathbb{P}_{X>T}$$

Proof Using the definition of N_T and Lemmas 7.11 and 7.12 we get

$$E[N_T^2 \mid N = n] = E\left[\left(\sum_{k=1}^{n} \mathbf{1}_T(X_k)\right)^2\right]$$

$$= \sum_{k=1}^{n} E[\mathbf{1}_T(X)^2] + \sum_{1 \leqslant i \neq j \leqslant n} E[\mathbf{1}_T(X_i)\mathbf{1}_T(X_j)]$$

$$= n\mathbb{P}_{X>T} + n(n-1)\theta_T\mathbb{P}_{X>T}$$

$\square$

Corollary 7.15.
$$\mathrm{var}[N_T \mid N = n] = \mathbb{P}_{X>T}(n + n(n-1)\theta_T - n^2\mathbb{P}_{X>T})$$

Proof This follows from Lemmas 7.13, 7.14, and the equality

$$\mathrm{var}[N_T \mid N = n] = E[N_T^2 \mid N = n] - E[N_T \mid N = n]^2$$

$\square$

Lemma 7.16.
$$E[N_T] = E[N]\mathbb{P}_{X>T}$$

Proof

$$E[N_T] = E\left[\sum_{i=1}^{N} I_T(X_i) \right] = E[N]E[I_T(X)] = E[N]\mathbb{P}_{X>T}$$

$\square$

Proposition 7.17. The second moment of N_T can be estimated as follows

$$E[N_T^2] = (E[N] + (E[N^2] - E[N])\theta_T)\mathbb{P}_{X>T}$$

Proof In order to prove the result we will use the law of total variance (Weiss 2005). Using the law, we can write

$$\text{var}[N_T] = \text{var}[E[N_T \mid N]] + E[\text{var}[N_T \mid N]] \qquad (7.1)$$

The variance gives the following (see Lemma 7.13)

$$\text{var}[E[N_T \mid N]] = \text{var}[\{\mathbb{P}_{X>T}n; p_n\}] = \mathbb{P}_{X>T}^2 \text{var}[N] \qquad (7.2)$$

The variance gives the following (see Corollary 7.15):

$$\begin{aligned}
E[\text{var}[N_T \mid N]] &= E[\{\text{var}[N_T \mid N = n]; p_n\}] \\
&= E[\{\mathbb{P}_{X>T}(n + n(n-1)\theta_T - n^2\mathbb{P}_{X>T}); p_n\}] \\
&= \mathbb{P}_{X>T}(E[N] + (E[N^2] - E[N])\theta_T - E[N^2]\mathbb{P}_{X>T})
\end{aligned}$$

$$(7.3)$$

Therefore, combining Equation 7.2 and Equation 7.3 together with the law of the total variance Equation 7.1, we obtain

$$\begin{aligned}
\text{var}[N_T] \\
&= \mathbb{P}_{X>T}^2 \text{var}[N] + \mathbb{P}_{X>T}(E[N] + (E[N^2] - E[N])\theta_T - E[N^2]\mathbb{P}_{X>T}) \\
&= E[N]\mathbb{P}_{X>T} + (E[N^2] - E[N])\theta_T\mathbb{P}_{X>T} - E[N]^2\mathbb{P}_{X>T}^2
\end{aligned}$$

Using Lemma 7.16, we obtain

$$\begin{aligned}
E[N_T^2] &= \text{var}[N_T] + E[N_T]^2 \\
&= E[N]\mathbb{P}_{X>T} + (E[N^2] - E[N])\theta_T\mathbb{P}_{X>T} \\
&\quad - E[N]^2\mathbb{P}_{X>T}^2 + E[N]^2\mathbb{P}_{X>T}^2 \\
&= E[N]\mathbb{P}_{X>T} + (E[N^2] - E[N])\theta_T\mathbb{P}_{X>T}
\end{aligned}$$

which proves the proposition. $\square$

The next theorem shows how the volatility curve captures dependencies.

Theorem 7.18. For a frequency/severity model with positively co-dependent losses

$$\tau_T = \theta_T \tau_0$$

Proof Using the definition of volatility τ

$$\tau_T = \frac{\text{var}[N_T]}{E[N_T]} + E[N_T] - 1$$

$$= \frac{\text{var}[N_T] + E[N_T]^2 - E[N_T]}{E[N_T]}$$

$$= \frac{E[N_T^2] - E[N_T]}{E[N_T]}$$

In particular

$$\tau_0 = \frac{E[N^2] - E[N]}{E[N]}$$

Using Proposition 7.17 and Lemma 7.16 we obtain

$$\tau_T = \frac{E[N_T^2] - E[N_T]}{E[N_T]}$$

$$= \frac{(E[N^2] - E[N])\theta_T \mathbb{P}_{X>T}}{E[N]\mathbb{P}_{X>T}}$$

$$= \theta_T \frac{E[N^2] - E[N]}{E[N]}$$

$$= \theta_T \tau_0$$

$\square$

Corollary 7.19. If the losses' impacts are independent, then

$$\tau_T = \mathbb{P}_{X>T} \tau_0$$

Corollary 7.20. If the losses' impacts are fully dependent, then

$$\tau_T = \tau_0$$

Theorem 7.18 establishes the connection between the tail dependence and the volatility curve. Moreover, it allows us to unify several approaches to dependence modelling such as large loss clustering, tail dependence and copulas for both severities and frequencies. Corollaries 7.19 and 7.20 explain the graphs in Figure 7.1.

7.5 VOLATILITY CURVE FOR INCOMPLETE DATA

In this section we show how we can estimate the volatility curve based on an incomplete data set of losses. We establish that, if we use an incomplete data set, the resulting volatility curve will be more conservative than the real one (Theorem 7.29).

In order to analyse an incomplete data source we will make an assumption on the nature of incompleteness.

Assumption 7.21. For each bank, the probability of a loss being reported depends only on the size of the loss (the probability may differ from one bank to another).

The assumption allows us to define reporting probabilities.

Definition 7.22. For a loss of size x, denote by $r(x)$ the probability that the loss will be reported.

For a loss given by a random variable X, denote by $R[X]$ the reporting random variable: $R[X] = 1$ if X is reported and $R[X] = 0$ if X is not reported.

Denote by N_T^* the number of reported losses excess of the threshold T (clearly $N_T^* \leqslant N_T$). Denote by $R_T = E[R[\mathbf{1}_T(X)]]$.

Similarly to the approach of the previous section, we would like to estimate $E[N_T^*]$ and $E[(N_T^*)^2]$ by analysing the indicator functions.

Lemma 7.23.

$$N_T^* = \sum_{k=1}^{N_T} R[\mathbf{1}_T(X_k)]$$

Lemma 7.23 establishes the connection between N_T^* and the indicator functions, while the lemmas below will proceed with estimation of $E[N_T^*]$ and $E[(N_T^*)^2]$.

Lemma 7.24.

$$E[N_T^*] = R_T E[N_T]$$

Proof

$$E[N_T^*] = E\left[\sum_{k=1}^{N_T} R[X_k, > T] \right] = R_T E[N_T]$$

$\square$

Lemma 7.25.

$$\mathrm{cov}[R[X], R[Y]] = \mathrm{cov}[r(X), r(Y)]$$

Proof By law of total covariance (Ross 2001)

$$\text{cov}[R[X], R[Y]] = E[\text{cov}[R[X], R[Y] \mid \{X, Y\}]]$$
$$+ \text{cov}[E[R[X] \mid \{X, Y\}], E[R[Y] \mid \{X, Y\}]]$$

As we have assumed that whether the loss is reported or not depends only on its size (and not whether another loss was reported)

$$E[\text{cov}[R[X], R[Y] \mid \{X, Y\}]] = 0$$

Next

$$\text{cov}[E[R[X] \mid \{X, Y\}], E[R[Y] \mid \{X, Y\}]]$$
$$= \text{cov}\, E[R[X] \mid X] E[R[Y] \mid Y]$$
$$= \text{cov}[r[X], R[Y]]$$

□

Proposition 7.26. If two random variables X and Y are positively codependent, then

$$\text{cov}[R[X], R[Y]] \geqslant 0$$

Proof Then

$$\text{cov}[I_a(X), I_b(Y)] = E[I_a(X) I_b(Y)] - E[I_a(X)] E[I_b(X)]$$
$$= \Pr[X > a, Y > b] - \Pr[X > a] \Pr[Y > b]$$
$$\geqslant 0$$

As we can approximate any $r(x)$ by a linear combination $r(x) \approx \sum c_i I_{a_i}(x)$ with $c_i > 0$ for all i, we can write

$$\text{cov}[R[X], R[Y]] = \text{cov}\, r(X) r(Y)$$
$$= \text{cov}\left[\sum_i c_i I_{a_i}(X), \sum_j c_j I_{a_j}(Y) \right]$$
$$= \sum_{i,j} c_i c_j \, \text{cov}[I_{a_i}(X), I_{a_j}(Y)] \geqslant 0$$

□

Lemma 7.27. If two random variables X and Y are positively codependent, then $X_{>T}$ and $Y_{>T}$ are positively codependent as well.

Proof By using the law of total probability (Zwillinger and Kokoska 2000) we can establish that

$$\Pr(X_{>T} > a, Y_{>T} > b) = E_{\{X,Y\}}[\Pr(X_{>T} > a, Y_{>T} > b \mid \{X,Y\})]$$

Note that

$$\Pr(X_{>T} > a, Y_{>T} > b \mid \{X,Y\}) = 1$$
$$\Leftrightarrow X > \max(a,T) \text{ and } Y > \max(b,T)$$

Therefore

$$E_{\{X,Y\}}[\Pr(X_{>T} > a, Y_{>T} > b \mid \{X,Y\})]$$
$$= \Pr[X > \max(a,T), Y > \max(b,T)]$$

Thus, as X and Y are positively codependent,

$$\Pr(X_{>T} > a, Y_{>T} > b) = \Pr[X > \max(a,T), Y > \max(b,T)]$$
$$> \Pr[X > \max(a,T)]\Pr[Y > \max(b,T)]$$

Clearly, $\Pr[X > \max(a,T)] = \Pr[X_{>T} > a]$ and $\Pr[Y > \max(b,T)] = \Pr[Y_{>T} > b]$. $\qquad\square$

Corollary 7.28. For any two losses X_i and X_j

$$\mathrm{cov}(R[X_i > T], R[X_j > T]) \geqslant 0$$

Theorem 7.29.

$$\tau_T^* \geqslant R_T \tau_T$$

Proof In order to prove the result we will use the law of total variance (Weiss 2005). Using the formula we can write

$$\mathrm{var}[N_T^*] = \mathrm{var}[E[N_T^* \mid N_T]] + E[\mathrm{var}[N_T^* \mid N_T]]$$

Denote by X_T the distribution of $X_k \geqslant T$. Then, for the variance between, we get

$$\mathrm{var}[E[N_T^* \mid N_T]] = \mathrm{var}\left[\left\{E\left[\sum_{k=1}^{n} R[X_k \geqslant T]\right]; p_n\right\}\right]$$
$$= \mathrm{var}[\{nE[R[X_T]]; p_n\}]$$
$$= E[R[X_T]]^2 \mathrm{var}[\{n; p_n\}]$$
$$= R_T^2 \mathrm{var}[N_T]$$

For the variance within, using Corollary 7.28, we get

$$E[\text{var}[N_T^* \mid N_T]] = E\left[\left\{\text{var}\left[\sum_{k=1}^{n} R[X_k \geqslant T]\right]; p_n\right\}\right]$$

$$\geqslant E[\{n\,\text{var}[R[X_T]]; p_n\}]$$

$$= \text{var}[R[X_T]]E[\{n; p_n\}]$$

$$= \text{var}[R[X_T]]E[N_T]$$

Note that

$$\text{var}[R[X_T]] = E[R[X_T]^2] - E[R[X_T]]^2 = E[R[X_T]] - E[R[X_T]]^2$$

$$= R_T - R_T^2$$

Therefore

$$\text{var}[N_T^*] \geqslant R_T^2\,\text{var}[N_T] + (R_T - R_T^2)E[N_T]$$

and

$$\tau_T^* = \frac{\text{var}[N_T^*]}{E[N_T^*]} - 1 + E[N_T^*]$$

$$\geqslant \frac{R_T^2\,\text{var}[N_T] + (R_T - R_T^2)E[N_T]}{R_T E[N_T]} - 1 + R_T E[N_T]$$

$$= R_T \tau_T$$

$\square$

Corollary 7.30.

$$\frac{\tau_T^*}{E[N_T^*]} \geqslant \frac{\tau_T}{E[N_T]}$$

Theorem 7.29 and Corollary 7.30 allow us to estimate the volatility curve based on incomplete data and to use the estimate as the upper bound for the volatility curve for the complete data.

7.6 CONCLUSION

The problem of estimating dependency coefficients is a difficult challenge for many operational risk models.

To tackle this problem, we suggest estimating dependence for large losses only. To make such an estimate in the case of two severities we would use the notion of the tail dependence coefficient. In this chapter we have introduced a new statistical tool – the volatility curve, which measures clustering of of the largest losses. We show that it generalises the notion of tail dependence from two severities to a frequency severity model with random number of severities and allows us to draw some conclusions about the copula type.

We demonstrate that the volatility curve approach addresses several challenges: it measures dependence both between and within units of measure, it is relatively stable with respect to copula choice and it can be used for incomplete data.

In this chapter we defined the volatility curve for the whole bank and one-year frequency. We can extend the approach by considering the volatility curve for specific units of measure and (given that Monte Carlo simulation assigns time to losses) by considering quarterly frequencies.

REFERENCES

Basel Committee on Banking Supervision, 2011, "Operational Risk: Supervisory Guidelines for the Advanced Measurement Approaches", Bank for International Settlements, June, URL: http://www.bis.org/publ/bcbs196.pdf.

Cope, E., and G. Antonini, 2008, "Observed Correlations and Dependencies Among Operational Losses in the ORX Consortium Database", 2008, *The Journal of Operational Risk* 3(4), pp. 47–76.

Vapnik, V., 1998, *Statistical Learning Theory* (New York: Wiley-Interscience).

Weiss, N. A., 2005, *A Course in Probability* (Addison Wesley)

Zwillinger, D., and S. Kokoska, (2000) *CRC Standard Probability and Statistics Tables and Formulae*, p. 31 (Boca Raton, FL: CRC Press).

Ross, S. M., 2001, *A First Course in Probability*, Sixth Edition (Englewood Cliffs, NJ: Prentice Hall).

8

External Data: More Love at Second Sight

Carsten Steinhoff, Marcel Monien

Norddeutsche Landesbank

Much has been written on external data in operational risk literature. In most cases rather technical papers can be found to answer
questions of how to mix internal and external data and how to make
the two comparable (Frachot and Roncalli 2002). The aim of this
chapter is to show what advantages external data can bring into
the operational risk management of the industry. Based on the German data initiatives DakOR and ÖffSchOR, we demonstrate in this
chapter how external data can be used to more closely examine
where operational risk really takes place and to get a deeper insight
into its consequences for the company. Therefore, in Section 8.1 we
describe our way of collecting two different types of external data
and how we combined both sources to accomplish scenario analysis.
In Section 8.2 we discuss the new international regulation on stress
tests and risk concentration and its impact on operational risk. The
requirement of the Committee of European Banking Supervisors
(CEBS) for stress tests affects all institutions, not just those with a
model in use. This being the case, our is aim to present some ideas
that can be used in basic indicator approach and the standardised
approach institutions as well. Practical approaches that are based on
external information will be shown.

8.1 THE USE OF EXTERNAL DATA
8.1.1 Scenario analysis with pooled data

Proper scenario analysis, whether it is qualitatively or quantitatively
driven, should be a key element of any operational risk framework. It

has become an important tool in risk management over the decade prior to the time of writing, although it has sometimes been used quite arbitrarily in operational risk. From our point of view there are two reasons for this. First, scenarios are generated by more or less qualified "brainstorming" rather than historical experience. Second, for the valuation, psychological insights are not considered. In particular, the work of Kahneman *et al* (1982) should be recognised. In 2002 Kahneman was awarded the Nobel Memorial Prize in Economics for his work.[1]

A key element of all operational risk efforts is to ensure that the current risk profile is properly analysed and that all data reflects the current situation of the business. The demand of joining different views of internal data, external data, scenarios and business environment and internal control factors is to draw the whole picture as completely as possible. Especially for small institutions it can be hard and time-consuming to verify that a set of scenarios in use is complete and that no risk has been overlooked. For that reason a workgroup of banks in the German data pool DakOR developed a way to extract even more use from their data and to supplement it by adding a public loss database and a validated scenario catalogue.

The data pool DakOR was founded as a non-profit-organisation in 2005 and at the time of writing it has ten members (see dakor.de or Steinhoff and Merchant (2007) for details). All of the members are banks that are approximately comparable in size and business activities. Beside this homogeneity, DakOR's strength is the description collected for any case. Only that way can the recipient of data comprehend what has happened, why and what kind of impact occurred. Because the losses are described in German (or English) it is perfectly qualified for scenario analysis within the participating German banks. Examples can be drawn directly from the database and given to the experts. Due to the description, the impact of the losses on the bank can be analysed directly by experts. The data is collected with a threshold of €5,000 and all institutions committed for a complete delivery of all their data fitting to the DakOR standards. At the end of 2011 the database contained more than 15,000 data points in total.

Due to its size and set-up, a natural weakness of the pool, compared with larger ones, is the relatively small number of very extreme events. For that reason the members decided in 2008 to set up an additional database of publicly recorded losses called ÖffSchOR where cases are collected that are relevant for banks in the German-speaking legislation. Here all events from the daily press exceeding €100,000 that could have a realistic impact on banks are collected according to the DakOR collection standard. Since data fields, categorisation and other rules are comparable, both sources perfectly complement each other. At the time of writing, the database contains more than 1,500 data points.

To make scenario analysis easier the DakOR workgroup developed a set of scenarios that are, on the one hand, directly derived from both databases and, on the other hand, combined with each single loss event in these sources. To get the initial scenarios all loss events were categorised logically by their description and a list of 50 "stories" generated. This catalogue is used as a mandatory field for any subsequent loss. If a case does not match one of the scenarios, it will be flagged as "other". These cases are used to update the catalogue regularly and make it more complete. The success of this method is compelling: even the first scenario list made it possible to categorise 95% of all cases clearly.

A complete set of cases is now available to all workgroup members for practical use. The common review of all participants assures quality and completeness of that catalogue. This data on hand makes it very easy to prepare a scenario workshop since concrete cases can easily be drawn directly from the databases to demonstrate the impact, discuss severities and take action.

No concrete values for scenarios are exchanged, since severity and frequency are highly connected to the internal control framework and values could promote anchoring effects. However, this catalogue is complemented by ideas for the valuation of any scenario including facilitators for the estimation of parameters, eg, studies or web links, technical background information and ideas of which variables could determinate the estimates. Possible internal controls or mitigation techniques are collected there in a structured manner as well (see Table 8.1 for an example).

8.1.2 Our approach to evaluating scenarios

Meta information as shown in Table 8.1 makes scenario analysis easier. We use this as a framework to prepare workshops and to choose experts to evaluate any scenario. It will be supported by a list of

Table 8.1 Facilitators for scenario analysis (example, abbreviated)

Scenario	Setup of trading positions exceeding own competencies
Description	A trader succeeds in concluding trading positions that technically are not counted towards the risk limit and/or are not within the scope of the trading limits or are not included in the product catalogue.
Cases	Here cases from DakOR and ÖffSchOR can be separated
Possible items of gross loss	• Trading loss (interest rates, price, currencies) • Litigation cost (court cost, attorney's fee) • Penalty
Triggers of frequency	People • Number of trading desks, traders … • Transaction parameters Environment • Number of used systems front to end (interface risks) • Competencies • Working conditions
Triggers of severity	Trading loss (interest rates, price, currencies) • Transaction volume • Time to discovery • Time to settle Litigation cost
Possible mitigation	Avoid/prevent • Technical securisation (eg, technical limits in transactions or volumes, four-eyes principles within the workflow) Reduce/transfer • unauthorised trading insurance
Sources to estimate severity and frequency	Internet links, statistics, press articles

cases and descriptions fitting to the situation. In any case, the analysis should be performed within a workshop and not only based on a questionnaire. The real power of external data only can be utilised if an interaction between an expert and the interviewer is possible, so the plausibility of all answers can be checked simultaneously. All workshop leaders are familiar with psychological and motivational biases a scenario analysis can have. Typical biases are as listed below.[2]

- Availability: an expert refers too much to a single event. For example, a big loss seen recently influences the estimation of a scenario ("I have just seen it happen, so it will happen often"). The bias can be reduced by asking the expert if/when they have already seen or referred to a similar event. They have to get a realistic valuation of their thoughts behind the situation and a good overview of the consequences the scenario really can have (the "story"). It can be reduced by making thoughts obvious and giving more examples from the database.

- Anchoring: the expert relies too much on one piece of information (eg, a severity given by an example) or sticking to an initial or prior estimate. People "anchor" too heavily on one trait. This can be reduced by not giving prior or peer-group estimates to the expert. However, the question technique helps to reduce anchoring. For example, we ask the expert to explain and evaluate a worst-case scenario first and then ask if they can imagine something even worse.

- Framing: presenting the scenario from only one particular point of view can alter people's decisions. To prevent framing, it is necessary to get a sound understanding of the situation and its impacts. External information can support this process as well and help to obtain the picture completed.

- Representativeness: this is a phenomenon where people judge the probability or frequency of a hypothesis by considering how much the hypothesis resembles available data. Obviously people overestimate a risk if the example given to them is too concrete. So we strive towards describing the scenario not too generally and not too specifically.

- Overconfidence/illusion of control: this bias describes the fact that experts tend to think of a situation as being under control. For example, the effectiveness of controls is overestimated and the risk is systematically underestimated. To reduce that bias we also work with external data, where in some cases the description tells us which control failed or was in place. Additionally, we consider audit findings and information from the internal control system to talk about the controls in place and their quality.

Additionally, strategic behaviour and overcautiousness can be seen. These motivational driven biases can be reduced by discussing external data, and used to challenge the expert.

Each of our scenario workshops is supported by a structured form. Experts first formulate at least three situations from the scenario for their department (worst, normal and lucky cases) and evaluate probability and severity for the cases. Furthermore, existing and necessary controls, mitigation activities and contingency plans are assessed.

No statistical models for scaling are needed when estimating scenario parameters this way. We are convinced that psychology is more useful for operational risk scaling than statistics and no unique scaling algorithm can catch all data, because it is too different. The story behind each single point has to be taken into account, especially for the low-frequency, high-impact losses.

8.1.3 Closer to the markets with external data: an operational risk philosophy

8.1.3.1 New chances for benchmarking with a linked scenario base

The additional information of a corresponding scenario for each loss sets up the opportunity for new benchmark methods. Based on the list of 50 different "stories" every scenario can be expressed by real-life loss exposures. It is possible to compare potential risk with the "market" that is represented by the losses from the institutions in DakOR. So we discuss a variety of concrete and similar situations with an empirical background. The exposure (eg, gross loss or net loss) for every loss that is linked with scenario *xyz* is added up. For the external data pool DakOR this sum has to be divided by a scaling factor to make the scenario exposure comparable to one institution. Possible scaling factors are the number of institutions or a ratio that characterises the size of the institution compared with the institutions in the data pool (in DakOR total assets, employees and gross yield from all institutions are available)

$$SE_1 = \frac{\sum_{i=1}^{|L_1|} L_{i,1}}{SF}$$

$$\vdots$$

$$SE_{50} = \frac{\sum_{i=1}^{|L_{50}|} L_{i,50}}{SF}$$

Where SE is the scenario exposure, L is loss and SF the is scaling factor. For market-related scenarios it is useful to subdivide the scenario exposure into business lines. An external fraud event in retail banking is generally less severe than in investment banking.

A scenario exposure, but without the scaling factor, for internal losses, can be calculated in the same way. In the data every institution gets back from DakOR the own losses are marked, which allows us to separate them. For this reason it is possible to compare internal and external data. The different scenario exposures can be compared and analysed for noticeable differences. Some of these can be explained because the institution is not particularly involved in a certain business. Most of the differences result from the fact that the institution has so far never recorded such high losses. This information is a valuable source with which to identify potential exposures that have not yet been observed. We illustrate this with an example.

Example 8.1. Connected with scenario A there are only two losses in the internal database with a total exposure of €10,000.

The external data contains 60 losses that are related to scenario A with a total exposure of €1.17 million. For simplicity we use the number of institutions as scaling factor, which is 9 because there are 10 members (including our own institution) delivering into the data pool

$$SE_A = \frac{\sum_{i=1}^{60} L_{i,1}}{SF}$$

$$= \frac{€1,170,000}{9}$$

$$= €130,000$$

So the scenario exposure of scenario A is €130,000, which is more than 10 times larger than the internally observed losses for this scenario. This shows that the potential risk for this scenario is probably larger than the observed internal losses so far. In advance of scenario analyses this should be regarded when estimating scenario A.

In the next step, the real scenario exposures from the internal and external data are compared with the exposures from the scenario analyses that have been estimated by experts. Furthermore, we validate the experts' scenario results by comparing on a scenario level to maximum and minimum single loss or quantiles from the pooled data. This comparison helps us to decide whether a scenario estimate is valid or not and to show if scenarios might be under- or overestimated.

According to the experts, the complete exposure for the scenario adds up to €500,000. Compared with those of the internal losses and the scenario exposure, it is by far the largest exposure. This is not necessarily biased. Maybe the experts have overestimated the exposure, but it is also possible that they have pushed the scenario to a possible maximum loss regarding the institution's specific business situation. It has to be ascertained whether the expert is right (eg, if internal processes are known to be error-prone or controls are weak) or wrong. The latter should be reviewed by psychological means as shown above.

8.1.3.2 Reporting/ad hoc analysis

External losses also help to make operational risk experts in the business lines more sensible. Losses that are relevant or interesting for the own business are routed to where such a loss is likely to occur. Managers will not only get the information given from the database. Under the scenario linked to this loss, a large amount of scenario data can also be delivered, and experts can recognise the variety of possible settings and outcomes regarding one scenario. This helps the experts to check if they have regarded the whole range of eventualities when estimating the scenario exposure and probability. If the loss shows a new situation with new circumstances then an ad hoc scenario analysis will be made to update the information. Moreover, current external events, which are relevant in the sense of gross loss, causes or their public interest, can be examined in a more effective way with regard to our own institution and a possible occurrence. The public database is updated daily and can also be triggered by the members. The decision-makers of the company can receive important information about these losses and, if necessary, are able to set measures in place quickly.

This continuous (rather than annual) back-testing of losses against scenario data ensures that the operational risk situation is always up-to-date, which is an important foundation for effective operational risk management.

8.2 STRESS-TESTING AND RISK CONCENTRATION

Stress-testing and risk concentration are challenges for the management and measurement of operational risks in financial institutions. For both topics the use of external data and scenario analyses can be helpful. Our particular concern is how we can identify the "right" and not only the most obvious situations regarding these terms.

As far as we are aware, research in this area is scarce and too closely linked with AMA frameworks and capital modelling. But this is only half the story, since regulatory demands apply to all institutions, non-model banks included. The role of stress in operational risk-related research is in most cases less significant and subordinated to other methodical topics. There does not seem to be a definitive stress-testing method. Stress is often the application of a "non-stress" methodology with adverse condition (Dutta and Babbel 2010, p. 23). But by creating a proper story for "adverse conditions" in operational risk, stress-testing can contribute an important element to operational risk management. We discuss this, to a lesser extent, in the following sections.

8.2.1 Stress-testing

The basic concept of stress-testing is to assess whether the company is prepared for extreme events as well as those under adverse conditions. A validated model is a good condition for stress-testing, but it is not absolutely essential, especially as looking into severe events, at least qualitatively, will give some insight into their effects. Scenarios will also help here and scenario methodology is a helpful tool. A good and comprehensive analysis not only should generate data for the model, but also provides an opportunity to talk about possible risks and necessary action.

In the first stress-testing-related publication of the CEBS in 2006 (Committee of European Banking Supervisors 2006) there was no separate section about stress tests for operational risks. In the context of the regeneration after the financial crisis, CEBS published revised guidelines on stress-testing in 2009 (Committee of European Banking Supervisors 2009b) that do contain a section about the application of stress tests to operational risk. The following quotes are important for the development and implementation of operational stress tests.

> [Stress tests should] address all the material risk types of an institution (eg, credit risk, market risk, operational risk, interest rate risk and liquidity risk). No material risk type should be left unstressed or unconsidered.
>
> (Committee of European Banking Supervisors 2009b, p. 11)

So a first question has to be how to identify drivers of "material (operational) risk". The external databases, as shown above, help to answer it.

> The stress assumptions [for operational risk] may be different from the ones used in credit and market risk stressed scenarios and should be based on external events (including a stock exchange crash scenario causing an increase in litigation)....
>
> The stress test should account for material changes within the institution, such as new products, systems, areas of business and outsourced activities. Especially in new areas with a lack of loss data, stress tests should be based on scenario analysis.
>
> (Committee of European Banking Supervisors 2009b, p. 33)

According to these CEBS statements, stress tests for operational risks should take into account adverse circumstances that are specific to the company and integrated into firm-wide stress test events together with all material risk categories. It is mentioned that the stress assumptions could be different. In our experience this is an important conclusion because the method of implementing operational risk specific (intra-risk) stress tests is basically different from the way of combining it with the other risk types (inter-risk). In the following subsection we explain and discuss ideas for both inter- and intra-risk tests.

8.2.1.1 Inter-risk stress-testing

While CEBS writes about risk-specific views, the implementation of inter-risk stress tests is less specifically defined. The latter should take into account the effects of certain events over all the important risk categories. The CEBS quotes above underline that stress tests for operational risks are different from credit or market risk stress tests. One reason is that it is difficult to find correlation between operational risk losses and the economic factors that are used for stress-testing of market or credit risk, such as interest rates or fluctuating stock prices.

Two exemplary effects of stress events are given from (Committee of European Banking Supervisors 2009b, pp. 33–34): first, an increase in litigation as a possible effect of a stock exchange crash; second, an increasing risk of fraud in an economic downturn. Both refer to the frequency, rather than the severity, of a loss. In the German regulatory guideline "MaRisk", which is the expectation of Pillar 2 from Basel II, stress tests explicitly have to consider the effects of a serious regression. The examples and the demand of the German regulation are probably based on the assumption that under a bad economic environment certain losses occur more often. These relations so far cannot be shown empirically in our external data. To the best of our knowledge, these causal explanations are not shown empirically in any source. The financial crisis in 2008, in particular, did not give a clear proof for them.[3]

The idea of including operational risk stress-testing in an inter-risk context without an internal model is to stress the assumption of scenario exposures by trying to find triggers of severity that are related to assumptions that are used to stress other risk categories. Based on the economic factors and their dependencies, event cascades are built up. For example, under adverse conditions the financial market is more volatile. Consequently, more transactions with a higher average volume take place. For the example in Table 8.1, the triggers for the transaction volume are raised by a factor and this leads to a higher exposure for this scenario. Another possible consequence of this situation could be that back-office processes are not adequate for such a high number of transactions. This could mean it takes a longer time to settle each trade and to discover processing errors and violations. Every scenario that is based on these triggers is also adjusted.

The average or maximum percentage difference between the original scenario exposures and the exposure after the adjustment can be calculated and used as a stress factor. The operational risk capital can thus be raised by this factor to get a stressed value that can be used for inter-risk stress-testing. For an internal model the results of the adjusted scenarios can be used as input factors to estimate a stressed value-at-risk.

Although the inter-risk stress tests are reasonable for a firm-wide overview of the risk situation, stress-testing for operational risk should definitely not be limited to this. There are lots of other, more important triggers that can lead to serious losses and that are not relevant for an inter-risk stress test examination. In addition to the regulatory examples, we advise enhancing any scenario analysis with a question like "will there be an effect on other risks?". That should be a good start to discussing certain stories from a holistic perspective.

8.2.1.2 Intra-risk stress-testing

The intra-risk aspect is focused on either a single cause or several independent or connected causes that could lead to large operational risk losses and/or to a crucial increase in the capital requirements. From the operational risk management perspective it is important to protect the institution as well as possible against these causes.

In Committee of European Banking Supervisors (2009b) it is explicitly noted that scenarios are an appropriate way to evaluate operational risk-specific stress tests. Practically speaking, it results in generating "stories" with different causes and under adverse or extreme circumstances. As mentioned above, the possible outcomes and effects of an event in the economy or the internal or external environment allow us to transfer stress test results into decisions for effective risk management.

We use our databases extensively here as well. Every scenario in the catalogue is caused by specified events and triggers (Table 8.1) that help the experts to estimate the exposure as accurately as possible. To enhance scenario analysis and make it useable for stress-testing, it is necessary to make a plausible "worst-case" assumption. What circumstances, what effects or what behaviour regarding the institution's specific internal and business activities could possibly raise the triggers of a scenario and, consequently, the exposure of a scenario event? The external data helps to prove that big losses are possible. The results of such an extremal analysis can be used to determine if one or more events can have "material" impact on an institution.

For stress-testing with an operational risk model, two fundamentally different approaches should be combined to get the whole picture for effective stress-testing. While the first is only possible in a model framework, we can apply the second in either case:

1. statistical model validation;
2. qualitative analysis of tail events.

A model has to be validated by statistical tools: a task known as sensitivity analysis. It is a precondition for learning about the model's reactions (Basel Committee on Banking Supervision 2011, pp. 14–17). During the statistical validation several modifications in the input data, the distributional and correlation assumptions are performed. The aim is to see how the value-at-risk reacts to single or multiple changes and to evaluate the limits of the model. The results from the validation process are helpful for stress tests, but the process is not a stress test on its own.

In a model framework the results of the scenario analysis are input factors for the internal model and in consequence part of the quantification process (Basel Committee on Banking Supervision 2011, pp. 9–10). The scenarios generated with the worst-case assumption mentioned above can be used. It is possible to exchange the existing scenarios when a worst-case assumption has not yet been realised. If the model already contains worst-case scenarios, then it is possible to convert scenario exposures and external losses to internal loss (leaving out scaling factors for internal data or increase probability for scenarios). Another possibility is to add losses that have not so far been part of the quantification data. We use real live losses from the public database ÖffSchOR.

It is important for us that these "additional" losses are plausible and used to perform stress-testing. When using big random events or when performing parameter shifts in the severity distribution the story and the cause are missing. This is the important trail to follow to transform the results of a stress test calculation into a significant stress report that helps the decision-makers to understand why it is so important to avoid certain events.

Thus, from our point of view, it is absolutely necessary to complement this model view with a qualitative analysis of events. It should be obvious that, in the interests of each operational risk manager, prevention is more important than capital figures and stress-testing has to support this analysis. Preconditions in operational risk are more progressed than in other risk categories, as it operates, since its "rebirth", in the context of Basel II with extreme events. The key to operational risk stress-testing, in our experience, is, in a nutshell, to tell the "right" story to discuss with scenario experts and draw conclusions from that. And "right" first of all means relevant and on the basis of objective facts such as those obtained from external data.

8.2.2 Risk concentration

Risk concentration is a relatively new regulatory topic for (operational) risk managers. It refers to multiple events that can lead to a common consequence. Some of these interconnections are obvious; others are not evident at first glance. A specific regulatory definition of risk concentration was published by CEBS in Consulting Paper 31 in December 2009:

> Operational risk concentration means any single operational risk exposure or group of operational risk exposures with the potential to produce losses large enough to worsen the institution's overall risk profile so that its financial health or its ability to maintain its core business is threatened.
>
> (Committee of European Banking Supervisors 2009a, p. 14)

The challenge here is also to identify it properly and to clarify how and which operational risk concentration is relevant for an institution. This depends on the business, organisation and system structure of the company. Here we can distinguish inter- and intra-risk types as well. The consideration of intra-risk concentration is a new regulatory demand regarding operational risks. Causes of market and credit risk loss can also arise from operational risks. In the measurement of the capital requirements they are mostly separate.

The regulatory definition shows that operational risk concentration is closely connected to scenario analysis and stress-testing. To identify its impact it is reasonable to look at the results of those stress tests that describe a real threat to the institution's business or risk-bearing ability. The above-mentioned worst-case assumption for scenario-analysis is also a possible way to identify operational risk concentration.

Possible correlations between the different worst-case scenarios can be discussed in separate workshops. It is useful to proceed in an object-oriented manner, to suggest connections and make them transparent. Objects can be, for instance, departments, products, processes, systems, (clusters of) customers or regions. While business continuity management (BCM) deals with breakdowns and interruptions in the infrastructure, including processes and systems, we consider absolutely necessary to link concentration analysis to the BCM of a bank. While clusters in products, markets/clients or regions are a second main source of concentration risk we also state a link to the banks (new) product process. For that external data as well provides helpful ideas.

The following example demonstrates a possible way to estimate and calculate operational risk concentration using the dependency of IT systems.

Example 8.2. The three main companies that set up a financial group have three main IT systems. During workshops experts estimate the possibility and maximum worst-case exposure for a breakdown of each system for more than 24 hours.

- System 1: €100 million with occurrence once in 20 years (0.05).

- System 2: €50 million with occurrence once in 10 years (0.1).

- System 3: €150 million with occurrence once in 50 years (0.02).

- The experts also estimate the correlation of a possible breakdown of two systems together on the same day. To simplify this they just have to say if there is a high (= 0.8), medium (= 0.5) or low (= 0.2) dependency.

- System 1 and 2: high dependency because they are applied by the same company on the same data centre.

- System 1 and 3, system 2 and 3: low dependency because they are from different companies and have a different IT infrastructure.

With these estimations it is possible to generate the risk concentration for these three main IT systems (Figure 8.1).

The sizes of the circles in Figure 8.1 illustrate the possibility of the breakdown of each system. The areas of overlap show the probability of a possible common breakdown. The interface area where all three circles overlap is the important one for operational risk concentration. Note that the probability of such an event is very small

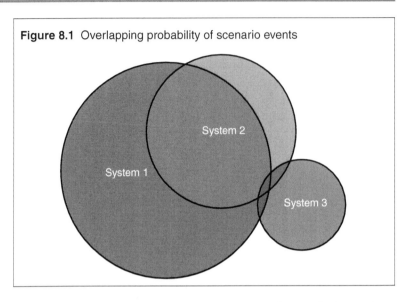

Figure 8.1 Overlapping probability of scenario events

but the overall exposure adds up to €300 million, which can be a crucial impact for the company.

In this way it is also possible to generate new data points for the internal model. Based on three independent scenario estimations, four additional loss exposures can be calculated:

- Systems 1 and 2: €150 million with probability[4]

$$0.04 (= \min(0.05; 0.1) \times 0.8)$$

- Systems 2 and 3: €200 million with probability

$$0.004 (= \min(0.02; 0.1) \times 0.2)$$

- Systems 1 and 3: €250 million with probability

$$0.004 (= \min(0.02; 0.05) \times 0.2)$$

- Systems 1, 2 and 3: €300 million with probability less than[5]

$$0.004 (= \min(0.4; 0.004; 0.004)$$

In the same way, it is possible to examine concentration risk between regions and business districts regarding impacts on buildings from natural disasters or on staff capacity, for example, from a pandemic or strikes in public transport.

Not every correlated risk exposure has to be a risk concentration. The measure of how large a loss has to be to worsen the institution's overall risk profile should be determined with respect to the risk-bearing ability of an institution.

8.3 CONCLUSION

Our aim has been to give a brief overview of how external data can be used and what power models can have if data is properly pooled. In particular, we have shown how case descriptions and scenarios can add value to operational risk management. These sources are useful not only for benchmarking but for scenario analysis and stress-testing. The concept we presented should provide risk analysts with ideas of how external data can be used. Furthermore, in using external data banks there will not only be a surplus on the risk management side, but there also will be an economic surplus if categorisation and additional information can be obtained directly from the database. Using this kind of transfer of tasks to a data pool or a service provider, risk management processes can be made sounder and more efficient.

Regarding scenario analysis and stress-testing, firstly we found that it is most important to talk about the "right" stories. "Right" means relevant in the sense of being appropriate for the bank's own business, but also being obtained objectively, eg, by an independent benchmarking to external data. Secondly, it will be crucial to get a sound quantitative estimate of the stories' impact. For the latter we have presented some biases known from psychology and shown how they can be reduced (in most cases by using external data as well).

Lastly, we addressed the regulatory requirements for stress-testing and operational risk concentration and showed a way of implementing them for operational risk. We see these ideas the basis of further discussion and are convinced that external data helps us to move to a best-practice approach within the industry.

The views presented in this paper are those of the authors and do not necessarily represent models or policies of Norddeutsche Landesbank.

1 Kahneman worked on behavioural models. In particular, he researched theories between alternatives that involve risk but where probabilities of outcomes are known. People make

decisions based on the potential (subjective) value of losses and gains rather than the (objective) final outcome. People use interesting heuristics and are biased in their statements. This can be transferred to the expert valuation of any type of risk and it is necessary to know about these heuristics to obtain sound estimates.

2 We only want to give a very brief overview here. See Kahneman *et al* (1982) for details.

3 A time lag in recognition of crisis-related cases is possible in external sources (eg, litigations). But internally we see no proof as well.

4 We use the minimum because to get a joint event both have to occur at least once.

5 Because the three events are overlapping it has to be less than the minimum. An estimation for this probability is appropriate.

REFERENCES

Basel Committee on Banking Supervision, 2011, "Operational Risk – Supervisory Guidelines for the Advanced Measurement Approaches", Bank for International Settlements, June, URL: http://www.bis.org/publ/bcbs196.pdf.

Committee of European Banking Supervisors, 2006, "Consultation Paper on stress Testing Under The Supervisory Review Process", Consultation Paper 12.

Committee of European Banking Supervisors, 2009a, "Guidelines on Aspects of the Management of Concentration Risk Under The Supervisory Review Process", Consultation Paper 31.

Committee of European Banking Supervisors, 2009b, "Revised Guidelines on Stress Testing", Consultation Paper 32.

Dutta, K. K., and D. F. Babbel, 2010, "Scenario Analysis in the Measurement of Operational Risk Capital: A Change of Measure Approach", Working Paper, Wharton Business School, University of Pennsylvania, September.

Frachot, A., and T. Roncalli, 2002, "Mixing Internal and External Date for Managing Operational Risk", Working Paper, http://ssrn.com/abstract=1032525.

Kahneman, D., P. Slovic and A. Tversky (eds), 1982, *Judgment under Uncertainty: Heuristics and Biases* (Cambridge University Press).

Steinhoff, C., and S. Merchant, 2007, "Exchanging Times", *Operational Risk and Compliance*, May, pp. 42–43.

9

Banks, Regulation and Rule-Bending

Roger Miles
King's College, London

Buy a policymaker a couple of drinks, and you may get them to admit privately to the uncomfortable truth: when you're trying to regulate any group activity, some of the group will always find ways to sidestep any rules that they see as inconvenient. In an age when rioting is a protest lifestyle option and when hackers club together to destroy brands, it seems that we're all becoming a bit more open-minded about how we choose and express our personal values. The latest research is finding that employees of large corporations, from board members downwards, also rather like the idea of a pick-and-mix approach to ethics. Surely, though, bankers were supposed to rise above that sort of behaviour?

Now we know otherwise. After conducting objective, academic-standard behavioural research, it has become clear that bankers can flex their ethics with the best of them, especially when it comes to public risk reporting. The research shows that we need to stop thinking about regulatory compliance as a simple black-and-white, binary decision (that is, "we are compliant" or "we are not"). It is time, instead, to re-conceive it as shades of grey.

9.1 STRUCTURE OF THIS CHAPTER

In the context of research studies into non-compliance in other business sectors, this chapter offers a glimpse of findings from newly completed research into bankers' distinctive relationships with their regulators. The research suggests that the real rules of engagement are more akin to Fight Club than to an old-boys' club (and we will be reminded of the relevant rules later in this chapter). We will see why a highly nuanced game of regulation unravelled, in a sector that was already far from easy to try to regulate. Related problems, including clashing concepts of "risk", were parked by bank boards on their hapless Chief Risk Officers (CROs), who struggled to make sense of what they should do. So here is what they did: under pressure from skewed incentives, more than one risk officer helped to manipulate risk reporting in various ways, some of which will be seen here. It is also clear that bankers were not the only players seated at the regulatory gaming table. This chapter concludes that, if we are serious about wanting to reassert control, it is time to move on from our industry's misguided fixation with inefficient proxy measures, especially econometric models. Instead, if we are serious about controlling conduct, we need to look directly at it. To track "what actually happens", rather than what the rules say, means that we have to directly observe human behaviour.

9.2 BANKS CANNOT BE TAMED LIKE OTHER CORPORATE ANIMALS

Studies have investigated how managers in various business sectors respond when the regulator's case officers come to call. The sectors studied included catering, logistics, health care and pharmaceuticals and, as of summer 2012, banking (Miles 2012).[1] The common theme of the studies was that past ways of designating compliant behaviour had been too simplistic to have much real value. Everyone concerned – but especially regulatory policymakers – had been guilty of narrowly defining how regulated people conceive compliance and how they act on this conception. Among other things, the research at the time of writing showed that old notions of compliance (that is, rules and obedience) were unfit for purpose. The true picture is more nuanced, more complex and ultimately a lot more personal.

Of course, no government feels comfortable questioning the premise that "(our) regulation works". Governments have to believe that it does, as the alternative is too politically horrible to contemplate. Hence the fashion, buoyed up by academic credentials, for the orthodoxy of enforced self-regulation (Ayres and Braithwaite 1992). This system has the political virtue of sounding vigorous and engaged, and was until the crisis the preferred way for governments to bind public-good interests to private risk-taking.

Banks' catastrophic failures of risk control showed how well-intended regulation can break down in practice: it failed the "what actually happens" test. And what actually happened, it seems, is that certain banks paved the way for their own downfall when they disengaged with the intent behind the rules and started to use "local definitions" of compliance and to manipulate risk reports.

9.3 BRAD PITT CAN EXPLAIN WHAT IS HAPPENING

Looking back over the longer history of banks' interactions with regulatory policy, we may discern a pattern: practitioners wanting to redefine rules, and any compliance with the rules, as whatever is commercially practicable. This approach requires everyone involved to keep adjusting their own expectations of what regulation is going to achieve: whether it is the policymakers, regulators or the regulated. In a bleak but recognisable assessment of what is going on, one academic (Cohen 2001) calls what is happening "The Game of No Game" (TGNG). What's that all about?

This game borrows a couple of cardinal rules from Brad Pitt's character in the film *Fight Club*:

> The first rule of Fight Club is: you do not talk about Fight Club.
> The second rule of Fight Club is: you DO NOT talk about Fight Club!

Other core rules of TGNG include that all players (for our purposes, bankers, regulatory staff and government) must mentally separate the facts that they know from the consequences of knowing them. Thus, a Treasury minister, a Financial Services Authority (FSA) case officer, a bank CEO, or CFO or, especially, a CRO, must simultaneously know of a risk and disown knowledge of its impact.

TGNG also requires that the control system itself must be designed to insulate a government from embarrassment. This is done by building in "firebreaks" of deniability (also known as agnotism, or "designed-in ignorance"; McGoey 2007); that is, ways to shift blame elsewhere in the event of a crisis. For as long as no crisis occurs, the players can all congratulate each other that the system works, or R. D. Laing, who first identified TGNG, put it (Laing 1970):

> They are playing a game. They are playing at not playing a game.
> If I show them I see they are, I shall break the rules and they will punish me. I must play their game, of not seeing that I see the game.

By 2007, it seems that this aspect of informal business culture – that a rule may be privately reinterpreted – had come to be seen as a general understanding between traders, government and regulators. The rules of TGNG barred open discussion of it (remember *Fight Club*), but the gist of what everybody understood was: rules themselves matter less than the general aim of keeping up public confidence, meaning keeping making money, even if this means that some lines of responsibility for risk-taking get blurred.

9.4 BANKERS AND ROCK STARS: ALL "SPECIAL PEOPLE" TOGETHER? (ACTUALLY, NO...)

When this author put this to them, many bankers recognised that they were playing TGNG. They also noticed echoes of a much older social rule, that the tribe allows admired people to break the rules as long as nobody gets publicly upset by this. That is, we like to make allowances for "special people", because they offer some higher form of value to us. Why do we not mind that this rock star takes drugs? Because we are too busy enjoying listening to their latest song (the old "don't break a butterfly on a wheel" argument, for those readers who remember it).[2] But does this mean that it is acceptable for bankers to say the rules should not apply to them either, because what they do is "special", in some similar way?

On the evidence, probably not. The trouble is, many did behave as if they deserved to be exempt from the rules. Over time, by believing in their own specialness, the chiefs of the City tribes (and their acolytes in Westminster) conditioned themselves to stop caring much about rule-breaking in general, focusing only on not being visible when breaking rules, that is, avoiding public embarrassment. We might decode this as a perverse way of applying the newly fashionable discipline of "reputation risk". What came to matter in banks' risk reporting was to be seen to be busily filing the reports, never mind the quality. As one CRO put it to the author at the time: "It's not that firms are getting more compliant, it's just that we're getting better at playing the game of regulatory reporting."

This suggests that, cynically, the only relevant concern was commercial rather than ethical: the problem was viewed as being less that risk reporting was being "gamed" and more that the game might have to be stopped if too many industry-side participants were seen to be profiting from it. A key reason for researching this topic in the first place was to gather first-hand accounts of "what actually happens", how banks process, or fail to process, regulators' formal demands into responsive action. Responses to the behavioural research, in the form of interviews with senior risk officers in banks, confirmed that this was a hunch worth pursuing: light-touch regulation encourages self-assured bankers to interpret rules creatively.

9.5 REGULATORY CHALLENGES: DESIGN, ENGAGEMENT AND RISK CULTURE

To be fair, the FSA was only using enforced self-regulation in the first place as the politically fashionable strategy for tackling the problems faced by pretty much every regulator: that the regulatees have all the information and all the resources. Why not try to co-opt these resources, especially if academic theory of regulation says this is the best thing you can do?

Bankers, being clever, of course quickly spotted the systemic flaw in this arrangement. Enforced self-regulation only works when information flow is strong and transparent, when there is at least a little bit of respect for the regulator and when everything is backed up by a credible threat of enforcement action. Instead of all that, as we found, bankers realised that the source of regulatory reporting demands was an agency that could never deploy the staff resources necessary to have full oversight over all banking activities. Banks appreciated keenly just how far the regulator's staff had to rely on them for practical know-how, product information and access to data. They also conceded, in our research interviews, that the FSA was aware of its own limitations, but was still scathing of the communication problems that this raised, which it saw as adversely affecting its work. Even as bankers accepted that the FSA's task was hard, they were frustrated that regulatory staff appeared unable to understand their own task.

Banks are of course unusually hard businesses to regulate, for a number of perfectly good reasons. No regulator's resources could hope to match what the banks can muster. On the one hand, for the banks, there is a cloud of complex, high-volume, high-value trades by time-pressed expert practitioners, using ever-evolving product platforms to generate enormous quantities of data, plus of course the political privileges that arise from their massive returns to the national coffers. Meanwhile, on the other hand, for the regulator, there would seem to be a relatively small number of technocratic staff clutching already out-of-date product briefings.

There is also a difference between expert cultures of the FSA and the banks regarding which risks are significant. This sometimes translates into the regulator's lack of resources, or apparent will, to enforce a new rule. As one interviewed CRO saw it (all quotes following are from the author's original research, conducted with King's College London, unless otherwise indicated):

> Regulators actually do understand that gaming of the rules goes on. Within the FSA there's a constant discussion about how to train their people, or get people in who understand where gaming's going to occur. Though it's not generally articulated in those terms – it's articulated as "how can we get the people in that will understand what this business is doing"!

9.6 SEEKING NEW UNDERSTANDING OF HOW RULES COME TO BE BENT

This research added to the growing stack of studies of regulatees' "bad behaviour", offering some insight into the version of a "game of compliance" (or TGNG) as played in banks, and in particular in their risk offices. Taken together, all of these studies begin to build up a picture of how bad behaviour comes to be accepted and even condoned in regulated organisations. Across a range of industries, including banks, we have a behavioural profile of informal groups of practitioners who respond with frustration, contempt or outright hostility towards any regulator who tries to interrupt their "business as usual". The study of banks' organisational behaviours in response to regulation – their "compliance culture" – is still emergent at the time of writing and offers fertile ground for new research initiatives. Some insights from this research now follow.

Although there are more academic names for this, like "information asymmetry" and "regulatory capture", in plain terms it looks more like a simple "stitch-up". Fair enough that, as the lobbyists argue, a bit of flexible interpretation of rules can be good for creating commercial opportunities. But this approach only works for as long as the underlying rules are both sound and generally accepted. Also, where the rules are defined with reference to wrongly applied risk models, things soon start to unravel.

As if the structural skews were not bad enough, let us also remember the culture that prevailed on the regulator's team. Up to 2008, regulators had been explicitly asked by government to exercise restraint, that is, not to intervene to disrupt trading activity if at all possible. The FSA accepted that high-profile raids or even announcements might cause market shocks, which would reflect poorly on its mandate to maintain "orderly markets". It seems, from the new research, that quite a few bankers interpreted this regulatory culture in a simple, commercially pragmatic way. As one risk officer put it to the author, "the trouble with principles-based regulation is that there are parts of the market which aren't very principled!".

A regulated person's intent to comply is affected by many factors but, overall, where the main aim of a market is to sell (as it tends to be), and when sales people see that there is a mismatch between what the rules say and what the money says, the money normally wins. Those in the way must step aside or stay and "cope", by rearranging their ethical compass.

9.7 WHAT DID "COPING" MEAN IN PRACTICE?

"Coping" is not a charter for fraud. Most traders claim to have a clear conscience, at least believing that they are rule-keepers in spirit, if not in fact. But, to sustain this belief, many of them need to use coping strategies such as "making our own sense of it", "this is how we do things around here, whatever 'they' say", and "let's tell them what they want to hear, so we can get back to doing what we want to do". Not that coping itself is a bad behaviour in the sense of implying clear criminal intent. It is, though, a fairly good early warning sign (or "pre-indicator") that some rule-bending may be about to happen, whether it be a short-term workaround or some more serious form of determined rule-breaking.

When asked about this, risk officers quite liked being able to lump together all kinds of coping strategies that they found useful for blurring the edges of rules, for "playing the grey" of compliance. They found it useful to be able to open up a conceptual space into which they could insert all sorts of new products, including, if they had a mind to, some barely plausible product pitches. For a long time before the reality check of 2008, it suited everyone to believe that this grey space was helpful – even regulators, who could see how it might insulate them from blame in the event of failure.

This author's research started with a simple hunch, that old systems of rules were unequal to the task of stopping coping strategies. A year in (2008), responses suddenly became much livelier as risk officers could no longer restrain themselves from talking about the gathering storm. The global credit crisis invigorated the research interviews no end, loosening the tongues of many professionals who earlier had been unwilling to admit any problem. While the research did not originally claim to predict a "coping game", under the spur of a crisis people seemed happy to speak freely about their anxieties and experiences, perhaps realising that the game was up, or at least that major rule changes were now inevitable.

9.8 PEOPLE'S INTENT TO COMPLY CAN VARY, AND MAY BE CONDITIONED

The default response to new rules in the past was a practical one, which we can summarise as: is it worth complying? (Supported by concerns of: how likely am I to get caught? What will it cost if I do get caught? Is this cost less than the cost of complying in the first place?)

As normal expectations were that regulators would not intervene much, and as the business culture associated risk-taking with profit, traders in particular were able to adopt the view that rules "needn't matter to us". The logic of this is simple, if perverse. If gaming the rules appears to pay, it will be reinforced as a useful choice. If a trader ignores a rule and gets away with it, they feel not only relieved of the burden of the rule but also freer to do what they like in future. Since most rule systems are constructed in a way that does not, in practice, inflict immediate pain on the person who breaks them, the rule-gamer's first lesson is often that rule-breaking "makes life easier".

As any forensic fraud investigator knows, where rule-breaking passes unchallenged, rule-gaming tends to become normal. By a similar effect, even among the most ethical of staff, compliance tends to decay over time. It certainly does not improve unaided. Add to this the fact that, in banks, the commercial culture of risk-taking is directly at odds with a public-service culture of risk-prevention and restraint. If commercial enterprise sees itself as running ahead of any social concerns – generate wealth first, sort out ethics later – so risk officers become expected to lag behind the development and marketing of the commercial products that they want to control. In fact, what we found in banks was more extreme: the culture is that fee-earning (market-making, bonus-entitled) jobs have top status, while back-office work such as auditing and running control systems is at best tolerated as a cost centre, and then only because it "keeps the regulators off our backs so we can get on with market-making".

9.9 IS COMPLIANCE JUST A PERFORMANCE TO REASSURE THE PUBLIC?

These views on the culture of risk-taking raise a challenging thought: is regulation real, or an elaborate game, a type of public performance calculated to reassure sceptical citizens and nervous politicians? Whenever new rules are issued, the people they affect understand that everyone is supposed to be seen to support the government's need to give public reassurances. Laws are, as one banker put it to the author, "rhetorical instruments". Over time, though, this rationale of needing to "put on a public show" encourages all kinds of perverse responses, including:

- interpreting definitions flexibly;
- excusing occasional rule-breaking (whether ignorant, accidental or planned);
- allowing profitable errors but ignoring loss-making ones;
- disregarding losses as "normal accidents";
- disregarding unfavourable test results.

Against this background, the scope of what is forgivable, or tolerable, may gradually widen until "playing the grey" shades off into something altogether murkier.

9.10 A CORE PROBLEM: ABUSE OF RISK MODELS

In one common example, risk officers described being willing to mount a technical challenge to the regulator based on the bank's use of proprietary risk models. Bankers' selective use of risk models and data was seen by everyone, including the FSA, as a major area of uncertainty, making banks vulnerable both to local manipulation and to wider market shocks. The author heard several confessions of "risk model abuse", such as "sure, we do stress-testing, but what a lot of people actually do is run the tests until they get the numbers they wanted to see".

It has also been common practice, apparently, to select a different risk model for each new product, based on how well the risk model supported the product's expected profit margin and regardless of whether this represented a balanced analysis of product risk. Even when a risk model was conceptually valid, its validity might be compromised by misapplying it to an irrelevant product. Bias in the selection of a risk model might be compounded by marketing staff's tendency to "cherry-pick" data when running the model. Some risk officers saw this not necessarily as a risky, or even unwelcome, activity but as an enjoyably interesting "creative–interpretative side of the job... reconciling compliance needs with marketing needs".

Models were also cynically deployed to respond narrowly to regulators' requests for specific types of information, ignoring wider concerns of whether they were measuring the appropriate categories of risk; that is, to "satisfy the regulator's evidence requirements rather than address the actual elements of risk".

Everyone complained about – but did not apparently do much to challenge – the tendency of salespeople to seek false comfort by producing econometric models and tests. Everyone knew that that test results could be derived from selectively gathered data. The author's favourite analogy for this was offered by a veteran CRO, saying that banks' biggest problem was always overconfidence in their own risk management systems, the "comforting myth that you can just kind of stick a 'risk probe' into any project, like checking a turkey in the oven".

Most risk officers did, at least privately, pause sometimes to question the nature of model-based rules and modelling assumptions. Many cited personal experience of situations where risk-modelled assumptions had to be called into question. Many also questioned the broader assumption implicit in the use of quantised risk models. As we all ought to ask: why would any policy designer expect that model-based rules would succeed in holding institutions to public account, when the regulated community itself selected both the risk models and the data that populates them? Most risk offices admitted to only developing "twenty-twenty hindsight after the crisis" and regretting that "so often the simple questions weren't asked because they were hidden by metrics".

The flexible use of risk models not only compromised risk reporting on transactions, but combined with manipulated data to destabilise the whole banking market. Many interviewees described aggregating risk data into a model that reported figures at group level within the bank, so concealing some significant risk exposures at divisional level. A bank's report showing an acceptable aggregated risk figure might have diluted some real concerns at operating level, albeit commercial problems that FSA case officers were "unqualified to advise on", smiled one respondent.

We also heard, forcefully argued, a completely opposite rationale, namely that the 2008 crisis, far from destroying risk-model assumptions, actually presented a great opportunity to further refine them:

> Our methodologies work as well as they're designed to. We need to … go back, check the assumptions and refine the models. I wouldn't say the stress-testing model is dead; it just needs some freshening up.

All the same, most respondents to our research, and indeed HM Government's own subsequent review (Turner Review 2009), argued that regulatory controls failed when bankers clung to the belief at sector level, until it was evidently too late, that all model-derived control systems worked as they were designed to:

> You'll never get to systemic risk by somehow going to each of the banks and trying to get the picture. You can't see the system at a component level. You've got to go to all of them together and call on them to face up to a systemic problem.

9.11 NOT SO MUCH THE MODELS AS THE GAMES BEING PLAYED WITH THEM

As CROs tended to concede, there is no point in blaming the risk models themselves for the abusive uses to which some were put:

> [Many] of the risk modelling requirements are driven by compliance in the minds of the risk team, and are not much discussed around the business.

Nor should a model be held to blame for being the carrier of corrupt data, as more than one back-office team admitted:

> It's easy enough to play with stress tests, you can run lots and lots of them until you get the numbers you wanted, then report those numbers. The regulator is happy of course because you can say you've done lots of runs of the test!

There were thus at least two types of "gaming" of risk models: first, that risk models based on sound assumptions may nevertheless be misapplied in the pursuit of profit, and second, that models could be used to carry data that has been manipulated and forced into them to give the appearance of an acceptable risk decision-making process. Reportedly, risk data could be combined or re-presented in ways that, though meaningless for practical commercial purposes, gave the appearance of a coherent risk-metric report. The CRO of a bank that subsequently failed told this author that such risk management "philosophies of presentation [were] themselves very serious risks".

Nor were banks the only players in the game. Bankers were concerned that the regulator was also keen to define models narrowly in order to exclude having to think about wider questions of risk exposure. Risk report formats were prescribed and:

> normally carried out at a senior level and using simplistic (and potentially misleading) top-down approaches. The process is highly prescriptive – I assume as the [FSA] want to standardise the results across banks – the top-down nature of these rules means that we can generate almost any result.

9.12 WHY RULES DO NOT CHANGE BEHAVIOUR

Unsurprisingly, we confirmed that the rule-makers tend not to succeed in changing behaviour, especially that of bankers, simply by issuing checklists of systems-operating standards. After all, the bankers' much-touted Basel II control regime spectacularly failed to anticipate the form of the crisis that occurred (liquidity, as of course we now know). Rules in general, and certainly in banking, are not formulated in such a way as to forcibly reject inappropriate moral norms. At a point where the fields of cognitive science and organisational behaviour meet, there remained a little empty area of research that we were very happy to occupy. The resulting research report is, in one sense, a happy outcome of choosing to pitch camp in a research field just as a storm was about to break.

The findings are not so much a completely new story as a revelation, with new evidence, that there are many earlier strands of thinking that can now be pulled together. For example, a relatively new theory of governance (Black and Rouch's (2008) "legitimacy criteria") says that any new rule will succeed or fail entirely according to whether the people it governs regard it as consistent with their own views: that is, whether it is democratic enough, constitutional, functional and in line with their own declared goals. Our bankers were generally pretty contemptuous of this as a "functional" point. They laughed at the (then) very New Labour requirement to broadcast detailed expressions of compliance and ethical probity, saying that this was in effect an invitation to respond perversely. As one said:

> There's a fundamental failure to recognise that a 700-page book of accounts is absolutely useless to anybody. Greater detail obviously hasn't created greater transparency; the accounts are in effect less informative rather than more. And so I think every now and again you hear a question now that I don't think you heard before, which is "OK, so that's what the regulator says; how much do we care? How much do we feel we actually have to go along with that?"

Our bankers understood that politicians like to announce new regulation because it "looks like 'doing something'", and so responds to the public's feeling that "something must be done" about a problem. They also understand that public administrators continue to delude themselves, or at least to be naively optimistic, when they think that a regulated group will simply "know what's good for it" and adapt to new rules without question. We already knew, from earlier research by distinguished colleagues (Bevan and Hood 2006; Goodhart 2006), that performance targets encourage game-playing, even among such blameless citizens as doctors and police officers, and we also knew that central target-setting also makes regulators themselves play coping games to "prove" their supposed social worth. All that our latest research has done is to show the same effect working in a banking context; but what a context, and what games!

9.13 TAKE A NEW APPROACH TO CONTROL

Crises have a useful way of destroying cosy assumptions. The banking crisis invited policymakers to reconsider whether it is safe, or wise, to import commercial risk principles into public sector regulatory design. In considering this, we can say that:

1. regulatory capital is not a reliable proxy indicator for good behaviour; and

2. no system based on self-reporting of "public good" risk will be effective in preventing aggressively self-interested risk-takers.

At the heart of banking, we must feel sorry in particular for the Chief Risk Officer. Their role is in itself a symbol of the tension between profit and public-interest reporting. In 2008, for many CROs, the role was, and perhaps even remains, irreconcilably conflicted.

Yet, now, the rules such as Basel III that replaced the old ones still rely on econometric indicators, not on observed behaviours. Our research makes a straightforward counterargument that the old commercial (and regulatory) culture needs a direct challenge. This culture appears to have valued the signalling of compliance far above the reality of playing by the rules. The only way to detect the gap between the two is to put econometric instruments back in their proper place, as just one part of a larger toolkit that offers a wider range of controls, and in particular the control of observing human behaviour on its own terms.

So let us now stop trying to measure behaviour (or rather, to pretend that behaviour can be measured) purely by the use of very poor proxies for it, such as the historical movements of money through ledgers. If risk control policy is really about modifying behaviour, any new rules need to define successful outcomes in terms of observed behaviour change, not how much effort or resources were expended. Now is the time to start applying this principle, if we are serious about effective regulation. Unfortunately, increased transparency brings political pain when things go wrong. Will our leaders have the moral courage to do this properly, to "feel the pain and do it anyway"? Sadly, looking at these findings, it does not seem likely.

---

1 For more information see the Web pages of King's College London, Hazards and Risk Group at http://www.kcl.ac.uk/sspp/departments/geography/research/hrg/, and London School of Economics, Analysis of Risk and Regulation at http://www2.lse.ac.uk/researchAndExpertise/units/CARR/research/Home.aspx.

2 In a now-notorious leader column, "Who breaks a butterfly on a wheel?" (*The Times*, July 1, 1967), editor William Rees-Mogg attacked the British justice system for sentencing Rolling Stones frontman Mick Jagger to prison for possession of four amphetamine pills. The editor argued forcefully that the sentence appeared to be motivated less by justice than by the "criticism and resentment his celebrity has aroused"; Jagger's sentence was quashed.

REFERENCES

Ayres, I., and J. Braithwaite, 1992, *Responsive Regulation: Transcending the Deregulation Debate* (Oxford University Press).

Bevan, G., and C. Hood, 2006, "What's Measured is What Matters: Targets and Gaming in the English Public Healthcare System", *Public Administration* 84(3), pp. 517–38.

Black, J., and D. Rouch, 2008 "The Development Of Global Markets As Rule-Makers: Engagement And Legitimacy", *Law and Financial Markets Review*, May, pp. 218–33.

Cohen, S., 2001, *States of Denial Polity Press* (Cambridge University Press).

Goodhart, C., 2006, "The ECB and the Conduct of Monetary Policy: Goodhart's Law and Issues from the Euro Area", *Journal of Common Market Studies* 44(4), p. 457.

Laing, R. D., 1970, *Knots* (London: Psychology Press).

McGoey, L., 2007, "On the Will to Ignorance in Bureaucracy", *Economy and Society* 36(2), pp. 212–35.

Miles, R. T., 2012, "From Compliance to Coping: Experiences of Chief Risk Officers in UK Banks 2007–2009", PhD Research Thesis, King's College London.

Turner Review, 2009, "A Regulatory Response to the Global Banking Crisis", Report, Financial Services Authority, December.

10

Evaluation of Risk Management Practices for Quantitative Models

Devon E. Brooks

Northern Trust Corporation

Over the decade or so that this author has been involved in the evaluation of quantitative models at financial services institutions, from smaller community banks to some of the largest institutions in the world, the words of Mark Twain have often been applicable, in the sense that "it ain't what you don't know that gets you into trouble; it's what you know for sure that just ain't so". When business executives asked whether or not a model worked, the "yes" answer was given in reference to the calculation engine, the computational process that combines assumptions, data inputs and a set of rules to produce an output. The validity and accuracy of the inputs, both data and business assumptions, was often assumed rather than being scrutinised with just as much rigour as the calculation engine.

One of the many lessons from the global financial crisis that took hold in 2008 is that the question of whether or not a model "works" encompasses more than just the calculation engine. The more holistic question being asked by executives is "can we rely on the information being provided to us such that we can feel confident that we are making the right decision?" Answering this question requires an evaluation not only of the calculation engine, but of all of the assumptions and data that make up the inputs to that engine. Challenges with any of these elements can negatively affect the model output and therefore the level of reliance that an executive can place on that output for decision-making purposes.

The field of operational risk modelling has been evolving since the final Basel II Capital Accord was published (Basel Committee on Banking Supervision 2006), and a significant amount of emphasis (appropriately so) has been placed on finding the most effective theories and quantitative techniques to build credible models. As the industry converges on a set of models and modelling techniques to quantify operational risk, it is imperative that there are no inappropriate assumptions about the validity and/or accuracy of the information being fed into these models. Vigilance should also be maintained in ensuring that operational risk model output is being used appropriately. No model is perfect, and failure to understand a model's limitations can lead to decisions that take an institution down the wrong path in terms of managing its operational risk profile effectively. Regulatory guidance has served as a catalyst to put more emphasis on all elements of model risk management, rather than solely focusing on whether or not a given model theory has been applied effectively.

In this chapter we will examine the impact of the aforementioned regulatory guidance, as well as some of the thornier issues that have arisen regarding the evaluation of risk management practices critical to assessing quantitative models and the level of confidence that executives should have in their output. We shall explore the various forms of model risk, along with different techniques for evaluating model risk management practices and who in a financial institution is qualified and responsible to offer the necessary challenge to model outputs and risk management effectiveness.

10.1   FROM MODEL VALIDATION TO MODEL RISK MANAGEMENT

On May 30, 2000, OCC Bulletin 2000-16 was issued by the US Office of the Comptroller of the Currency (OCC) to provide guidance on controlling model risk (Comptroller of the Currency 2000). The bulletin was focused on regulatory expectations of model validation processes, particularly validation procedures relative to the information input, processing and reporting components. Elements that would be more prominent in later regulatory guidance, such as an understanding of model limitations and data input controls, were only touched on in 2000, when the processing component took centre stage.

This emphasis changed with the issuance of OCC 2011-12 (and its twin, Supervisory Letter 11-7 (SR 11-7)) on April 4, 2011, by the

OCC and the Board of Governors of the Federal Reserve System.[1] The scope of the guidance was broadened to include all aspects of model risk management. Specifically, model risk, defined in SR 11-7 as "the potential for adverse consequences from decisions based on incorrect or misused model outputs and reports", was articulated as a risk that should be managed no differently from other risks, such as credit and market risk, in the sense that the risk should be effectively identified and quantified. Governance, policies and controls were considered critical to modelling risk management effectiveness.

The guidance's impact was powerful because it expanded responsibility for model risk management beyond an institution's model validation function. The model risk management framework is expected to be established by the board of directors and senior management. There should be a firm-wide model inventory that sets the foundation for the evaluation of individual and aggregate model risk. The guidance addressed formal policies and procedures more directly by highlighting the documentation of

- roles and responsibilities relative to model risk management, including business unit responsibilities,
- model approval,
- model validation,
- model performance monitoring,
- model reporting, and
- operational controls (change management, security, data and inputs, assumptions and limitations, outputs and reporting).

The model validation and internal audit functions were addressed in the guidance, with an emphasis on avoiding overlap between the two functions. Audit was considered responsible for the evaluation of the model risk management framework rather than duplicating activities already performed by the model validation function. None of this absolved audit of its responsibilities to test the design and effectiveness of controls, but it did raise some interesting questions regarding where audit and the model validation function may overlap and how those overlaps could be avoided. We address those questions in more detail later in this chapter, along with how the procurement (also known as strategic sourcing) function fits into the picture.

The 2011 regulatory guidance introduced the important concept of "effective challenge" as "critical analysis by objective, informed parties who can identify model limitations and assumptions". The guidance made it clear that, in addition to identifying potential concerns, these "objective, informed parties" should also have the influence and stature necessary to drive appropriate changes. It makes sense that the value of raising concerns is greatly diminished if no one can be compelled to address those concerns. "Effective challenge" can take many forms, affecting model identification and the evaluation of inherent and residual model risk. Before delving into the different manifestations of effective challenge, we should start with the forms of model risk that evaluators might encounter.

10.2 FORMS OF MODEL RISK

The regulatory guidance issued in 2011 broadened the landscape of model risk management beyond the theory, analytics and mathematics normally reviewed in many institutions by a model validation function. This in turn raised the question of how to delineate responsibility between internal audit and model validation relative to the evaluation of model risk. This question cannot be fully answered without first identifying all of the forms that model risk can take in an organisation.

One of the thorniest questions that an organisation faces may seem to be relatively straightforward: what is a model? The question of model identification becomes challenging because the regulatory definitions of a model could potentially lead to the belief that any spreadsheet or application that calculates anything is a model. The regulatory definition of a model, per OCC 2011-12 and SR 11-7, is

> a quantitative method, system, or approach that applies statistical, economic, financial, or mathematical theories, techniques, and assumptions to process input data into quantitative estimates.

While the definition cannot be considered inaccurate, imagine having a model validation function spending its time evaluating every spreadsheet that calculates something and produces output. The impractical nature of such an endeavour becomes clear pretty quickly. Where over-identification of models may lead to a resource allocation nightmare, models that go unidentified may not receive the attention necessary to establish appropriate controls, thereby increasing the risk that decisions based on output from these models are uninformed or that model output is misused.

A clear model definition is critical as it enables the appropriate identification of models and assessment of an organisation's model risk profile. Casting a wide net is most useful when identifying model candidates, because it increases the likelihood that models in use or under development will be properly identified. Potential model owners can be educated on how to effectively evaluate whether or not their spreadsheet, tool or application qualifies as a model. In working with various institutions, it has proven most effective for the potential model owners, rather than a centralised function, to conduct this evaluation because it is ultimately the model owners that will own the model risk and any necessary mitigating actions. Centralised functions are then in a better position to challenge model identification as appropriate.

An annual certification process is one way of organising this effort. The certification process helps to ensure the integrity of an organisation's model inventory. The inventory is an important tool supporting the assessment of an organisation's model risk profile. A typical certification process involves personnel throughout the institution each identifying models using the organisation's model definition. The model name and owner, along with a rationale for the model owner's decisions, are provided to a centralised function, where the centralised function has the opportunity to provide challenge. The nature of the interaction between the centralised function and the model owners is at least partly dependent on an organisation's culture and size. In some organisations this interaction consists of face-to-face meetings where the identification of models is essentially a joint effort between potential model owners and the model risk management experts. For other organisations, it may be impractical for a small number of model risk experts to meet with every potential model owner to walk them through the model-identification process. Instead, potential model owners may be on their own for the initial identification effort and the model risk experts will only engage if they disagree with a decision or require additional information before adding a model to the institution's model inventory. Regardless of the details, it is essential for the process to include all business functions and geographies to minimise the risk of excluding models that represent material inherent risk to the institution.

Material inherent risk, defined in alignment with SR 11-7, is the risk, before the application of controls, of incorrect model output or output misuse leading to a certain level of financial loss, negative impact on business and strategic decision-making or damage to an institution's reputation. When thinking of models that represent material inherent risk to a firm, "complex models" typically come to mind. The question is what constitutes "complexity". Does it only include models that utilise higher order mathematics in their calculations (as opposed to basic addition, subtraction, multiplication and division)? There are two types of complexity that are useful to understand: assumption complexity and computational complexity. Computational complexity seems to be better understood and is most often associated with a "complex model", so let us first address the lesser discussed assumption complexity.

Assumption complexity reflects the level of uncertainty in the data and/or parameters that ultimately become model inputs. Sometimes the term "expert judgement" will be used in reference to this type of complexity because without a clear empirical basis for these inputs, it is necessary to tap into the collective experience and knowledge of executives who can best estimate the data and/or parameters for modelling purposes. Assumptions are part of any model, but examples of more "complex" assumptions include certain forecasted macroeconomic factors and operational loss frequency and severity distributions. Data limitations may necessitate a greater reliance on the judgement of those deemed to be "experts" in any given institution.

An important distinction should be made regarding assumptions, especially when thinking about the evaluation of a model's inherent risk. For our purposes, "model assumptions" are those parameters that are embedded within the model theory being applied in the calculation engine. These are the parameters often evaluated by a model validation function. "Business assumptions", such as business growth rates over time, are established by company management and serve as inputs into a model, either as dynamic inputs that change periodically, or as hard-coded inputs that represent a management decision. The evaluation of these assumptions will be explored again later in the chapter as effective challenge could originate from different sources.

By comparison, computational complexity seems clear-cut in its definition and responsibility for its evaluation. When thinking about the level of mathematics employed in a model, lower complexity models tend to utilise basic mathematical operations and higher complexity models tend to be associated with higher order mathematics (eg, calculus), simulation approaches (eg, Monte Carlo), and/or multi-stage calculations involving various algorithms.

There is one distinction that needs to be kept in mind when thinking about computational complexity. Institutions sometimes confuse computational complexity with what should be thought of instead as "processing complexity". Think of this as the notion that not every spreadsheet with multiple tabs and calculations is a model. Although it is true that there is an increased risk of error in situations where manual spreadsheets have multiple linked tabs with various calculations, the determination of whether or not something is a model, and is therefore subject to model risk, should be focused on the basic questions of assumption complexity and computational complexity. For example, if a spreadsheet has 50 different linked tabs, all of which are calculating something with some calculations dependent on the result of other calculations, the fact that there is no uncertainty in the data and that the calculations are all basic mathematical operations should lead to the conclusion that the spreadsheet is not a model, regardless of the risk of processing error. This type of "tool" or "application" would typically be evaluated by a group other than an institution's model validation team in order to ensure that model validation resources are allocated to models that warrant the application of the group's unique skill set.

To clarify, models can have either complex assumptions or complex mathematics. It is not necessary for a model to have both, although it is not uncommon for that to be the case. The determination of complexity level is critical to understanding whether or not the tool, application or spreadsheet is a model that requires further assessment. Once this has been assessed, there is one more important element required to set the stage for an effective evaluation of a model's inherent risk.

Output criticality does not affect model identification, but once something is identified as a model, it has a profound impact on the inherent risk that a model represents for an institution. To state it plainly, the criticality of a model's output hinges on what business decisions or activities are driven by that output. Examples of high criticality outputs include those that directly influence strategic decision-making, management reporting and/or allocation of capital, and regulatory required reporting such as financial statements. In contrast, examples of low criticality outputs include those that increase awareness for an institution's management without serving as the basis for key decisions or external reporting. We may hear the term "reasonableness check" used in those cases where a decision is made based on other information or factors, but the model output provides extra information that may prompt additional questions or dialogue.

The term "directly influence" is being used in the context of output criticality because no model is a replacement for management judgement, and management due diligence to question the information with which it is provided continues to be vital. However, management is paying its qualified staff to provide reliable information upon which it can base its decisions; therefore, the higher the stakes associated with those decisions, the higher inherent risk a model represents to a firm, and the more focus and resources should be placed on the controls around such models.

Operational risk models developed to estimate Basel II regulatory capital requirements have tended to fall into the high output criticality bucket, and are ultimately considered to be high inherent risk models. If a firm decides to have a separate operational risk model that calculates economic capital, then a solid argument could be made that the output of such a model would be used by management to make capital use/allocation decisions and therefore should also be considered high inherent risk.

Note, then, that the determination of a model's inherent risk comes in two stages:

1. model identification using an assessment of assumption and computational complexity; and

2. determination of output criticality for identified models.

This is not meant to diminish the output criticality of applications and spreadsheets that are not models. These tools simply fall outside of the model risk management framework and will tend to be evaluated by a group other than the firm's model validation function.

A discussion of output criticality can be expanded to the important concept of "appropriate use", or model output being utilised in accordance with its intended purpose. Although model risk management received a tremendous amount of scrutiny as a result of the financial crisis, another insight from the crisis was that in many cases the models were not "broken", but executive management took messages from the output that should have been challenged and ultimately corrected via effective communication of the models' intended use and limitations related to that use.

Model risk in the context of appropriate use can arise in the form of disconnects between a model developer's perspective on the business need for a model and the information that business management is seeking to inform decision-making. One example involves the hiring of external specialists (ie, consultants) to develop a model where a "cookie cutter" approach is taken to model building. As a result, an insufficient understanding of the business leads to the building of a model that may work well for most of the specialist's clients, but fails to take the nuances of a specific client into consideration and leads to output that is misleading regarding the decisions the client has to make. This disconnect can also happen when all of the parties are internal, but that is less common.

A more common type of disconnect that occurs internal to a given institution stems from operating in silos. A model owner may understand a model's theory, operations and output in depth for a certain part of the business, but as the use of the model expands to other parts of the business, adjustments are not appropriately made to adapt the model for use in the other areas. Ineffective or nonexistent communication between the different business areas is the culprit in this case and can typically be improved by instituting robust change management processes to ensure model changes in response to changing conditions are appropriately analysed, tested and implemented.

Generally speaking, there are six controls that can facilitate appropriate model use:

1. clear statement of a model's purpose within the model documentation;

2. a model validation function that evaluates whether or not model development is consistent with the model's purpose;

3. requirement for models to undergo independent model validation prior to initial implementation, as well as prior to the implementation of significant changes;[2]

4. performance monitoring that involves analysis of model output uncertainty and responsibility for defining concrete actions to adjust for this uncertainty;

5. clear and comprehensible reports for decision-makers;

6. periodic communication of model assumptions and limitations to enhance management's understanding of the output being relied upon for decision-making.

10.3 FORMS OF EFFECTIVE CHALLENGE

The value of clear reporting and communication of model information to senior management includes enabling effective challenge. Effective challenge can take several forms and be provided by different areas of an organisation. It is valuable to look at effective challenge in the context of model risk management process points: model identification; inherent risk evaluation; model validation; and escalation.

An institution's definition of a model is critical as it will influence the size of its ultimate model inventory and how many resources need to be allocated to model risk management activities. Although model definitions may differ to some extent from one institution to the next, the definitions should all be aligned with the definition articulated in regulatory guidance (SR 11-7/OCC 2011-12), and can be calibrated by thinking through the concepts of assumption and computational complexity mentioned earlier in this chapter. A model's definition should be challenged in the context of any perceived misalignment with the organisation's view of assumption and computational complexity and regulatory expectations.

When thinking about the effectiveness of a model definition, there are two main pitfalls to be avoided. The first is the notion mentioned earlier that anything that uses inputs to calculate a result and produce output is a model. Yes, there may be quite a few spreadsheets that end up meeting the definition of a model, but it is also highly probable that many are still just plain old spreadsheets. A model definition that is too broad may, depending on an institution's size, result in hundreds or even thousands of models that will require resources to implement heightened levels of control and to validate that those controls are designed and operating effectively. Risk management overkill can be just as ineffective as the absence of appropriate risk management practices.

The other extreme is the thought that only "complex" applications are models. This is often based on the perception that phrases like "Monte Carlo simulation" or "lognormal distribution" serve as indicators that something is a model and anything simpler could not possibly fit the bill. Another misconception is that models are things that only people with advanced degrees (eg, PhDs) can understand. Although a high level of complexity is definitely associated with models, simpler models do exist and should not be overlooked. Simpler models could have a profound impact on management decision-making and neglecting to control them properly could therefore yield significant negative consequences.

To strike the appropriate balance, a wide net should be cast to capture everything in the institution that could possibly be a model. This includes every spreadsheet and application that has an input, calculation and output component. The list can then be narrowed using the assumption and computational complexity filters described earlier. Documentation should be prepared to record what was evaluated against the model definition and the rationale for determining what qualified as a model and what did not. The documentation establishes the foundation for effective challenge of management's decision-making by the institution's model risk and control experts, with challenge focused on accurate application of the firm's model definition and the reasonableness of model assumption and computational complexity analysis.

Vendor applications pose a unique challenge because applying the computational complexity filter can be inhibited by an inability to obtain a vendor's proprietary code. Regardless of whether a model is developed and maintained in-house or externally, management of risk posed by the model remains the responsibility of the organisation using the model's output to drive business decisions. Therefore, it is worth the effort to find a solution to the challenge of vendor model identification. Often, there is no difficulty because a vendor is specifically advertising its application as a model. In these cases, the challenge is in the model-validation arena, which will be addressed in more detail later in this chapter.

Vendor model identification is most effective when there is a strong partnership between business units and the procurement/ strategic sourcing functions. Procurement's expertise in vendor selection and management is useful in discussions regarding a vendor tool's capabilities. Procurement may also be able to provide assistance in obtaining vendor documentation related to product components, design and intended use. In situations where day-to-day vendor management is owned by business unit personnel, procurement may be more advisory in nature after a vendor contract is signed, and obtaining vendor documentation may be a business unit responsibility. In either case, obtaining the necessary documentation enables effective challenge regarding to vendor model identification.

Once a model has been identified, the importance of the model's output should be used to evaluate the inherent risk of the model to the institution. The higher the output criticality, the higher a model's inherent risk. Documentation supporting the output criticality analysis is essential to enabling independent, objective challenge of the inherent risk determination. When challenging the determination of inherent model risk, effective challenge consists of evaluating the use of model output as well as the materiality of output impact (eg, dollar thresholds). For example, a bank may identify a model as having high inherent risk because it directly influences external reporting or financial statements; however, the model may only have a minimal impact on reported figures, and therefore a determination of high inherent risk to the bank should be reconsidered.

Consistency in the evaluation of inherent model risk is important, as information on models across the corporation can be compiled into a model inventory that provides insight into an institution's model risk profile. Institutions can facilitate this consistency by tasking a central, corporate-level function with challenging the evaluation of inherent model risk throughout the organisation.

Another advantage in having a consistent view of inherent model risk is that it maximises the value of a model inventory in driving the prioritisation of model validation efforts. A model validation function can use the inventory to focus its initial efforts on those models that pose the highest inherent risk to the institution. Model validation frequency can then be determined using a risk-based approach. The highest risk models are typically reviewed at least annually, or more frequently, depending on the level and extent of model changes. The model validation function is critical to an organisation's model risk management framework and serves as one source of effective challenge, particularly as it relates to model theory, analytics and mathematics.

Now, what does it mean to effectively challenge model theory, analytics and mathematics? It is important for an institution to define this in the context of its model risk profile, but there are certain principles that should be kept in mind. A risk-based approach to the frequency and depth of model validations should be based on a solid understanding of model inherent risk and will help to ensure optimal allocation of validation resources. Standard validation procedures and reporting templates should include, but not necessarily be limited to, a model's conceptual soundness, ongoing performance monitoring and outcome analysis.

Recognising that models are unique and validation approaches may vary, model validation procedures should allow for the documentation of explanations regarding situations where certain testing approaches are not applicable or standards do not apply. One example is back-testing over operational risk quantification models because a credible back-testing approach has yet to emerge and, therefore, refraining from testing back-testing efforts in this situation may be justified.

Standards accounting for differences between the validation of an in-house model and a vendor model should also be established. As mentioned earlier, validating vendor models can be especially challenging because vendors will be reluctant to share their source code or other details that may be considered proprietary. Vendor managers should obtain independent model validation results from the vendor if available. Alternatively, vendors could be required to provide documentation on their development processes so that model experts can review the documentation and raise any questions or concerns. If none of this documentation can be obtained, then an institution has to evaluate whether or not it is in its best interests to continue the vendor relationship in light of the risk involved in relying on the vendor model output to drive decision-making.

In addition, vendor managers should be obtaining periodic reports from vendors identifying any model changes and ongoing model performance monitoring. Vendor managers should then leverage model owner expertise in evaluating the adequacy of the reports provided. According to SR 11-7

> Banks should expect vendors to conduct ongoing performance monitoring and outcomes analysis, with disclosure to their clients, and to make appropriate modifications and updates over time.

Despite the challenges associated with vendor models, SR 11-7 is clear that vendor models

> should nevertheless be incorporated into a bank's broader model risk management framework following the same principles as applied to in-house models, although the process may be somewhat modified.

Model validation functions may need to rely more on sensitivity analysis and benchmarking for vendor models in the absence of some of the information from vendors mentioned above. The modified approach that a validation function decides to take with vendor models should be fully documented along with the rationale for the decisions made. Regardless of whether a model validation function is evaluating an in-house or vendor model, testing should result in a statement of the residual risk that a model represents for the institution. Defined risk ratings should reflect the level of confidence that senior management should have in a model's output.

Ultimately, effective challenge manifests itself in the interaction between the model owner and evaluators. Once testing is completed, it is critical that evaluators are able to effectively negotiate action plans with model owners. The most successful negotiators in this space are able to frame an issue in the context of the issue's potential impact on model output. Once agreement is reached on this point, attention can be focused on crafting actions that directly address the issue at hand and reinforce accountability for addressing issues in a timely manner. It is actionable responses with due dates that directly address risk in a reasonable timeframe that evidence the effectiveness of the challenge that occurred during the model validation process. Consistent evidence of this effectiveness over several model validations is indicative of a model validation function that has the appropriate level of influence and stature in an institution, something stressed in SR 11-7.

The establishment of appropriate and timely action plans is not the end of driving accountability. Effective challenge extends from the actual validation effort and delivery of results to holding model owners accountable for following through on their commitments. Issue closure should be tracked, including the date a model owner asserts that an issue is addressed, or when a model owner delays delivery dates of action plans. A pattern of delays in delivery could be indicative of a model owner who is not committed to addressing issues in a timely manner, or needs assistance in getting the support or resources needed to move forwards with remedial actions. One way to promote accountability is to report overdue validation issues to senior management, particularly issues that represent a high risk to the institution. Senior management actions driven by this reporting are indicative of the importance it places on effective model risk management, and by extension the influence and stature of the model validation function.

Regardless of an evaluator's influence and stature, it is important to have a defined and useful escalation process. The escalation process should be established to address exceptional circumstances that arise from the challenge process when agreements cannot be reached on model identification, inherent risk rating, validation issues and residual risk ratings, or remedial action plans.

Depending on the size of an organisation, the Chief Risk Officer (CRO) or an appropriate delegate may be the best authority to resolve disagreements. Additionally, organisations typically require exception approval for models that are implemented prior to being validated, and the CRO of the organisation is generally considered to be a qualified approver. In these situations, it is advisable for the users of the model's output to be informed of the risk associated with using output from a model that has not yet been validated.

Immediate escalation to the CRO may not always be advisable, practical or even possible (if, for instance, an organisation does not have a CRO). Disagreements between a model owner and a model validation function can be escalated in a variety of ways. A couple of methods of note include an independent committee of model risk experts representing various risk disciplines, or a panel of model developers from across the corporation who serve as quantitative experts that have the authority to resolve disputes. In both cases, procedures should be in place to ensure that experts abstain from voting if there is a potential conflict of interest regarding certain disputes. Regardless of how the escalation occurs, an independent and effective escalation point should have the following characteristics:

- escalation is used only for exceptional circumstances;

- individuals/committee membership is independent of the model development process and the model validation function; and

- individuals or committee comprised of quantitative peers that will understand the technical issue(s) at hand.

10.4 ROLES AND RESPONSIBILITIES: WHO IS ON THE HOOK FOR PROVIDING EFFECTIVE CHALLENGE?

This chapter has outlined the various forms of model risk and effective challenge relating to model risk management. One of the challenges faced by various institutions is the question of who is going to be responsible for challenging the full spectrum of model risk management practices. The Basel II Capital Accord has brought this challenge front and centre for the largest banking institutions, with the spotlight shining most brightly on the model validation and internal audit functions. Scrutiny of the role played by the procurement/strategic sourcing function has also been increasing.

Let us start with model validation and internal audit, which may be separate functions in an institution or be combined with quantitatively focused personnel reporting up through internal audit. When the model validation and internal audit functions are separate, there is a natural separation between audit's evaluation of model risk management effectiveness and the areas of model theory, analytics and mathematics that fall under the purview of model validation. Audit under this structure will tend to focus more on data input integrity, model security, the reasonableness of business assumptions (as opposed to assumptions embedded within the model), communication of model limitations to senior management and the board, change management processes, model documentation and appropriate use of outputs and reporting. Audit will also test calculations under circumstances where the calculations are relatively simple (eg, basic operations such as addition, subtraction, multiplication and division), but note that overlap between audit testing and model validation testing should be kept to a minimum.

When model validation and internal audit are separate functions, internal audit can gain full coverage by evaluating the effectiveness of model validation processes, with specific focus on model validation's role in evaluating inherent model risk, planning and executing its model validations and reporting on model risk to senior management. Audit could also engage consultants to augment its skill set and re-perform certain model validations to gain comfort with the effectiveness of the institution's model validation function.

Questions have arisen within financial services about what qualifications are necessary to effectively evaluate model risk management practices, particularly for auditors. Regulatory guidance focuses on independence and expertise, but there is not much guidance on whether or not an advanced degree is necessary, or if that advanced degree has to be a PhD. However, it is worth noting that, in the model risk arena, those with advanced degrees, particularly PhDs, may often have an easier time gaining influence in an institution, which helps the process of negotiating with model owners who may have similar PhD credentials. This tends to be especially true for members of the model validation function that are evaluating technical modelling aspects. For auditors, mathematical and analytical orientation is helpful, but it typically does not require an advanced degree to understand the process testing that is necessary for audit to assess control environment effectiveness.

Considering model validation and internal audit as separate functions, the responsibilities with regard to assessing model risk management practices could break down as follows.

1. Model validation:

- challenge of model identification;

- corporate-wide evaluation of model inherent risk ratings;

- validation of relevant model theory, analytics and mathematics, as well as performance testing, stress-testing and back-testing;

- obtaining management responses to validation findings;

- tracking and testing remediation of validation findings; monitoring and validating significant model changes; and

- reporting aggregate and individual model risks to senior management (for example, dispersion of inherent and residual model risk, overdue high priority model remediation actions, rationale for deviations from the model validation schedule, etc).

2. Internal audit:

- assess effectiveness of model risk management policies and corporate oversight, including

  - corporate-level model risk governance (framework review and approval, independence of the model validation function, design and effectiveness of oversight committees),
  - completeness and effectiveness of firm-wide model inventory maintenance processes (identification, inherent risk rating and model ownership),
  - validation frequency and coverage of model validation procedures, as evidenced by model validation supporting documentation and deliverables, and
  - comprehensiveness and clarity of model risk reporting to oversight committees;

- challenge model identification in alignment with the corporate and regulatory definitions of a model (executed as part of process reviews where models are part of the process, which may reveal the existence of certain spreadsheets or applications that should have been classified as models but were not).

- evaluate effectiveness of operational controls supporting models and business unit/model owner adherence to model risk management policies and procedures, including

  - model documentation,
  - change management,
  - security,

- data and inputs,
- assumptions and limitations (note that audit should be equipped to assess the reasonableness of business assumptions, while model validation should have the expertise to evaluate the assumptions embedded within models), and
- outputs and reporting.

It is worth noting that the delineation of responsibility over the aforementioned operational controls should be clear to both the audit and model validation functions in order to minimise unnecessary duplication of effort. It should also be kept in mind that the internal audit and model validation functions are not the whole story when it comes to evaluating model risk management practices.

Procurement/strategic sourcing has a role to play in assisting business units with building requirements and identifying vendor model candidates. Procurement should also adhere to model risk management policies and set standards to help business unit vendor managers do the same. One key standard for vendor managers is the expectation that they request and obtain vendor model documentation as appropriate. If requested documentation cannot be obtained from vendors, there should be an "acceptance of risk" process where continuing with a certain vendor is deemed appropriate despite the inability to obtain the documentation necessary to facilitate model validation efforts. The procurement group would be responsible for monitoring vendor manager performance against these expectations.

10.5   NEXT STEPS TO ENSURE EFFECTIVE CHALLENGE

Every institution should evaluate its practices regarding the evaluation of model risk. Operational risk modelling is still evolving, so it is understandable that certain practices relating to the evaluation of operational risk quantitative models may continue to change over time. However, the establishment of basic principles and practices relative to model risk management will allow that evolution to progress more smoothly. Using the guidelines in this chapter, any institution should be able to start the evaluation of its model risk management practices and set the stage for effective operational risk quantification models that produce output that senior management can rely on to make informed business decisions. It is important that the groups tasked with evaluating model risk management practices have the appropriate stature and influence to drive positive change in the institution, with the full support of appropriate "tone at the top" from the CRO (if there is one) and business unit senior management. It is this partnership between business units, model owners and evaluators that will help to ensure that operational risk models remain well controlled as the tools and techniques used to measure operational risk become more sophisticated and regulatory requirements relative to these models continue to solidify.

> The views expressed herein are those of the author alone and should not be attributed to Northern Trust Corporation, any of its affiliates or subsidiaries or any of their respective officers or employees. The author's affiliation is given for identification purposes only.

1 See Comptroller of the Currency (2011) and Board of Governors of the Federal Reserve System and the Office of the Comptroller of the Currency (2011).

2 Note that what constitutes a "significant change" should be well defined; this could be done at the corporate level, or at different levels of the firm all the way down to individual model owners, depending on what makes the most sense from a risk management perspective.

REFERENCES

Basel Committee on Banking Supervision, 2006, "Basel II: International Convergence of Capital Measurement and Capital Standards: A Revised Framework", Bank for International Settlements, June, URL: http://www.bis.org/publ/bcbs128.pdf.

Board of Governors of the Federal Reserve System and the Office of the Comptroller of the Currency, 2011, "SR Letter 11-7: Supervisory Guidance on Model Risk Management", Board of Governors of the Federal Reserve System, URL: http://www.federalreserve.gov/bankinforeg/srletters/sr1107a1.pdf.

Comptroller of the Currency, Administrator of National Banks, US Department of the Treasury, 2000, "OCC 2000-16: Description: Model Validation", Office of the Comptroller of the Currency, URL http://www.occ.gov/news-issuances/bulletins/2000/bulletin-2000-16.html.

Comptroller of the Currency, Administrator of National Banks, US Department of the Treasury, 2011, "OCC 2011-12 – Description: Supervisory Guidance on Model Risk Management", Office of the Comptroller of the Currency, URL: http://www.occ.gov/news-issuances/bulletins/2011/bulletin-2011-12.html.

11

How Much Credit Risk Is There Really in a Loan? An Analysis of Credit Defaults to Determine the Contributing Factors

Nasreen al Qaseer; Hansruedi Schütter

Kuwait International Bank; Risk*Business* International Ltd

Operational risk has received increasing attention from both financial institutions and policymakers, as large losses have resulted in either failure or bailout of large banks and investment firms, as well as a massive evaporation of market capitalisation of a variety of well-known firms. The importance of understanding and measuring operational risk is heightened by the fact that an operational event's impact frequently extends well beyond the direct impact and often beyond the bank where the loss occurred.

The financial crisis of 2008, through its impact on the cost of inputs, outputs and substitute goods, played a significant role in determining the competitive position of companies with no direct international operations relative to foreign firms.

In view of the entangled events of the crisis years and Basel III's subsequent focus on the effects of the crisis, the desire to investigate the dilution of credit risk by other factors grew. In this chapter we will present the results from a thorough analysis of real life credit default data and its meaning in the context of how we define credit risk.

In its justification for a new capital accord, the Basel Committee on Banking Supervision argued that operational risk was, up to that point, embedded in the credit risk capital charge and was henceforth to be separated. There were high hopes for the very young discipline of operational risk management. In the course of the Basel II consultation process, and upon the insistence of the Working Group on Operational Risk, the Institute of International Finance arranged a meeting in Rome between credit risk and operational risk representatives. But it may have been too early for a major paradigm shift. Credit risk capital kept its operational risk components without the promised segregation.

This chapter deals with a study undertaken in 2010 and 2011 to examine the magnitude of operational risk in the lending process. The study was largely based on the views of senior managers of 12 lending organisations, as well as data from real life loss events contributed by lenders, most of them on an anonymous basis. In addition, the study aimed to address the prevalent issues related to operational risk in the lending cycle. The result depicts a snapshot of the effectiveness of credit risk assessments and procedural activities in the organisations concerned and their effect on the economic progress of banks and lending organisations.

The research managed to examine issues relating to losses booked as a result of loan defaults, typically recorded as credit losses, and the underlying root causes attributed to the affected lending institutions. The study sought to determine the extent to which the operational risks in various lending processes contributed to these credit losses, and the potential effect on capital allocation for the individual risk types.

The lending process in financial institutions is, like any other activity, subject to human error, misjudgement, negligence and other improper practices and, last but not least, fraud. The regulatory community has acknowledged this fact but requires regulatory capital for the loan portfolio exclusively as credit risk capital. While this method may be simple and practical, it contradicts Basel II's expressed aim of creating a risk-sensitive capital charge.

Fundamentally, credit risk refers to the risk of loss due to a debtor's non-payment of a loan or other form of credit. Therefore, strictly speaking, loan losses attributable to a lender's own internal problems or mistakes should be classified not as credit losses but rather as operational losses.

Credit risk is apparent in loans, trading facilities, guarantees and other related activities. To this effect, lenders engage credit analysts, who approve or reject credit limits and specify loan conditions and, if appropriate, collateral required.

The global financial crisis severely interrupted the commercial lending process due to both liquidity issues in the financial markets and a widespread fear of customers defaulting, leading in turn to exactly such dreaded commercial defaults, as refinancing became impossible for many firms despite solid business activity. In the aftermath of the crisis, the financial industry is challenged with re-establishing confidence to reassure the public that both financial institutions and financial systems in general are safe and do not simply rely on financial emergency aid by governments and central banks. Part of this confidence rebuilding should be a thorough look at corporate governance and risk management practices.

The increasing complexity of banking activities has been partly responsible for the increase in events resulting from operational risk. Operational risk is defined by the Basel Committee on Banking Supervision (Basel Committee on Banking Supervision 2006) as:

> the risk of loss resulting from inadequate or failed internal pro-cesses, people and systems or from external events. This definition includes legal risk but excludes strategic and reputational risk.

This definition by the Basel Committee is fundamentally focused on operational events and underlying causes, but boundary issues and cross-risk-type effects are essentially ignored.

11.1 RISK MANAGEMENT FAILURE

The financial meltdown of 2008 exemplifies risk management fail-ure. It was not just subprime lending and most participants' limited understanding of the concept that caused the crisis. A general atti-tude of cutting corners in due diligence and risk assessment played a major role in this drama.

Regulators have been working hard to make enhancements to the Basel II framework in order to get a better grip on the stability of the financial system. Disappointingly, the new Basel III Capital Accord says almost nothing about operational risk. Instead, its main concern is recalibrating credit risk to accommodate complex instruments and to keep banks from being tainted by moral hazard. This implies that Basel III merely touches on new reserve requirements for operational risk as an afterthought. Operational risk is too young a discipline for

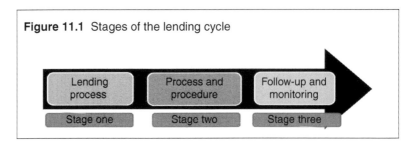

Figure 11.1 Stages of the lending cycle

Lending process · Process and procedure · Follow-up and monitoring

Stage one · Stage two · Stage three

many (particularly regulators), and available industry data on what contributes to losses is still too sketchy to give bankers much in the way of meaningful, predictive information that can be acted upon.

Our research examined the risk indicators and the value of risk at various stages of a loan, evaluating and analysing the relationship cycle as defined by the Basel Committee and by sound banking principles. The study focused on the lending stages by using Risk*Business* International Ltd's model in testing the relationship. It examined pre- and post-acquisition risks in the lending relationship (Figure 11.1). The analysis was based on 120 loan default cases received from banks who volunteered to participate in this survey to examine the magnitude of operational risk in the lending process. This further defines and investigates factors and underlying causes of risk within the three main stages of the lending process.

The detailed activities in these stages are described in Figures 11.2–11.4.

11.1.1 Disclosure of limitations

There were some limitations to our study that need to be disclosed and highlighted. As defined by the Basel Committee, various risks affect the organisational strategy and capital. This research was limited to banks and was based on primary research, with support from secondary materials. Collecting data for this research was the most difficult part, due to the highly confidential and sometimes embarrassing nature of data and the absolute anonymity required by banks with respect to both the loss events and the impact on their clients. As a consequence, the survey was limited to a few cooperating banks located in Gulf Cooperation Council (GCC) countries and a few international banks willing to participate and share their data.

It was extremely difficult to administer the questionnaires to obtain the necessary information from participating organisations and

which helped in delving further into the analysis of the size of operational risks in the lending process. Surveys were used to gather information on actual default cases and this became the primary method of data collection. The survey was restricted to employees of banks and lending organisations who had been working for their respective employers for at least a year, so as to ensure that they were familiar with their organisations' procedures. The criterion for a case to be considered was repayment failure. The survey was limited because of cost and time constraints. Due to confidentiality of survey information, most banks approached by mail did not respond or share information on credit default cases. Through networking and personal relationships, positive responses and contributions were received from some banks in Bahrain, Qatar, the UAE, China, Japan, Thailand and India. Due to the anonymous submission mechanism, it cannot be excluded that default cases from other countries were included in the data set.

In the analysis, the collected data was divided into two categories; these are:

1. test pre-acquisition on operational and credit risk as defined under stage 1 in the lending process;

2. closed response survey questionnaires that detail information pertaining to loan loss event questions under stage 2, covering regulator and Basel II guidelines and principles to meet best practice.

In addition, semi-structured interviews with selected key risk professionals and external consultants were used to interpret and support the results and recommendations. A discussion with risk managers and consultants was arranged to present the research concept to the regulator in Bahrain. This method was employed to solicit risk professional views on the research topic, and the results helped in concluding the findings and recommendations.

The survey questionnaire was defined on the basis of the three stages in Figure 11.1, which helped the respondents to identify, examine and include different aspects of defaults in their answers. The three stages in the process are presented in Figures 11.2–11.4.

In addition, a separate survey with a single question on the allocation of regulatory risk capital defined by Basel II was sent to selected banks in the GCC. Their licenses varied from retail banks to wholesale banks and investment banks. The banks chosen are located in

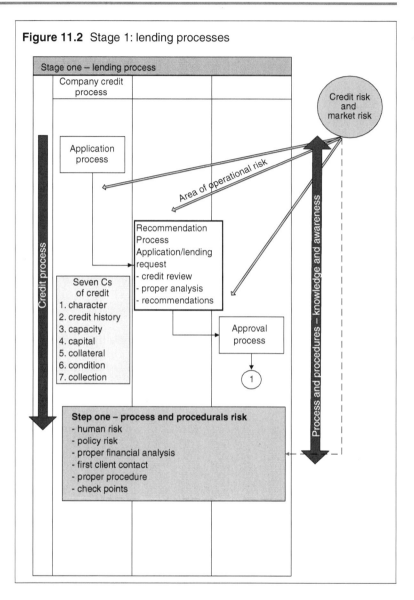

Figure 11.2 Stage 1: lending processes

Bahrain, Qatar, Kuwait and the UAE. Banks were selected based on ease of access and on personal contacts ensuring support for the project and cooperation. A group of 50 risk professionals, external auditors and consultants were contacted to share their opinions and views. This separate survey addressed personal experiences and views on distribution and allocation of risk across their respective organisations, as well as the scale of the main risk incorporated in

Figure 11.3 Stage 2: lending processes and procedures

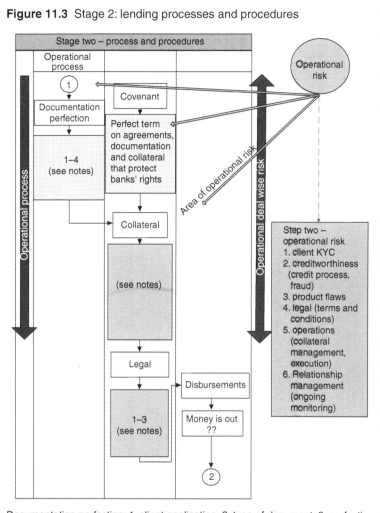

Documentation perfection: 1. client application; 2. type of document; 3. perfection of collateral; 4. perfection of document.

Collateral – perfect terms, legal clause on documentation for collateral and notarisation. Proper legal review with good agreements and contracts.

Issues: 1. collateral linked with more than one bank; 2. collateral sold without notification.

Legal: 1. proper legal documents/opinion; 2. proper legal reviews prior to lending; 3. proper legal review on lending to sector, banks, companies and countries.

the calculation of the capital adequacy ratio of those organisations. Out of the distributed single question, responses from 35 addressees were received, which is a 70% response to the qualitative questions (Table 11.3).

Figure 11.4 Stage 3: follow-up and monitoring

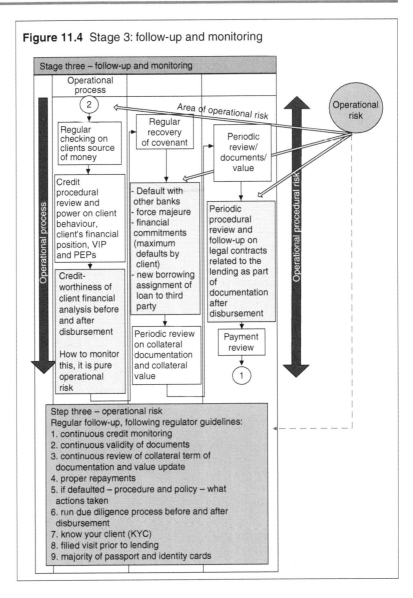

To ensure the reliability of submissions received, statistical analysis was employed (Table 11.4). Allen and Yen (2002) stated that they were able to assess the reliability of data using Cronbach's α to test the reliability of the constructed research instrument. The instruments in this study were the statements made by the respondents to quantify their perception of the magnitude of operational risk in the lending process.

Table 11.2 Survey questionnaire returns from personal relationships

Group	Distributed questionnaires	Returned questionnaires	%
Risk managers	6	6	100
Credit managers	5	5	100
External auditors	6	6	100
Consultants	2	2	100
Total	20	20	100

Table 11.3 Professionals' responses to allocation question

Country	Distributed questionnaires	Returned questionnaires	%
Bahrain	25	18	72
Qatar	15	10	66
Kuwait	5	3	60
UAE	5	4	80
Total	50	35	70

Table 11.4 Reliability statistics

Cronbach's alpha	N of items
0.835	8

Estimating internal consistency, ie, reliability, from the average correlation, the formula for alpha also takes into account the number of items, based on the theory that more items will result in a more reliable scale, and that the more consistent within-subject responses are, and the greater the variability between subjects in the sample, the higher Cronbach's alpha will be. Cronbach's alpha is a reliability coefficient formula. The formula used to calculate the coefficient is

$$\left(\frac{N}{N-1}\right)\left(\frac{\text{total variance} - \sum \text{individual variances}}{\text{total variance}}\right)$$

In addition to the surveys, semi-structured interviews were conducted. These interviews were arranged by phone with two key risk professionals and a consultant. The aim of the interviews was to collect the interview partners' views in light of the survey findings and to understand their opinions on the capital allocation in general and for operational risk in particular. In addition, three semi-structured face-to-face interviews were conducted to collect data for the pilot study. These interviews consisted of two parts, the first part related to measurement methods and the second part related to loss data collection. The interviews were arranged with a head of risk management, a head of operational risk and an external consultant based on the knowledge and experience required to critically respond to the questions on measuring and managing overall operational risk capital across an organisation.

11.1.5 Key results

The ultimate reason for the investigated defaults lay in counterparty insolvency and only 29% of defaults were attributed to credit fraud. This, however, only represented the final straw. The history and trail of causes leading to the point of default is well worth looking at.

We would naturally assume that more care is applied to large loans than to smaller deals and, as a consequence, procedural failures in the lending process should be less frequent for large amounts. The research results, however, show that the average root cause responses by risk managers from wholesale banks were similar to those of their peers from the retail sector. This means that operational risks that ultimately lead to credit loss events in a wholesale lending environment are similar to those in retail banks. The loan size does not appear to be a significant factor, nor is there much of a difference between the two business segments when it comes to causes like fraud or insolvency that lead to loan defaults. We may add that banks typically require some sort of security against the issuance of a loan; therefore, the size of the loans affected by a lending failure does not appear to matter that much. We therefore conclude that large loans are not necessarily subject to more careful processing.

Talking of security, it was surprising to see that 67% of loan defaults were not collateralised but granted on the basis of a business relationship. Where collateral was a condition, it was often not received or secured before disbursement of the loan. It also appears that in three quarters of all defaulting cases, the collateral was not regularly revalued. One reason for this seemingly excessive trust may lie in the socioeconomic environment of the Middle East, and it would be interesting to see whether this finding holds true in other

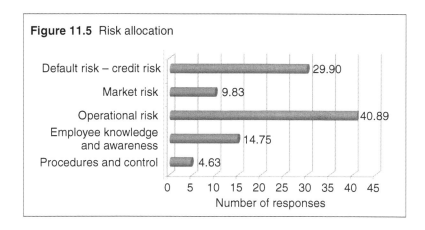

Figure 11.5 Risk allocation

parts of the world. Other reasons have been identified as weak credit policies and/or adherence to them, or in all of the above together. Where bank internal causes have been identified with respect to policy adherence and operational procedures, operational risks are dominant.

For every reported loan default, respondents were asked if the loss could have been prevented. According to their answers, the majority of losses were believed to have been preventable if proper operational risk management and controls had been imposed. The figures say that, in the opinion of the responding managers, 62% of credit losses could have been avoided and only 38% were considered unforeseeable.

In 70 cases out of the 120 samples, respondents admitted that procedures in either the credit approval process or the subsequent disbursement were not properly followed, even if the majority of credit procedures were deemed to be adequate.

More surprising than anything else was the revelation that only 54% of defaulting loans were properly documented. Again, it would be interesting to compare this figure with data from other parts of the world.

Results from the default analysis point massively in the direction of the following operational failures.

- Inadequate procedures and employee knowledge, together with a host of other operational risks, account for 60.27% of the reasons contributing to the defaults.

- Another 9.83% of default reasons were attributed to market risks, where property, stock or currency markets negatively affected the credit exposure.
- A mere 29.9% of all the contributing factors in sampled loan defaults were considered genuine and unforeseeable borrower defaults where the lender could not find any blame in its own operation.

To summarise, a typical average loan that eventually defaulted carried 60.27% operational risk, 9.83% market risk and 29.90% genuine credit risk.

11.2 CONCLUSION

Judging from the results, many organisations should review their procedures for both secured and unsecured lending, and the periodic collateral adequacy review may have to be reinforced.

To put the lending process weaknesses pointed out in this study in perspective, participant responses also confirm that there are no fundamental problems in their respective firms. Lending procedures typically comply with prevailing laws, and where properly produced, legal documentation is deemed to be appropriate.

Even though the problem of operational risk brought on by the lending process may be small in the overall context of a bank's balance-sheet activities, it has a direct impact on the business operation. Greater awareness of internally initiated debtor default may lead to better quality of loan assessments and fewer mistakes in transaction processing and the subsequent maintenance until final repayment.

It may be time to officially break down credit into its real components: true and unexpected borrower default (credit risk), internal issues (operational risk) and market fluctuations affecting the value of collateral or the viability of a business or property for which the loan was extended (market risk). While we cannot expect regulators to implement such a breakdown of risk in the near future, banks can make a start in their own economic capital allocation frameworks and thus migrate towards a more risk-aware operation.

REFERENCES

Allen, M. J., and W. M. Yen, 2002, *Introduction to Measurement Theory* (Long Grove, IL: Waveland Press).

Basel Committee on Banking Supervision, 2006, "Basel II: International Convergence of Capital Measurement and Capital Standards: A Revised Framework", Bank for International Settlements, June, URL: http://www.bis.org/publ/bcbs128.pdf.

Collis, J., and R. Hussey, 2003, *Business Research: A Practical Guide for Undergraduate and Postgraduate Students*, Second Edition (Basingstoke: Palgrave Macmillan).

Guba, E. G., and Y. S. Lincoln, 1994, "Competing Paradigms in Qualitative Research", in N. K. Denzin and Y. S. Lincoln (eds), *Handbook of Qualitative Research*, pp. 105–17 (Thousand Oaks, CA: Sage).

Index

(page numbers in italic type relate to tables or figures)